Samuel Andrews

Our great writers; or, Popular chapters on some leading authors

Samuel Andrews

Our great writers; or, Popular chapters on some leading authors

ISBN/EAN: 9783743658042

Printed in Europe, USA, Canada, Australia, Japan

Cover: Foto ©Thomas Meinert / pixelio.de

More available books at **www.hansebooks.com**

OUR GREAT WRITERS;

OR,

POPULAR CHAPTERS ON SOME

LEADING AUTHORS.

BY

SAMUEL ANDREWS, M.A.

LONDON:
ELLIOT STOCK, 62, PATERNOSTER ROW, E.C.
1884.

PREFACE.

THE multitude of different texts to be found in the acts and thoughts of our Literary Men is so great, that the commentary never needs to be a repetition of what was formerly written. And were it otherwise, this little book seeks to occupy a vacant place, by acting as an interpreter between higher authors and the ordinary reader, who is sometimes repelled by the dryness of literary history, as found in compendiums, and even in essays written in a learned or technical style. The aim of the Author of this Work has been, by avoiding unnecessary detail, difficult language, or involved phraseology, to interest English readers in the lives and thoughts of some of our greatest Writers, who are indeed familiar names, but often nothing more. Those who have not received a collegiate education sometimes take it for granted that the great classics of our tongue are too high and difficult for them. This book aims at making such persons feel that those Great Writers might all have one motto describing themselves and their works—'I am a man, and everything human interests me.'

It is also hoped that the Book will demonstrate that the

cultivation of our literature should not be placed under the ban which it is placed under by some 'serious' people; as literature (with that mixture of evil which belongs to all human things) is neither more nor less than a record of the 'noblest and best thoughts of the best and noblest minds.'

Though many labourers have worked in this field, it is still rich enough to repay not one, but many, more. The treatment in the present instance is biographical, with an expository aim —the incidents and characteristics of the author being set in connection with the thoughts found in his works.

Two chapters are of an entirely expository kind, dealing only with the works of the authors—one on 'HAMLET,' the other on 'IN MEMORIAM.' These are attempts to popularize the highest thinking of SHAKESPEARE and TENNYSON, which it is hoped will prove acceptable.

Sectarian bias is, of course, excluded; the Author holding that the works of our great men, whatever be their faults, should be treated, not in a strait-laced or dogmatic, but in a considerate and liberal, spirit.

PORTADOWN, *Christmas*, 1883.

OUR GREAT WRITERS.

INTRODUCTORY.

LITERATURE AND CULTURE.

THERE are those in this northern Province who will ask, What has a man, whose life is devoted to pastoral work, to do with literature? It is true there still exists among us a certain kind of religion that repels literary culture as a thing antagonistic to its very nature; but; whatever may be the sentiment on this subject in my own or in other churches, I am one of those who deplore and condemn the divorce of agencies which were married 'in the beginning.' I regard religion as the highest kind of culture, and something more; but I reckon it a reproach and injury done to religion when, by bigotry and narrowness, it is severed from subordinate kinds of culture. I know well the narrow, exclusive, and gloomy spirit in which religious people in this country are sometimes brought up. I know why the religious spirit has sometimes proscribed the works of genius. I can to some degree respect the motive while deploring the act. Whatever in works of genius may be styled divine, there is nothing in these works so divine as duty; and those who cannot reconcile the use of works of genius with their sense of duty, are bound at all risks to preserve the latter. But they are bound also to make progress and acquire broader and higher views of duty—views which will enable them to recognise and accept the divine in all things, wherever it is manifested.

I accept the principle, All light is good. It was simply a mistake to say:

'The light that led astray was light from heaven.'

It is an unworthy fear and a hurtful prejudice which makes us unwilling to have Nature's as well as the Bible's exposition of God. Let us regard Athens and Jerusalem as two great original lights (of different kinds) still shining on the world. In different senses both are ordinances of God. Neither light is to be condemned—rather the two are to be blended, and thus we shall neither neglect our highest faculty nor deprive the lower faculties of cultivation.

Mr. Arnold, while admitting that the churches do good by making life orderly, moral, and serious, accuses them of starving more than half of the finest faculties of human nature. We do not make so grave an accusation, but think the churches should be zealous in striving to give not even the slightest ground for the charge. As all true knowledge is resolved at last into the knowledge of God, when men, by refusing wider intelligence, refuse to remove what obscures the divine image, are they not in this akin to idolaters? We are simple beginners—we have not left behind us the 'beggarly elements'—unless we acknowledge that scientific truth and religious truth are both emanations from the same Divine source of light; and surely, in presence of Him who is the Maker of all, it becomes us to say we fear not, but are grateful for, every true source of knowledge, every true help towards the advancement of our immortal natures!

It is, I believe, quite possible to show that there is no opposition, but a divine harmony between true religion and true literary culture. Indeed, one might think, since we use a Bible containing what literary men have described as the very highest specimens of literature, the proof is scarcely necessary. Nevertheless, whatever we say, there exists a lurking suspicion among religious men; and often by those who are reputed to be pre-eminently evangelical the pursuit of literature is frowned upon. However unwilling to learn, such persons must be taught that they cannot take such a course without causing results disastrous even to the faith and morality which they seek to conserve. Let them know that the mind in which a true literary ardour has been created, will read *with* the sanction of religion or *without* it; and if the latter happens, what is the result? Then you have that sad spectacle, the cultivated man without faith and without reverence; one delighting in all forms of intellectual beauty, but, unhappily, shut out from contemplating the very highest, feeling the sweetness and light which stream from all books but one, that has infinite riches of sweetness and light. It is evil for such a one to be exiled from the luminous circle which we call the Church, it is evil also for the Church that has banished him. By such an action the Church grows poorer, less interesting, less verdant, less powerful; and her literary exiles are left in the company of strumpet Pleasure instead of maiden Virtue, and to wear on haggard faces the hollow sceptic sneer, instead of beaming with the true celestial smile of hope.

Thoughts of this kind should somewhat mollify even our sternest religionists in their disposition towards literature. They should be reminded, too, of its humanizing influence diffusing itself where religion cannot enter. Sects and parties are places fenced in, grounds rendered private. Only the family and its friends are permitted to walk there. If I wear the habiliments of a Capulet, will the Montagues receive me? If I disguise myself as a Montague, I am not honest, and among the Montagues I shall get into danger, and do harm where I wish to do good. A sectary myself, I cannot cure sectarianism. I cannot persuade all the other sects to come over to mine. The only hope at present for all the sects and parties, is in all being more highly educated. To whatever sect or party you belong, you may rise in the scale of being, by bringing your mind into contact with whatever of greatest and best is to be found in the writings of literary men. No man is educated who is not being educated all his life long. No man is educated unless he has apprehended and felt in sympathy with the highest thoughts and best sentiments in literature— say, if you like, in English literature; for if you know the best things in that language you know what is best in all languages. There is a softening, moderating power in such study. It makes mutual forbearance, justice, and tolerance possible between parties and sects. Religious and political fanaticism, the bane of our country, finds its congenial home among those who are utterly unacquainted with such culture. The fiercest political fanatics on either side, were they addicted to reading a little true poetry, would beat their drums in a milder spirit. There is a troubled atmosphere of dogmatic controversy—there is an equally troubled atmosphere of political warfare: the home of literature is far from both. Amid those dreary storms the human spirit does not put forth its tender and delicate blossoms, fragrant of immortality; let us for a season retire to a calmer region. By way of introduction to some literary studies, let me ask you first to pause on this question: *What is Literature?*

I. In an age which produces such floods of books, papers, pamphlets, and magazines—in an age in which almost every one reads, in which every railway-carriage is filled with students—the question may seem unnecessary. All reading, however, is not reading of literature. The reading that is done to find out the price of wheat, the rise or fall of stocks, the prizes of the racecourse, the victory of certain electors, or the name of a dear friend in some presentation paragraph, has little or nothing to do with literature. In a loose way, you may term everything that is printed literature; but the name properly belongs to a special product of that kind. That special product is the work of an artist, just as a picture on canvas, or a statue which makes the cold marble speak, is artistic work. The literary artist uses language as the others use colours or stone, to present to us the conception of genius;

for genius, or the genial element, is in a greater or less degree manifested in all true literature. Like any other living natural product, literature is difficult to define. It would be hard to give a perfect definition of a tree; it is pleasanter and more satisfactory to take your child to the wood and show him one. If you have learned to distinguish the true literary product when you meet it, it matters little whether you can define it or not. One can perhaps best do that directly by making the acquaintance of some of our literary kings, Shakespeare, Milton, Wordsworth, getting into sympathy with the author, and waiting patiently till the impression of the literary product is gradually formed in the mind.

Some define literature as the beautiful realized in language. In this sense the beautiful includes the good and the true. Deformity is the result of some imperfection, or want, or disease. The beautiful is 'the true in all its truth, in all its light, and with all its reflections.' It is the complex and most perfect expression of nature. Literature is therefore a truer expression of nature than science, just as the artist's painting is truer, because fuller of nature, than the mere plan of the architect. The common idea that poetry is composed more or less of falsehood is therefore wrong, and it is the highest praise of a poet to say he is true to nature. Literature has been referred to as the expression of superior mind in writing —superior meaning what is removed from the commonplace. The quality which is essential in literature is originality. The mere communication of facts, or the imitation of a style which you have studied, is not literature. As without heat in the animal world, without originality in the literary world, nothing can live. The literary man fuses in his own soul as in a furnace the matter he receives, and when it comes forth it has the glow of his own life-heat. Originality can be seen and known, but is difficult to describe. Carlyle somewhere speaks of original men as those who do not go blindly by formula, but have an eye, and can see into the heart of things, with a fresh natural piercing glance of their own. 'When the word that will express the thing follows of itself from your clear intense sight of the thing,' what you write is original, creative—in a word, literary.

In another aspect, we might say that literature is pre-eminently human. It is the revelation of man to man. Its special branch of knowledge is human nature and human life. Hence it is so generally interesting. Hence it is a power of such widespread influence. The word genius is related to genial. Pure literature at once impresses the mind as easy and pleasing; and men call the man a genius who brings them good new thoughts so easily. Not every one can present truth as he does, so that its perception is pleasant. The thoughts of the literary man come home to the heart, and we have pleasure from their beauty as well as from their truth. M. Taine says: 'They are instructive, because they are beautiful'—as if the complete truth could not be communicated except under the forms of beauty. The most gifted minds have the power of producing the most quickening and most beautiful thoughts; and because they are attractive, they are universally instructive. Thus, by the arrangement of the all-wise Creator, beauty and truth, pleasure and usefulness, are made inseparable in the thoughts that most widely influence mankind.

Again, literature is eminently the expression of sentiment. Thus it gives a sense of brotherhood to all who read the same language; for the true brotherhood is that of sentiment. A late excellent series of literary works therefore bears the appropriate motto: 'One touch of nature makes the whole world kin.' M. Taine says: 'The more a work makes sentiment visible, the more it is literary; for the proper business of literature is to note sentiments. The more a book notes important sentiments, the higher is its place in literature; for it is in representing the mode of being of a whole nation and of a whole age that a writer rallies round him the sympathies of the whole age and the whole nation. . . . Therefore,' adds M. Taine, 'of all documents placing before us the sentiments of preceding generations, a literature, and especially a great literature, is incomparably the best. Laws and catechisms only represent the human spirit in gross and without delicacy; we want documents in which politics and dogma are living.' This demand of M. Taine reminds us of that grand old Hebrew literature which we call the Bible—it is not a mere book, but a national literature—from which, indeed, many laws and dogmas have been drawn; but which, we are thankful, is not given us in the form of a creed or a code of laws. 'We want documents in which politics and dogma are living.' We want the transparent language of literature, through which we can clearly discern human sentiment just as it rose, though it rose three thousands years ago. We want this poetic, natural language of the Bible, because the truth we get from it is so human, and touches us nearer than all the definitions of the catechism or the logic of the schools. We want this divine, blessed, saving truth always to wear the human garb which our great Father put upon it!

Lastly. We wind up these remarks on literature by an observation or two on its relation to morals. Charged with sentiments, literature, like a perfume, reveals the internal state of our civilization. Vinet says: 'It seizes only whatever society adopts. It is the echo of life, the expression of society.' It was Milton's opinion that you cannot have the highest literature apart from the purest morality. Contemplating in the far distance the writing of 'Paradise Lost,' he saw and confessed that the first requisite for writing a great and noble poem was the leading of a pure and noble life. And now we know that we could not have had his sublime epic but for the victory which in his life that stern Puritan poet obtained over the sensual and sordid, the unworthy and the false. For the reason just indicated, it is chiefly by the study of literature that (as M. Taine remarks) the moral history of man can be written, and the spiritual laws on which events depend arrived at. Common history is not so candid as literature, and therefore a great poem, a beautiful romance, or the confessions of a superior man, will often be more instructive than the best work of the historian. Hence M. Taine asserts he would 'give a hundred volumes of diplomacy for the memoirs of a Cellini, for the letters of St. Paul, for the table-talk of Luther, or for the comedies of Aristophanes.' 'The scholar,' says Emerson, 'may at some crisis represent a nation;' by a rich literary document one may interpret a whole age; and there is a profound philosophy in the well-known saying of Andrew Fletcher: 'Let me make a nation's songs, who will may make its laws.' It is in the power of literature to create pure, and lofty, and noble sentiments; therefore, it is in your power and mine, by striving to maintain such sentiments in our hearts, to help to create a good literature, and so make the influence of our pure and high sentiments perpetual.

II. We shall see the force of this by a careful consideration of our second question: *What is Culture?*

The word refers us for its meaning to the tilling of the ground. The land has certain properties or capacities, and it is the business of the cultivator to cause the land to act according to its proper nature, and according to the purpose for which it was made. It will bear either weeds or grain, but his business is to see that it bear grain and not weeds. By removing obstructions, by loosening and mixing the soil, he must keep it in natural working order. He has not to make the soil originally, but only to keep it in a condition in which it will fulfil the required end. He cannot himself make grain, the soil only has the property which does that; but he must establish the proper connection between the grain and the soil. Culture is therefore simply bringing out into full action and effect the natural powers, which, by the original gift of the Creator, we all possess. One may, indeed, render a comparatively barren soil fruitful, but he cannot give to any soil the seed-bearing property. Carlyle tells the story of the stern old school-master, who, when a new pupil was presented, used to ask, 'But are you sure he is not a dunce?' Culture, as the old educator knew, can confer on the mind no new power which it had not naturally; but it can raise dormant powers into exercise—it can increase their strength—it can remove obstructions. Must the field come into contact with the intelligence of man, in order that it may be properly fruit-bearing? Your mind, in like manner, must come into contact with the intelligence contained in a powerful literature.

It is a question whether, without literature, there could be any culture of the mind. I am, however, far from holding books to be the only means of culture. There is, we all know, much to be learned besides what we get from books. The world rightly suspects the wisdom of the merely bookish man as neither sound nor practical. Shakespeare, the greatest of all literary men, was a student of men and things directly as well as through the medium of the printed page. It is he who speaks of finding 'books in running brooks, sermons in stones, and good in everything.' Even Pope, the greatest literary man of another age, did not depend on reading alone, but, as he says, tried to 'catch the manners living as they rise.' There are other means of culture besides literature. Every man who knows well his trade or business, and can do it, is, so far, a cultured man. His intelligent faculties, his judgment, memory, and imagination, have been to some extent developed and strengthened. There is a culture in the family where becoming manners, good taste, and sincere religion prevail: moral purity, sweetness of temper, all-embracing charity, heavenly faith, are the plants which grow up under *that* blessed culture. And there is a *scientific* culture—the knowledge of the laws of nature—for which some great men are now claiming the highest place.

We all know something of Mr. Huxley's views, and they well deserve to be known and considered. With consummate power, this great, and earnest, and honest thinker puts forward the claims of scientific culture. To him the whole of education is comprehended in 'learning the laws of nature, and training one's self to obey them.' His striking illustration is from a game of chess. In such a game we all engage. While you play, there is opposite you a great unseen player, whose playing is always fair, just, and patient. But you must know the laws of the game, and play well, else you suffer. The unseen player never overlooks a mistake, or makes the slightest allowance for ignorance. Such is the rough education of nature, or of the world; judging merely from facts, ignorance is treated like wilful disobedience, incapacity is punished like a crime. 'It is not even "a word and a blow,"' says Huxley, 'but the blow first without the word.' While we all know, and know to our cost, that here Mr. Huxley is right, yet we think we have good reasons for objecting to an absolute predominance of the scientific spirit. But we thank Mr. Huxley for pointing out to us so forcibly the necessity for studying the laws of nature, and learning to obey them. Some men who neglect or carelessly violate the laws of health may continue to see in sickness only a special interposition of Providence; but the world is fast moving out of that state of ignorant wickedness and blind superstition. Farmers on the ancient system, who lay the blame of their bad crops on Providence, are becoming extinct. Business men not up to the mark, who think their failures are caused by want of luck, are now rarer than they used to be. Thanks to such men as Huxley, who have taught us to look rationally at the world. But we are not yet prepared to allow even Mr. Huxley to rob us of a higher education than what is to be obtained in playing a game for the highest stakes. However, let us hear Mr. Huxley's famous description of an educated man.

He says: 'That man, I think, has a liberal education who has been so trained in youth that his body is the ready servant of his will, and does with ease and pleasure all the work that, as a mechanism, it is capable of; whose intellect is a clear, cold, logic engine, with all its parts of equal strength, and in smooth working order; ready like a steam engine to be turned to any kind of work, and spin the gossamers as well as forge the anchors of the mind; whose mind is stored with a knowledge of the great fundamental truths of nature, and of the laws of her operations; one who, no stunted ascetic, is full of life and fire, but whose passions are trained to come to heel by a vigorous will, the servant of a tender conscience; who has learned to love all beauty, whether of nature or art, to hate all vileness, and to respect others as himself.'

From this fine picture of an educated man it is evident Mr. Huxley includes under 'learning the laws of nature,' learning obedience to the moral laws of our constitution. With all his scientific study, man is not educated unless 'his will is the servant of a tender conscience,' nor unless he has learned 'to respect others as himself.' Now, we submit, this is a part of education which the study of the laws of nature cannot give. Huxley's picture, therefore, is defective—his theory of education is faulty in one respect. To the end which he proposes he does not furnish adequate means. Learning the rules of the game—learning to be a good player in the game of life— has *this* a tendency to make a man 'respect others as himself,' or to produce a 'tender conscience'? Does not everyone know that the tendency of the struggle of life is to make men intensely selfish? With only the prize in view, in the excitement produced by the prospect of winning, *do* men learn to 'respect others as themselves'? *Do* they cultivate a tender conscience thus? Mr. Huxley is too great and too noble a man to be content with a liberal education which does not include moral training; but on his own showing he has no means of giving this. If what we know of the great unseen Opposite is to be wholly learned from nature, we must find but little moral impulse in our knowledge. To judge simply from what we experience in daily life, Providence does not always sanction the highest morality. Success and happiness do not always follow it. And if I as a player imitate the character of my unseen Opponent as displayed in His doings, am I not likely to swerve from the highest morality as impracticable, and to care mainly about outward success? It is plain, that in order to arrive at the education described by Huxley, there is required a higher knowledge of God than Huxley proposes to give. We must know Him as a Being of absolutely perfect moral excellence. We must know something more than these fixed natural laws, which encompass us externally and rule us within. We must know something more than some indefinite force or power that works behind these laws. Yes; we must know that old doctrine of his Fatherhood—perfect righteousness and infinite mercy, unspeakable grace and truth. In a word, we think that Huxley's ideal of an educated man cannot be realized without the knowledge of the Father as He is revealed in Jesus Christ. Without this, who has a 'vigorous will—the servant of a tender conscience'? Let Mr. Huxley tell us who, without this, 'loves all beauty, hates all vileness, and respects others as himself'? If Mr. Huxley himself does it without belief in Christianity, that is because he lives on a heritage from the past, because his mother was a Christian, because he has breathed from childhood a Christian atmosphere, and because a Christian element, often unnoticed, permeates like an odour every page of all our best literature.

Huxley's theory of culture is defective in its spiritual aspect. It falls in with the tendency of these busy times towards mere outward success. What position does it give to the high heroic souls who have never counted the cost of adherence to a principle of morality or faith? They are failures—'players who played badly, who were ignorant of the rules of the game.' Huxley's theory encourages, not a high ideal, but an average market morality. It produces no sympathy for martyrs and heroes, and those whom men have been taught to esteem the noblest spirits of all time. We think Huxley's view of education too exclusively scientific. We advocate a large literary element as requisite for a perfect education. Literature is more human, and it is certainly more humanizing, than science. It also contains the noblest, and highest, and most spiritual thoughts; therefore, we think it is even *superior* to science as an instrument of culture. This leads to our third question: *What is the value of literary culture?*

III. The value of literary studies is well indicated in the following passage from Hood: 'Infirm health, and a natural love of reading, threw me into the society of poets, philosophers, and sages—to me, good angels and ministers of peace. From these silent instructors, who often do more than fathers, and always more than godfathers, for our temporal interests, from these mild monitors, delightful associates, I learned something of the divine, and more of the human religion. They were my interpreters in the House Beautiful of God, and my guides among the Delectable Mountains. These reformed my prejudices, chastened my passions, tempered my heart, purified my taste, elevated my mind, and directed my aspirations. I was lost in a chaos of undigested problems, false theories, crude fancies, when those bright intelligences called my mental world out of darkness, and gave it two great lights, Hope and Memory—the past for a moon, and the future for a sun.

> ' Hence have I genial seasons, hence have I
> Smooth passions, smooth discourse, and joyous thoughts ;
> And thus from day to day my little boat
> Rocks in its harbour-lodging peaceably.
> Blessings be with them and eternal praise,
> Who gave us nobler loves and nobler cares,
> The poets who on earth have made us heirs
> Of truth and pure delight by heavenly lays.
> Oh ! might my name be numbered among theirs,
> How gladly would I end my mortal days.'*

In a speech made by Lord Derby, at Liverpool, some time ago, I find some useful remarks on this subject, and as they come from a 'man of affairs,' and a statesman rather than a literary man or a poet, they are likely to be more heeded. Referring to the effect of a 'profession or business in which the mind is necessarily for the most part conversant with the means by which money may be made—legitimately and honourably made, of course—but still where the prize set before you is pecuniary gain,' Lord Derby said : ' I think a man so circumstanced, unless he is one of a thousand, will be a little apt to look at most things in their material aspect, which is not always their most real aspect ; that those three

* Wordsworth.

most familiar letters, "£ s. d.," will get rather too deeply impressed on his brain; that he will be inclined to let his thoughts run too much on interests and too little on ideas; and for that very natural and excusable bias, he may find a corrective either in the speculations of great thinkers, in the historical documents which bring home to him how microscopically small are his own concerns in comparison with those of the world in general, or, better still, in the records of those eminent men, of whatever country and age, by whom health, and comfort, and life itself were accounted as nothing when public duty, or private honour, or even love of fame, drew them in an opposite direction. . . . Put it at lowest,' said Lord Derby; 'a man who has the habit of reading, to whom books are the best company, finds in them a distraction from anxiety, a comfort in petty troubles, a protection against weariness and ennui, a society which he can take up when he will, and leave without giving offence, and above all, an escape from the vulgar interests and mean details of private life, into the healthier air of thoughts and ideas which concern mankind in general. We could not, if we were foolish enough to wish it, remain absolutely and exclusively absorbed in our affairs; but we have the choice in our power, whether we will participate, if only as lookers on, in the great intellectual movements which influence our race, or whether the interest in that which is external to ourselves shall be confined to the petty gossip of the parish or town where we live.'

We do not think that more needful words than these of Lord Derby could be spoken in the present age—an age in which we worship wealth, as men have done in all ages, but as competent witness testifies, never before in the world's history with such unanimity and strength and consistency of devotion as at this time in this land. A taste for literature would save many a heart from that stony desolation caused by continual mammon-worship, often making the wealthy pitiable in comparison with the poor. 'Consider,' says Mr. Arnold, ' consider these people, their way of life, their habits, their manners, the very tones of their voice. Look at them attentively, observe the literature they read (if any), the things that give them pleasure, the words that come forth from their mouths, the thoughts that make the furniture of their minds :—would any amount of wealth be worth having with the condition that one was to become like these people by having it?'

In these days, as of old, there are multitudes of Pharisees within and Sadducees without the Church, who deny that man's inward and spiritual condition transcends in value all his outward goods—deny this so absolutely, that even did the Divine Preacher come among us and again announce His doctrine in person, it would be rejected as before. Yet, surely it is not desirable that the cultivation of the human faculties should be strictly confined to what is needful for money-making. But where is man's inner life, and what is the amount of its growth, if his ideas never rise above his trade, and if he can find no easy resource of pleasure but sensual indulgence? if his highest aims are those of mere mechanical improvement and material civilization? if, while the means of living 'are chased with unparalleled energy,' the ideas of beauty, of harmony, and of completely rounded human excellence have faded from the minds of men?

In an age 'when the jingling of the guinea heals the hurt that honour feels,' and when everything is valued by its use, it may be needful to speak of *the use* of literature too. Some would not stoop to do that. Carlyle scornfully tells you he does not value the sun by the quantity of gas-light it saves him; and somewhat fiercely he announces that literature 'shall be invaluable or of no value.' But, surely it will be admitted that a good book is one of the lights of the world shining on the affairs and nature of man eternally as the stars; and if men can value a star for no other reason, they may value it for keeping them out of the ditches. Among the articles of value prized by practical men, is not 'distinction' a somewhat notable one? Are not nations 'distinguished' by superior literary productions? What distinction have Greece and Rome superior to that of their splendid feats of war and legislation? Is it not the deathless pages which their famous authors have left? Carlyle proposes the question : 'Will you give up your Indian Empire or your Shakespeare, you English?' He says it were a grave question, and that we should be forced to answer, 'Indian Empire or no Indian Empire—we cannot do without Shakespeare!'

Yes! men who would have scorned the company of Shakespeare had they lived in his time, are now proud of their nation because his name gives it a high distinction. Truly, the way in which a nation acquires such distinctions is not of the noblest. Why should you, O nations! always treat your literary kings as the accidents and waifs of society while they are with you, and then, when they are dead—perhaps of starvation—struggle for the honour of their tombs, and grasp through mere vulgar greed the distinction which their genius confers? Could not something be done to produce a state of society in which such men would not be accidents and waifs? Where, in this country, for example, is the literary atmosphere in which such men, if they rose among us, could find a congenial home? Where are there any attempts to create such a social condition? A plan for such reform is not to be found in the programme of candidates for election, or of our rising politicians.

Yet we seriously believe in the cultivation of a taste for pure literature as one of the best means to be used for the nation's true advancement and reform. Literature is that easy and agreeable channel by which gifted minds communicate with those less nobly endowed. And even as an army moves forward at the word of its general, a nation will sometimes advance at the word of its gifted man. Thus, by means of literature, the noble impulses of a few minds may swiftly animate all; and on the faithfulness of great minds to this their awful function, the true progress and happiness of the race chiefly depend.

We talk of British freedom, freedom of the press, our exceptional privileges as a nation—why do we not use them?

Why do we let all those grand old authors—kings of thought—lie slumbering on our shelves? What is liberty but scope for our growth in all that is good, for enlargement of energy, intellect, sentiment, virtue? And what is the use of this constant boasting that we have scope for our growth, if we never grow? What is the use of liberty of the press, if we never enter into the thoughts and sentiments to which there is such free access? If education be, as the old Greek master affirmed, 'learning to like and to dislike the right things,' we have need of literature to help us to that. Are the things we most like always worthy of our liking? Are the things we dislike always deserving of dislike? Have we overcome prejudice? With our 'glorious constitution,' and with all our educational institutions, we are yet far from that higher education which was understood by the old Greek. By the discipline of life, of 'losses and crosses,' by much earnest painstaking and self government, and much fellowship with high intellects and truth-loving souls, a few have been led in these last days to some dim idea of it. It is not the idea of those who seek education simply as a means of making a living. It is not the idea of the poor workman, who gets his son taught to read and write and cast accounts, that he may earn more with ease than his father could earn with difficulty. We must try to think of our education as something higher than that. It is a poor and shallow soul that can be satisfied with simply winning what are termed the comforts and luxuries of life. The immortal spirit may have wide connections, and when it awakes to fuller consciousness and knows itself the heir of all things, it will not stoop to be the body's drudge, or a mere professional machine. It glories in expansive sympathies, it longs for fuller disfranchisement, it sets up and contemplates a higher and an unselfish ideal; it therefore gives itself freely and often to *books*, to hold delightful fellowship with mighty and exalted minds,

> 'The dead but sceptred sovereigns who still rule
> Our spirits from their urns.'

If you would be among those who possess a higher than mere mercenary culture, you must allow the great actions of the past to strike and thrill your spirit; the life of the high thoughts of dead men must vibrate within you; and the beautiful creations of the gifted of all ages must rise on your inward sight as the fresh bright world rose at the Creator's fiat through the drowsy blankness of Chaos. Thus all the beauty and strength that slumber within you may be drawn into exercise as spiritual gifts; and while in this way *some* arrive at the bright possession of culture, to *others* there may be even a higher reward—not only the appreciating soul, but the 'cunning hand to make that which is seen in the mount.' Yes! Thrilled and illuminated by gazing on the great pictures of the masters, you may receive power to say with rapture, ' I, too, am a painter!'

Some may think I have spoken dangerous words in the ears of young enthusiasts; let such listen to a few wise sentences from Principal Shairp. 'Not even the most ethereal being,' he remarks, 'can live wholly upon sunbeams, and most lives are far enough removed from sunbeams. Yet sunshine, light, is necessary for every man, and though most are immersed in business and battling all life through with tough conditions, yet if we are not to sink into mere selfish animality we must needs have some master light to guide us, something that may dwell upon the heart, though it be not named upon the tongue. For if there be sometimes a danger lest the young enthusiast, through too great devotion to an abstract ideal, should essay the impossible and break himself against the walls of destiny that hem him in, far more common is it for men to be so crushed under manhood's burdens, that they abandon all the high aims of their youth, and submit to be driven like gin-horses,

"Round the daily scene
Of sad subjection and of sick routine." '

It is possible, therefore, that our wise practical people may fear poetry too much. They have a good deal to say about their preference for 'plain facts and sober realities,' while hinting they are too severely busy in physical and mental labours to have any relish for 'ideal dreams.' But before we hastily dismiss the ideal, it is to be considered whether it is possible, without some ideal, rightly to attend to the real. Without something beyond the real, some 'master light' in the soul, men will flag in the commonest tasks. Certainly men may carry their practical wisdom too far, and pride themselves on their 'plain common sense' too exclusively. What you consider an act of practical reason may be caused by the want of a higher understanding. After all, what is poetry but (as one says) 'the most lively comprehension of things, their most intimate as well as their highest truth?' We do not need to justify God for making His works so beautiful, neither do we need to justify the human soul for admiring that beauty which He has made, or for expressing its admiration in the flowing and musical words which feeling or emotion naturally adopts. Poetry is not beauty, but our feeling of beauty expressed in such a vivid manner, that the expression has the power of producing a similar feeling in the mind of the reader or hearer. It is to be hoped that in our days only children make the mistake of fancying that the thing essential to poetry is that jingling of like sounds called rhyme. The chief value of poetry is quite independent of this. The thought, the sentiment, is the chief thing, yet we do not make of no account the *form* in which the thought or sentiment is put. There is also some power in the form. True, form endures only on a solid substance, but a powerful thought is made still more powerful by an appropriate form of expression.

I do not deny that literature has its dangers to the young: it may excite false hopes, it may stir unworthy passions. Those who descend into the mine to find gems will find some soilure. Genius sometimes lends its charms to what is evil. Of this we have due notice, and this we shall disregard at our peril. You can always know, if you are faithful to yourself, *what* it is you are seeking in the book which you love—

whether it is higher thought, more light, or—something else which you dare not name. I should say, as a rule, the higher the genius of the writer, the less the danger to your morality. Shakespeare is too great a man to sneer at religion or undermine morality, as Byron does. We should constantly remember that life is short—'art is long, and time is fleeting,'—and since none of us can give to all the first-class authors sufficient attention, there is no reason for wasting time with meaner lights. While despising prudery, you will not forget to cultivate a healthy and vigorous morality. Not even for the sake of genius will we forget our manhood or our womanhood, by which we are 'conscious of the utter worthlessness of all outward distinctions compared with what is treasured up in the soul.' Let your intellectual love be something great and noble, and you will disdain to feed on what one has well termed these modern 'garbage fields of vulgar and brutal fiction.'

It is said to be the fault of literary culture that it tends to make men exclusive and unsympathetic, fastidious, and easily repelled by the common herd. This must be in some measure the case with those who make their own highest improvement their chief end, and to whom religion and virtue are only branches of culture. The virtuous love virtue on its own account, and religion admits of no higher aim than itself. Any theory of culture that refuses to give to religion and to virtue this position, must be evil. But, religion being allowed its proper place, the egotism and self-consciousness of culture are kept in check; and certainly there is no better sign of true spiritual progress than your ability to forget yourself in One higher, to merge all mere self-interest in the cause of God. In that case, acquaintance with books only increases your admiration of *The Book;* and you find the image of Christ, beheld with ever increasing beauty, power, and blessing in the pages of the Four Gospels, to be incomparably superior to all other instruments of literary culture.

CHAUCER.

THE mighty stream of English literature has been flowing for five hundred years, growing broader from age to age. We go to the source of this great river; we observe the first living water gushing from the bosom of the earth; we call it CHAUCER —'pure well of English undefiled.' Of all the travellers who cross the river by bridges, or walk by the margin of its deep, quiet water, beholding its forest of masts and its little barques shooting to and fro, few ever care to think of its source. Yet it might prove something exhilarating, or even romantic, to go in search of it. Should you find less splendour and luxury amid those bleak, barren hills where the water rises, there at least you will be far from the flat commonplace, and your heart may be stirred by the austere simplicity of nature.

That fourteenth century of which Chaucer lived his sixty or seventy years has many attractions for the student of the present day. Ere its close the three races—Britons, Saxons, Normans —were thoroughly blended in one—the English which we see. Wat Tyler's rebellion may be considered the last protest of the vanquished Saxons against their Norman lords. It was in the fourteenth century the House of Commons rose to power, and in it the three races long hostile rejoiced to recognise the palladium and representative of English union and English liberty. Then were those heroic days whose memory has so often evoked the martial spirit of England—of Crécy and Poitiers, battles of the Black Prince, 'that young Mars of men.' Then was felt by the nations the breath of spring after the dark, dead winter of centuries; a more than ordinary 'zephyr' seemed to blow

> 'Her clarion o'er the dreaming earth, and fill
> With living hues and odours plain and hill.'

Dante had sung in Italy; a literary revival was beginning to be felt thoughout Europe; Wycliffe awoke the Church; and then appeared

> 'The morning-star of song, who made
> His music heard below.
> Dan Chaucer, the first warbler whose sweet breath
> Preluded those melodious bursts that fill
> The spacious times of great Elizabeth
> With sounds that echo still.'

It is fitly said that Chaucer's song 'preluded' that of SHAKESPEARE; for, after Chaucer none like him, or only one, his equal came, till the lord and king of all poets of all times made England, by his advent, a glorious land.

The greatest man between Chaucer and Shakespeare is Spenser, who is well named 'the Poets' Poet,' but never has been and never will be the poet of the people. There are but few poets who have written well for all classes, and Spenser is not one of them. With all its wonders of imagination, his famous allegory, the 'Faërie Queene,' has never been found very readable by the ordinary mind with the ordinary education. You may, indeed, use Spenser's poem as a test to discover whether a true poetic vein be imbedded in your nature; for it requires some natural possession of this sort, as well as considerable culture, to enable one to enjoy the 'Faërie Queene.' Now I set Chaucer and Shakespeare—I might add Burns and Byron—in contrast to this kind of writing. These writers dwell more in the region of the real as it is generally apprehended—they are more obvious—they wear the air of everyday life. You can get at their meaning without analyzing their sentences, or without reading them twice. You have not to pay for the beauty you behold in them by mental fatigue or headache.

To some it may sound strange to hear Chaucer named as

one of the most readable of poets. Perhaps it would be more strictly correct to say he *was* one of the most readable. To our modern eyes his page, when first seen, presents, it is true, a rather uncouth and forbidding appearance. The spelling and pronunciation of words have altered since his day, and many words used by him are now no longer in use. Five hundred years bring about changes: how many new fashions in your bonnets, ladies, have come and gone during that portion of time? It is, I believe, Pope who says:

> 'In words, as fashions, the same rule will hold,
> Alike fantastic if too new, or old.'

Yet the young ladies who wore farthingales and bonnets like coal-boxes were, after all, young ladies in their time. Notwithstanding what you call their old-fashioned, stiff-looking, formal dress, they were no mummies. They had human hearts and tender souls. They could sing, and preserve dignity, and even, I suppose, flirt a little, as in modern times. Would you be surprised to discover that one of these old-fashioned 'bonnets' was passionately, deeply, even desperately in love? And, notwithstanding his ancient dress, with a little trouble you may touch the living heart, eternally fresh and young, which beats under Chaucer's peculiar apparel. Through all the strangeness of his verbiage you can clearly see that he 'writes all like a man'—like an able and experienced, a shrewd and humorous, a noble and liberal-minded man. Do not let your imagination deprive you of his acquaintance by exaggerating the difficulties of his language. The ear finds something peculiarly sweet in infant lispings; and it is both pleasant and instructive to observe the first imperfect modes of our dear mother-tongue.

Since the Norman invasion the literary men of England, such as they were, had generally written in French, the language of the court, of the nobility, of the schools, of good society in general. But at the time when the Black Prince was conquering Frenchmen at Crécy, the Saxons at home were gaining over them a victory of another kind and of more importance. The

Saxon tongue then drove the French language out of England. As we have to thank the Black Prince for the one victory, we have, perhaps as much, to thank Chaucer for the other. At a time when it was more fashionable to write in French, he resolved to write in the language of the common people; he stamped the English language as established among the languages of the civilized world by writing in it his works of genius.

Here are his own bold words (bold in their age) prefixed to one of those works: 'Let, then, clerks endite in Latin, for they have the property and the knowing in that faculty; and let Frenchmen in their French also endite their quaint terms, for it is kindly to their mouths; and let *us* show our fantasies in such words as we learned of our dames' tongue.'

But, as one would expect from the circumstances of the time, Chaucer's English is a good deal sprinkled with French words, and requires a good deal of French pronunciation. The circles in which Chaucer moved were accustomed to the alternate use of the two languages; nor is it a misfortune for the English, but an advantage, that it has thus become possessed of a large stock of French words. The silent *e* in such words as *fate, write, love,* was generally sounded in Chaucer's time, so that in reading him to preserve the metre you must pronounce *fatë, writë, lovë.* Also a great many words which now have no final *e* had it in the days of our poet. The knowledge of a few facts of this kind, and a few rules of Saxon grammar, will enable any one to read him easily and with pleasure in an evening or two. Burns's poems are quite as hard to the Englishman who has never heard Scotch. And it is wonderful how many lines of Chaucer read like good modern English at the present day, as our quotations, by-and-by, will show.

Meantime, let us try to make the poet's personal acquaintance. A rhymed photograph, by Robert Greene, may help us to form some conception of Chaucer.

' His stature was not very tall;
Lean he was, his legs were small,

> Hosed within a stock of red,
> A buttoned bonnet on his head,
> From under which did hang, I ween,
> Silver hair both bright and sheen.
> His beard was white, trimmèd round,
> His countenance blithe and merry found;
> A sleeveless jacket, large and wide,
> With many plaits, and skirtes-side
> Of water camlet he did wear,
> A whittle by his belt he bare,
> His shoes were cornèd broad before,
> His ink-horn at his side he wore,
> And in his hand he bore a book—
> Thus did this ancient poet look.'

Chaucer's father, it is now believed, was a London vintner, from whom young Geoffrey had, for the times, a good education at school, and probably also at college (Cambridge). His writings manifest acquaintance with astrology, divinity, philosophy, logic, and other scholastic learning of the time. But, though always a student of books, Chaucer was to a much greater extent a student of men and things. And for such study he had good opportunity, having been successively a page at court, a valet of the King's household, soldier abroad, knight of the shire, and ambassador. He shared the experiences of Edward III.'s conquering army, and appears to have borne arms for twenty-seven years. In the vicissitudes of war he once suffered imprisonment. He married a knight's daughter, and had the greatest lord in England, John of Gaunt, for brother-in-law, protector, and friend. He was long Comptroller of the Customs in London, and thus mixed with all sorts of affairs and all classes of men. The greatest military genius of the age (the Black Prince) and the greatest literary genius of the age (Chaucer) were personal friends, and appreciated each other's character. All this, however, did not save the poet from poverty, or from exile, which in his old age he suffered in Zealand. In the State papers there are still to be seen records of the salaries and pensions which he received, and of the allowance of wine with which he was served—not for his poetry, however; he was no laureate like Tennyson—but for good, steady, sober work done in his office—for writing in ledgers done with his own hand. Is he anything less a poet in your eyes for this? If you think that prolonged and close application to business is inconsistent with the flights of genius, you may find, on making due inquiry, that your theory will not apply to any of the great or first-class poets. Milton, as Cromwell's Latin secretary, did daily an amount of plain matter-of-fact work which would astonish some whose idea of a poet seems to be that of one who needs to be held down by weights lest he should 'leave dull earth behind him.' Shakespeare, while he was writing 'Macbeth,' could look after his debts in a very successful and business-like way. A first-class poet will be found on examination to be a man who could succeed and excel in any business or calling which he might undertake. So much for the popular, thoughtless notion, that men who can make poetry are good for nothing else.

So far was Chaucer from being considered unpractical or lacking in plain, saving common-sense, he was elected knight of the shire, and thus represented Kent in the House of Commons, which was just then taking shape as a national institution, its members receiving payment for attendance at the rate of four pounds sterling per day. For, in addition to his other studies, Chaucer had pursued that of law, in the Inner Temple, where there is a record showing that on one occasion he was fined two shillings—for what? For 'no good,' you may be sure; yet the act is none the less interesting because it is ill—for beating a friar, with whom he quarrelled somewhere about those venerable courts. Alas, the poor friars! it is long since they began to be drubbed, and Chaucer gave them worse than physical flagellation, as we shall see.

By a change of Government the poet was dismissed from his offices, and lost his salary at the age of fifty-seven; and as he had not then saved money, he was for some time very poor. But he was now liberated for a task which he liked better than money-making. It was when old and poor, like Milton, that he began to compose his greatest work, the fruit of his ripe experience and ripe genius—in point of time the first undoubtedly great work of an English author, and still in its way unsurpassed—the 'Canterbury Tales.' Though fortune afterwards smiled on him, and by royal favour he died in possession of a large pension, it was nevertheless the lot of that masterpiece, as of so many others since, to grow to maturity in the sharp air of poverty and an outcast condition. Let us note this, and also the kindly genial spirit of the book, and remember how independent of external circumstances a great soul always is. He died within hearing of the bells of St. Paul's, and, the beginning of a glorious galaxy of genius, was buried in Westminster Abbey, in the first year of the fifteenth century, when his contemporary, the tedious old poet Gower, had grown blind with age.

Two events in Chaucer's life deserve particular notice in connection with his writings. One was his visit to Italy. Sent by the king on an embassy to Genoa, he visited Florence and various other Italian towns, particularly Padua. Italy was then the seat of the Muses in a sense which it would be extravagance to apply to England. The celebrated Petrarch had a short time before been crowned poet laureate at Rome. Dante's immortal poem was enjoying the full fervour of a nation's worship, and a true literary spirit strongly pervaded Italian society. Long afterwards, Milton's visit to Italy produced important consequences on *his* character as a poet; but Chaucer's visit to that wondrous land was even more important. His works, in fact, show two divisions: *one* composed of tedious allegories and tales of chivalry, full of frigid conceits—under the French influence; *the other* division, totally different, rich and strong, real and natural, formed under the influence of Italy. Chaucer seems to have had the good fortune to meet Petrarch in Padua, and to learn from him the substance of one of his tenderest and most pathetic tales—the story of Griselda, which is told by the Clerk (or scholar) among the Canterbury pilgrims. The language used by this personage in introducing the tale is supposed to contain a reminiscence of Chaucer's own visit to Italy:

> 'I wol you tell a talë, which that I
> Learned at Padua of a worthy clerk,
> As provëd by his wordës and his work—
> He now is dead and nailed in his cheste—
> I pray to God so give his soulë reste—
> Francis Petrarch, the laureate poete,
> Hight this clerk, whose rhetoric swete
> Enlumined all Itaille of poetry.'

The importance of Chaucer's visit to Italy in relation to his writings is equalled, or surpassed, by one other event in his chequered career. The glorious Ayrshire ploughman, though a born poet, though gifted at birth with fire and faculty divine, tells us he would have lived and died undistinguished, but for *an occasion* which revealed to himself and others the treasure contained in his breast. We shall let Burns tell his own story, for it is essentially Chaucer's story, and the story of most, if not all, writers of genius. Burns says that in his early youth he felt an impulse, an internal prompting, towards some indefinite literary product:

> ' Even then a wish (I mind its power)
> A wish that to my latest hour
>   Shall strongly heave my breast,
> That I for poor auld Scotland's sake
> Some usefu' plan or buik could make,
>   Or sing a sang at least.'

Years after he was first conscious of this obscure inward intimation, a certain event made its meaning clear. He continues:

> 'But still the elements of sang
> In formless jumble, right and wrang,
>   Wild floated in my brain,
> *Till on that hairst I said before*
> *My partner in the merry core*
>   *She roused the forming strain :*
> I see thee yet, the soucie quean,
>   That lighted up my jingle,
> Her witching smile, her pauky e'en
>   That gart my heartstrings tingle.'

The event which Burns here points to as determining his literary career, is similar to that by which a large section of Chaucer's poetry must be explained; but, unfortunately, Chaucer's passion was not radiant with mirth and gladness as the Ayrshire poet's was. Chaucer's literary life began 'with bitterly disappointed love, and its pangs shot through him for many a year before he could write the merry lines which laugh with gladness still.' In one of those earlier poems he tells us 'he has been ill for eight years, and yet his cure is no nearer, for there is but one physician who can heal him. But that is done. Pass on. What will not be must needs be left.' In another poem—the 'Complaint to Pity,' apparently written when his rejection was yet fresh—he pours out 'the passionate, sad pleadings of his early love.' 'He tells us that when, after the lapse of certain years, during which he had sought to speak to his love, at last, even before he could speak, he saw all pity for him dead in her heart; and down he fell, dead as a stone while the swoon lasted. Then he arose, and to her in all her beauty he still prayed for mercy and for love.'

> 'Have mercy on me, thou heaven's queen,
> Who has sought you so tenderly and yore,
> Let some stream of your life on me be seen,
> That love and dread you ever longer more!
> For Goddes love have mercy on my pain,—
> My pain is this, that what I do desire
> That have I not, ne nothing like thereto,
> And ever setteth desire mine heart on fire;
> Also on every side, where'er I go,
> I find still ready, unsought, everywhere,
> Things that remind me, and increase my woe :—
> Me lacketh but my death, and then my bier.'

One who wishes fully to appreciate Chaucer's ripest and richest writing, should first learn his experiences as expressed in the poems which precede his last great work, the 'Canterbury Tales.' The poetry is the man always, when it is poetry of the first order, and, therefore, to do Chaucer justice, we should read him in chronological order. We should 'start with him in his sorrow, walk with him through it into the fresh sunshine of his later life [when his love was revived after a reconciliation] and then down to the chill and poverty of his old age.'*

It is chiefly on account of his 'Canterbury Tales' that Chaucer has been styled the 'poet of character and manners.' Only Shakespeare has surpassed him, if even he has surpassed him, in this kind of work. It appears to have been Chaucer's design to give the world, ere he left it, a full and faithful picture of human life as he had seen it with his own eyes. In doing this he did not write a drama, as Shakespeare afterwards did; for in Chaucer's time the English drama was unknown. But though he did not give to his great work the exact form of a play, it is truly dramatic in spirit.

> 'All the world's a stage, and all the men and women
> Only players,'

said Shakespeare; and by that rule he did his work of instruction and delight for the human race. Chaucer's idea was slightly, but not substantially, different. 'All the world is a pilgrimage,' said he, adopting a Scriptural idea. So he sat down to compose the 'Canterbury Tales.' 'Mere pictures of life,' you cry, 'what can they teach us? We want to know its end.' Yet we are mistaken if we fancy the purpose of these great minds in projecting their masterpieces was one of mere amusement. The idea under which they worked seems to have been, that they who best comprehend the character of life are nearest the knowledge of its end.

Such a company of pilgrims as Chaucer had often seen travelling to the shrine of Thomas à Becket in Canterbury, he somewhat modifies in his representation, and makes the account which he gives of it the vehicle of his wit and wisdom. There are, in the interesting company described by Chaucer, twenty-nine persons of different sexes and of all ranks of society. The Prologue to the Tales contains a life-like picture of each, such as only a consummate artist could make; the Tales themselves are told during the journey by each person in turn for the amusement of the rest, and the shortening of the way. The

* Furnivall.

pilgrims all met at the since world-famous inn, the Tabard, in Southwark, London, from which they were to travel to Canterbury to get the blessing of St. Thomas : and Chaucer himself is one of the company. It was not considered inconsistent with the religious purpose of the journey to have plenty of mirth and laughter by the way. One of the pilgrims, the Miller, has brought his bagpipes with him. And if anyone thinks such music and the singing which accompanied it unbecoming the errand of the pilgrims, here is a justification thereof in the very words of an Archbishop of those days. Archbishop Arundel says, ' When one of them that goeth barefoot striketh his toe upon a stone and maketh it bleed, it is well done that he or his fellow begin then a song, or else take out of his bosom a bagpipe for to drive away with such mirth the hurt of his fellow.' The jolly Host of the Tabard, who proposes to guide and rule the company as to the story-telling and its results, views this matter of mirth-making in a light not less liberal than that in which it is seen by the Archbishop. In his good-humoured address to the pilgrims, he says :

> ' Ye gon to Canterbury, God you speed,—
> The blissful martyr quite you your meed !
> And well I wot as ye gon by the way
> Ye shapen you to talken and to play ;
> For truëly comfòrt, ne mirth is none
> To riden by the way domb as a stone.'

This Host, who appears throughout the book at the end of every story, making gay or shrewd remarks, and arranging who shall speak next, is one of the best characters Chaucer has drawn ; most genial and humorous is he ; and he is understood to be the original of Shakespeare's famous Host of the Garter in the ' Merry Wives.'

But the drawing in the other characters is equally felicitous. Take one or two examples. The spirit of chivalry illustrated in so many old romances that ring with tilt and tournament, battles with giants and other monsters, encounters with the infidel in Palestine, and cries of fair ladies about to be rescued —the spirit of chivalry, which was finally extinguished amid laughter by the publication of the immortal follies of Don Quixote, obtains an excellent embodiment in Chaucer's Knight. This worthy man represents the upper class of society in the fourteenth century; and though we join with Cervantes in his laugh at knight-errantry, we may well believe that for these modern days something not so good has come in its stead. There is this meaningless infatuation of wealth-hunting which is worse than the quest of the Holy Grail, for it brutalizes and degrades, while knight-errantry developed some of the noblest traits of human nature—both pursuits as to their object being equally shadowy. The kingdom which Don Quixote expected, and the governorship of the island which Sancho hoped for, were not more unreal than the blessing which modern infatuated gentlemen are seeking in the enormous accumulation of money. We can hardly afford to despise that old age of chivalry to which modern society mainly owes its regulative code of politeness, which, it is feared, may soon be the only morality extant.

Chaucer's Knight is one who, 'from the time at which he first began to riden out loved chivalry, honour and truth, freedom and courtesy.' He had been in fifteen mortal battles, had fought in lists thrice and always slain his foe. Though no man had ridden farther than he, and though he was most worthy, he was wise and modest.

> 'And of his port as meek as is a maid,
> He never yet no villainy ne said
> In all his life unto no maner wight—
> He was a very perfect gentle knight.'

The Knight's tale is certainly one of the best, if not the best, in the collection. It is concerning two young knights who were taken prisoners in battle, and who, while in prison, both fell in love with the daughter of their conqueror, whom they saw every morning through their prison-bars tending her garden. They managed both to escape from prison, to engage in a duel, and afterwards a battle, about the lady. One of the knights (Arcite) is wounded, but is gratified by marrying Emilia on his deathbed, bequeathing her immediately after to Palamon, the friend whom love had turned to foe. HALLAM, who in general gives Chaucer faint praise, accusing him of want of 'grandeur both in conception and in language,' admits that 'the Knight's Tale is abundantly sufficient to immortalize Chaucer, since it would be difficult to find anywhere a story better conducted or told with more animation and strength of fancy.' This is great praise from Hallam, who is not easily pleased, and seems to have had an unaccountable dislike to Chaucer, as is evidenced by the absurdly insignificant space allotted to him in that otherwise noble work, the 'History of European Literature.'

Chaucer's Knight has a Squire who attends on him. This young man is, of course, a lover, and a lusty bachelor who has borne him well in Flanders and in Picardy in hope to stand well in his lady's grace.

> 'Embroidered was he, as it were a mead
> All full of freshest flowers, white and red,
> Singing he was or fluting all the day,
> And he was fresh as is the month of May :
> He couldë songës make, and well endite,
> Just, and eke dance, and well pourtray and write :
> So hot he lovëd, that by nightirtale
> He slep no more than doth the nightingale.'

The picture of the Yeoman who waits on the Squire is equally vivid; and after him the Nun is introduced. She is described with great delicacy, and with some of the quiet, good-humoured, delightful sarcasm for which Chaucer is remarkable. This is still more powerfully exercised upon the Monk, the Friar, the Pardoner, and other clerical personages. It is a curious fact that the literature of all countries is strongly spiced with satire on men of religion. But though abundant examples of this are found in Chaucer's writings, he is not necessarily a Lollard on that account. Probably Chaucer did not consider it inconsistent with membership in the Church in which he was born to show up the human follies of some of its officers. Laughter is most easily excited on a solemn subject, and poets in their treatment of the clergy have shown that they understood this. But where reverence is justly due, Chaucer is by no means wanting in reverence. He can see the faults of religious men, while in his eyes religion itself is none the worse. There is no hateful prejudice or rancour, but the most genial and kindly spirit, in his representations, even when he attacks hypocrisy itself. And if he sometimes delineates a Monk or a Friar, who is not exactly what he ought to be, it must be admitted that he has drawn at least one clerical character of matchless excellence—his Parish Priest. Certainly if this be drawn from life, the Church in Chaucer's day was not so corrupt as it is sometimes described. Chaucer probably knew something of Wiclif, but there is no proof that he had embraced his doctrines. In true dramatic spirit the poet makes his characters express various opinions, but his own is reserved. Who can tell what confession of faith he or Shakespeare would have signed? By imputing to them the sentiments of their characters you might make both either orthodox or heterodox, as you wished. The following passage by this method would prove Chaucer a *foe* to Lollardism. It occurs at the end of one of the tales (where some conversation usually takes place among the Pilgrims), when the Parish Priest has occasion to reprove the Host for profane swearing, and receives a humorous retort from both the Host and the Shipman:

> '" Now, good men," quoth our Host, " hearkneth to me—
> I smell a loller in the wind," quoth he.
> " Wait, and we'll have a predication. . . .
> This loller here [namely, the Priest] will prechen us somewhat."
>
> '" Nay, by my fader soul, that shall he nat!"
> Saidë the Shipman; " here shall he nat preach,
> He shall no Gospel glosen here, nor teach!
> He wouldë sowen some difficultee,
> Or sprinkle cockle in our cleanë corn." '

It may indeed be argued that, inasmuch as to the Parish Priest the highest excellencies of character are given by Chaucer, and as he gives to the Host and Shipman very inferior qualities, the objections made by the latter to the former indicate that the poet was friendly to the Lollards. Otherwise, why should his best character be objected to by inferior characters as a Lollard? Yet the popular feeling against the followers of Wiclif is forcibly presented in the extract just quoted. It is evidently an anti-puritan feeling, anticipating times to come; it expresses dislike of anything tending to disturb settled beliefs, and some suspicion of evil intentions on the part of those who spread the new opinions. They are likened to the 'enemy' who came to the field by night and 'sowed tares' among the wheat. This was one side of the question, which is appropriately taken by the Host and the Shipman—the latter from proverbial superstition, and the former from his business, being keener than others in support of the existing religion. But Chaucer also allows the other side of the question to be seen. He exposes hypocrisy with a purpose as moral and earnest as Wiclif's, but with less despair of human improvement. Like all great natures, he hoped well for his race—the most excellent work of the great God. He had genuine goodwill towards humanity, and a true sense of his own part in it. He could, therefore, enter fully into every character, dealing with all good-humouredly, with the wise tolerance which is obtained by enlarged views of life. One sees in him 'a healthy English sense both of the serious and the ridiculous.' So that his severest satire has no undue austerity, but is always felt to be the product of a shrewd, sound, able man who knows the world and understands true religion. And we think many men in condemning such poets have been strangely blind to the fact that a truly religious spirit may be shown in satirizing the abuses of religion ; and in such cases the poet, even in his gayest mood, may be as truly religious (or loyal to God) as the most serious preacher.

Chaucer's criticism of a class is, like a quintessence, briefly and elegantly embodied in his picture of a single case. His portrait of the Monk enables us to see what he thought of the monks of his time. Their lives were not so austere, their morals were not quite so strict, as the original founders of their orders would have wished.

> 'The rule of Saint Maure and of Saint Beneit [Benedict],
> Because that it was old and somdel strait,'

was largely ignored. One may as well be out of the world as out of the fashion, and fashions had changed since Benedict's day. Therefore,

> 'This ilkë monk let oldë thingës pass,
> And held after the newë world the trace.'

He would not give a straw for the text which condemned his practice of hunting. Chaucer comments on this with sly humour.

> 'And I say his opinion was good !
> What [why] should he study and make himselven wood [mad]?
> His boots were souple, his horse in great estate—
> Now certainly he was a fair prelàte !
> He was not pale as a forepinëd ghost—
> A fat swan loved he best of any roast.'

The Friar gets a longer portrait, for the friars, as a class of Churchmen, were those against whom the most complaints were made. Indeed, it would be difficult to mention any defect of the clerical character which is not glanced at in this powerful picture, which shows that Chaucer could be exquisitely life-like and good-humoured, without losing the keen edge of his satire. The Friar, we are told, knew more than anybody else of 'dalliance and fair language.' He was on the best of terms— 'beloved and familiar'—with all the wealthy farmers and worthy women of the district.

> 'Full sweetly heardë he confessïon,
> And pleasant was his absolutïon;
> He was an easy man to give penànce
> Where he was sure to have a good pittànce.'

For the best proof that a man has properly received the last rites of the Church is the fact that he has left something to a poor Order of friars. If he gave, this friar was well assured that his repentance was genuine:

> 'For many a man so hard is of his heart,
> He may not weep, although him sorë smart;

> Therefore, instead of weeping and of prayers,
> Men must give silver to the poorë frères.'

He did not think it becoming, or for his advancement, to know poor fellows as well as he knew the rich and the inn-keepers :

> 'And still wherever profit should arise
> Courteous he was, and lowly of service.
> There was no man nowhere so virtuous.
> He was the bestë beggar in his House.'

On certain occasions, when he entered the congregation in his official capacity, he could assume great pomp and authority.

> 'Then was he like a maister or a pope . . .
> Somewhat he lisped for his wantoness
> To make his English sweet upon his tongue . . .
> His eyen twinkled in his head aright
> As do the starrës in a frosty night.'

On two other ecclesiastical characters, the Summoner, an officer of the bishop's court, and the Pardoner, a full-blown Tetzel, the poet is still more severe. Of the Summoner, Chaucer says :

> ' He was a gentle harlot and a kind,
> A better fellow shouldë men not find.'

He was far from total abstinence :

> 'He loved to drink strong wine, as red as blood,
> Then would he speak, and cry as he were wood,
> And when that he well drunken had the wine,
> Then wouldë he speak no word but Latÿn :
> A fewë termës had he, two or three,
> Which he had learned out of some decree. . . .

If any one wished more Latin :

> 'Then had he spent all his philosophy—
> Aye *Questio quid juris* would he cry.'

His way of easing a troubled conscience cannot be commended. If he found anywhere a good fellow who had transgressed, for a quart of wine he would relieve him of all fears; he would teach him to have 'none awe'

> ' In such case of the archëdeacon's curse,
> Unless a manës soul were in his purse ;
> For in his purse he should ÿ punished be.
> "Purse is the archëdeacon's hell," quoth he.'

Though Chaucer does not always think it necessary to protest against a wrong sentiment uttered by one of his characters, he puts in a *caveat* here. But there is an irony in his protest which doubles his offence of repeating the Summoner's irreverent words.

> ' But well I wot he lïed right indeed !
> Of cursing *ought* each guilty man him dread !
> For curse will slay, right as assoiling saveth. . . .'

He slyly affirms that the curse has as much power in the one direction as the assoiling in the other—how much that is, is left to the reader to imagine.

The Pardoner is treated with greater freedom—with direct and open censure, as doubtless this class of clerics was more openly condemned by the popular voice.

> ' This Pardoner haddë hair yellow as wax,
> But smooth it hang as doth a strike of flax. . . .
> Such glaring eyën had he as a hare. . . .
> A vernicle had he sewed upon his cap,
> His wallet lay before him in his lap ;
> Bret-full of pardons come from Rome all hot.
> A voice he had as small as any goat. . . .
> He had a cross of laton full of stones,
> And in a glass *he haddë piggës bones*. . . .
> But with these reliquës, whan that he found
> A poorë parson dwelling upon lond,
> Upon a day he gat him more monèy
> Than that the parson got in monthës twey :
> And thus with feigned flattery and japes
> He made the parson and the people his apes.'

We would rather hear of the ' poor Parson.' Let us, therefore, turn from these characters, more or less discreditable to the Church, and look at another also found in it, but, alas ! not frequently in those days, or in these !

The ' poor Parson ' is described as one who was ' rich of holy thought and work.'

> ' He also was a learnèd man, a clerk,
> That Christès gospel truëly would preach,
> His parishens devoutly would he teach.
> Benign he was, and wondrous diligent,
> And in adversity full patïent. . . .

> Full loth were he to cursen for his tithes,
> But rather would he given, out of doubt,
> Unto his poorë parishens about.'

He could be contented with little, but he did not spare himself in visiting his flock :

> 'Wide was his parish, and houses far asunder,
> But he neglected none for rain or thunder. . . .
> Upon his feet, and in his hand a staff—
> This noble example to his sheep he gave,
> That first he wrought and afterward he taught,
> Out of the Gospel he tho wordës caught ;
> And this figùre he added yet thereto,
> That if gold rustë, what should iron do ? . . .
> He was a shepherd, and no mercenarie [hireling].'

He was not overbearing or scornful in his dealing with poor sinners:

> ' To drawen folk to heaven with fairëness,
> By good example, was his business;'

but if he met an obstinate one, be he of low estate or high,

> 'Him would he snibben sharply for the nonës.'

In short, he was independent because he was honest; sincerity knows its prescriptive right, and truth feels it can afford to go alone.

> ' He waited after no pomp nor reverence,
> Ne makèd him no spicëd conscience,
> But Christës love, and His Apostles twelve,
> He taught, but first he followed it himselve.'

Chaucer has a wonderful power of hitting off a character by a word or two, as when he says of the Man of Law :

> ' Nowhere so busy a man as he there n' as,
> And yet he seemed busier than he was.'

But far greater than this was his power of entering thoroughly into every character, and, for the time, breathing, as it were, the very soul and spirit of each. In this, the secret and source of dramatic power, he is not far surpassed by Shakespeare himself. The unrefined mirth of the Wife of Bath, and the over-refined delicacy of the Prioress, appear with equal distinctness on Chaucer's ever-living page. He enters into the soul of the

Shipman or the Reeve as fully, and by turns possesses their spirit as absolutely, as he does that Clerk, the character that represents himself—who would rather have at his bed's head

> 'A twenty bookës clothed in black or red
> Of Aristotle and his philosophy
> Than robës rich, or fiddle, or sautrie. . . .
> Of study took he mostë care and heed,
> Not a word spake he morë than was need,
> And that was said in form and reverence,
> And short and quick, and full of high sentènce.'

The stories which Chaucer puts in the mouths of these characters are in every case admirably suited to the tellers. The stories are not original, or new inventions, in the sense in which many of our modern novels are. Chaucer, indeed, makes no pretence to that sort of originality. He avowedly takes his tales from the Italian or French or Latin sources; yet they are *his* tales all the same. He makes them his by his manner of narrating, and especially by his wondrous power of realizing the scenes and incidents, the outward appearance and inward mental working of the actors. It would be foolish to object to Shakespeare, that his dramas are founded on old tales which he found somewhere. The skeleton composed of dry bones, and the man clothed in flesh and blood, breathing spirit, and full of action, are different things. It is true, the clothing process as it appears in Shakespeare's dramas and in Chaucer's stories is very different, but to a certain extent it is the same. Creative imagination, dramatic spirit, and felicity of situation, are seen in both; and it is for these things, and things like these, not for the mere story, that the productions of genius are valued and enjoyed.

Chaucer's learning, for his age, is truly wonderful; yet, if he had not had some of that native power which puts life into learning, he would be forgotten long ago. We feel him tedious at times, when he allows the scholasticism of the age to become an element in the discourse; but of what he writes in his own best manner, the interest is vivid and unfading. In the time-defying freshness of his pictures we see something exactly like what we recognise in the paintings of old masters —an indescribable quality which we can only point to and say, 'That is genius.' Chaucer could not only put life into his learning in using it for a literary purpose, he was also able to use for the same purpose his acquaintance with men and things, his vast and varied knowledge of life. He had been the companion of the ablest and noblest in the land, because his rare spiritual endowments were seen and acknowledged. His wit and humour are natural, flowing, as a limpid streamlet flows freely from its source. He has that perfect ease which marks the consummate artist. We do not say he reaches the 'highest heaven of invention'—the sublime which Milton sometimes touches—the grandeur of some of the great Shakespearian scenes. But he has the art of presenting the interesting points of a scene or of a subject in a manner which no artist has excelled—in language which, notwithstanding its archaism, is rich and interesting, and sweetly melodious still. And for accurate penetrating observation of human character and life, for insight into motives, for pathos most touching, for keenness of satire, for richness of fancy, for simplicity of incident and feeling, and above all for powerful and delicious humour, he has, after Shakespeare, no superior or equal. Though five hundred years old, such is the power of true genius, his poetry is found to-day among the freshest and greenest of all poetry. It forcibly reminds us of the fact that antiquity was the youth of the world. And to one who wishes to understand the age in which Chaucer lived, the value of his writings is incalculable. How much more we can learn of the real state of things in that time from *his* pictures, than from the pages of any formal history! Chaucer, as we possess him, is indeed the 'abstract and brief chronicle of his time.' Mr. Furnival has well pointed out the advantage of studying Chaucer's works in chronological order :

'Thus you will see Chaucer not only *outwardly* as he was in the flesh—page, soldier, squire, diplomatist, custom-house officer, member of Parliament, then a suppliant for protection and favour, a beggar for money; but *inwardly*, as he was in the spirit—clear of all his early nonsense of courts of love, etc., gentle and loving, early timid and in despair, sharing others' sorrows, and by comforting them losing part of his own; yet long dwelling on the sadness of forsaken love, seeking the 'consolation of philosophy,' watching the stars, praying to the 'Mother of God;' studying books, and, more still, woman's nature; his eye open to all the beauties of the world around him, his ear to the heavenly harmony of the birds' songs; at length becoming the most gracious and tender spirit, the sweetest singer, the best portrayer, the most pathetic, and withal the most genial and humourful healthy-souled man that England had ever seen.'

SHAKESPEARE.

Though two centuries divide Chaucer from Shakespeare, the literary products between these two great names are comparatively inconsiderable. And in English literature the age of Shakespeare was as fertile as that of Chaucer was barren. Chaucer, our 'morning star of song,' is solitary and distant, but Shakespeare is conspicuous in the midst of a galaxy which is still distinctly visible—the well-known, eminently English 'Elizabethan authors'—and in which blazes at least one splendid star of the first magnitude, though inferior to Shakespeare—I mean Edmund Spenser.

The sudden profusion of rich literary products which astonishes the student of English literature when he comes to the times of Elizabeth has been variously accounted for. Precedent natural causes in the history of the nation have been pointed to. The long, deep rest which the nation enjoyed after a tremendous agitation and exercise of energy in the Wars of the Roses—the mental awakening connected with that mighty outburst of religious earnestness and religious scepticism which is called the Reformation—the social, political, and spiritual freedom enjoyed by the English at a time when other European nations were in comparative bondage—the feeling of contrast and superiority engendered by their condition—all this helped to create the vast literary impulse which gives character to that age. Though Chaucer was before them, he was so distant from them that those great Elizabethan authors may be said to have been also thrilled by a *primitive* enthusiasm—they felt they were workers in a glorious dawn—that they were founding a national literature: and one is forced to notice in those who occupy such position—whether as founders of a religion, a science, a government, or a literature—a something indicative of extraordinary, almost superhuman energy.

But none of the historical causes we have mentioned, nor any other natural cause known to us, will account for the appearance of SHAKESPEARE. 'In regard to the real mystery of this man's power, both criticism and philosophy are mute. His appearance is simply a fact in the world's intellectual history which can be connected with no preceding facts, nor with the history of the age.' History would but stultify herself did she call him the product of his age, for he would have been a miracle in any age. One might as well undertake to sail round Africa in an hour, as to treat fully in a single lecture the mighty continent of Shakespeare's works. But respecting what every one sees and feels a slight hint is as eloquent as a long discourse. We do not attempt describing to each other the great ocean, or the azure fields of air—we simply look at them together, earnestly, and in silence. Or if we speak, a very few words will serve to recall a scene which has deeply impressed us or excited our highest admiration. Like others, I have for many years found recreation and instruction in walking through the multitudinous world of creations which we call 'Shakespeare,' and may do so occasionally in years to come. I have learnt something, but have not learnt, and do not expect *ever* to learn, *all* that is taught there; for in Shakespeare instruction is infinitely multiplied, even as in nature itself. Before giving any more special account of what has struck me in reading Shakespeare, let me say a few words on his life.

Almost all we know of it, in the words of De Quincey, is 'that he lived, that he died, and that he was "a little lower than the angels."' Though there are two centuries and the Wars of the Roses between Chaucer and Shakespeare, yet, as De Quincey remarks, we know more of the personal history of the former than of the latter. Much natural regret has been expressed that so little of Shakespeare's private life has been preserved; our comfort must be that in the various disguises which he has chosen to assume we are perfectly familiar with him. Though we know little of Shakespeare personally, we know—millions of human beings know—old Jack Falstaff well. Though we cannot boast of an extensive biography of our great poet, we can be intimately acquainted with the inner workings of Hamlet's soul—we can sympathize with the terrible throes of the jealous, though honourable and mighty Othello—with the madness, and grief, and despair-driven eloquence of Lear. And what little we do know of Shakespeare's life will ever be profoundly interesting, because of its connexion with those sublime and original creations which the cultured in all lands have hailed with wonder and delight.

Shakespeare's father, like Chaucer's, though not a lord or aristocrat, was a man of respectable position in the business world, and was able to give his son the advantage of the grammar school in Stratford. By his mother's side Shakespeare was of knightly descent, and the maiden, who before her marriage bore the pretty name of Mary Arden, deserves, as the mother of Shakespeare, the full benefit of the remark which is commonly made respecting the mothers of great men. Shakespeare owed more to her than his gentle blood. The boy was an early lover of books, and an early lover of the sweet quiet scenery round Stratford. He was, it appears, an early lover of something else, namely, a certain Ann Hathaway, who, however, was seven years older than himself. Perhaps it would have been better if he had not married her so early, that is, when he was but eighteen years of age; and I need not try to conceal the fact that Miss Hathaway has got a share of blame in this business.

It has been said there is no heart pure except it be passionate—passion, when noble, is a purifying element like fire. Shakespeare knew this, for he felt and acted like a man before he wrote like a poet. Out of the fulness of his first great imprudent love, by the aid of recent memories, he was able to make Romeo speak words of such entranced fervour and dream-like sweetness; but from a dear-bought experience he was then also able, by the mouth of the Friar, to utter a warning:

'These violent delights have violent ends.'

For better or for worse, Shakespeare had the important knot tied at eighteen. If the infinite passion which dwelt in him, and afterwards became the inexhaustible fund of his poetry, had led him into what is called an imprudence, such was his nature, even in that immature stage, that it would rebound and touch again the top of honour, though with the sacrifice of himself. His only three children were born before he was twenty-two; and then, when his domestic life, alas! had defaced and for ever dissipated the rosy-tinted vision of his youthful love—perhaps fleeing from family broils (the mention of which in connexion with his illustrious name sounds like profanation), or simply seeking employment by which he might support his household, he went to London with some respectable actors whom he probably had met at his father's house when they came to play at Stratford. But observe, he was not, first or last, the poor needy strolling player that some have imagined. His father had a good position in Stratford—had even been mayor of the town; and when his son, following his natural bent and his poetic instinct, chose the profession of an actor, it is likely there was an arrangement with the London company in terms advantageous to young Shakespeare. We may conclude as much from the fact that in 1589, three years after Shakespeare went to London, he was a shareholder in one of the leading London theatres. The connexions of the firm with Stratford had procured him a favourable reception, and he was found on trial to be a valuable accession to the staff, even as an actor. At first he undertook the additional work of improving old plays and adapting them to the stage. He was distinguished by unwearied industry as well as mighty genius, and soon advanced to higher work. With the modesty which ever distinguishes true worth, he did ¦not disdain this poor employment of patching up old plays of an inferior sort, and his reward was that in this work, in due time, he became conscious of the latent powers which nature had lodged within him. Therefore, instead of this cobbling work he soon began to send forward new pieces, which instantly made all other English dramas look mean and worthless in comparison. From these first outbursts of his youthful fire—the 'Two Gentlemen,' 'Romeo,' and others—he proceeded to efforts yet more wonderful and glorious. He had the magnanimity to set before him the approval of the great artists and high intellects of his acquaintance, not mere popular applause, as the mark to be hit, and despising a momentary gain, he worked for an eternal crown. For twenty-five years he thus continued to write in London, occasionally paying visits to his wife, who lived all this time in Stratford; and finished by giving to the world 'Hamlet,' 'Lear,' 'Macbeth,' 'Othello,' and the 'Tempest,' at the end of a series of thirty-seven dramas, which are now universally acknowledged to contain the very highest literary work which has yet been accomplished by the unaided intellect of man.

Some have thought that Shakespeare was, like other geniuses, not appreciated in his time; but this appears to be a mistake. His pre-eminence was fully acknowledged by the best intellects of his day; he was a success even in a pecuniary point of view, and he retired to Stratford rich. Geniuses of a lower order are frequently unpractical and improvident; it is not so with those in the highest class. It is on record that Shakespeare, during the time when he was engaged on one of his grandest dramas ('Macbeth'), sued Philip Rogers in the borough court of Stratford for 35s. 10d. for corn delivered to him at various times. To Shakespeare it was given, in doing his own needful work as a bread-winner, to do a work of glory and delight for all mankind and for all ages. Yet there is evidence of his possessing such admirable balance, as to prefer his quiet retirement at Stratford, and the enjoyment of his earnings among his friends in his native place, to all those results of his wondrous artistic skill, and the fame which he knew would be immortal. His pecuniary success had been such as to raise him even to affluence; he is said to have retired with an income of £1,500 a year. He had kept his wife and children in comfort. He had done the part of a dutiful son, by re-establishing his father's fallen fortunes. He had purchased the 'best house in Stratford,' with one hundred and seven acres of land adjoining, in which he passed the four or five last years of his life in dignified ease and profound meditation, and in which, in the year 1616, he died on his birthday, at the early age of fifty-two.

In the adieu of his own Prospero his spirit seems prophetic of its departure from the stage of time. You remember the scene in which that benevolent and wise magician, having accomplished the restoration of right, the conversion of evil-doers, and the happiness of a noble pair of lovers, abjures his art, casts off his magic robe, and breaks his wonder-working staff. Prospero's address to the 'elves,' or spirits, by whom he had wrought his wonders, may be taken for Shakespeare's own 'Farewell' to the multitudinous creations of his fancy, which had become almost real beings to him, as they are to all who read his book.

> 'Ye elves of hills, brooks, standing lakes, and groves,
> And ye that on the sands with printless foot
> Do chase the ebbing Neptune, and do fly him
> When he comes back; you demi-puppets that
> By moonshine do the green and sour ringlets make,
> Whereof the ewe not bites, and you whose pastime
> Is to make midnight mushrooms, that rejoice
> To hear the solemn curfew; by whose aid,
> Weak masters though ye be,'—

imagine Shakespeare here pointing to the poor contrivances of stage characters by which he did his work—

> 'I have bedimm'd
> The noon-tide sun, call'd forth the mutinous winds
> And 'twixt the green sea and the azured vault
> Set roaring war: to the dread rattling thunder
> Have I given fire, and rifted Jove's stout oak
> With his own bolt; the strong-based promontory

> Have I made shake, and by the spurs plucked up
> The pine and cedar : graves at my command
> Have waked their sleepers, oped, and let them forth
> By my so potent art. But this rough magic
> I here abjure, and when I have required
> Some heavenly music, which even now I do,
> To work mine end upon their senses that
> This airy charm is for, I'll break my staff,
> Bury it certain fathoms in the earth,
> And deeper than did ever plummet sound,
> I'll drown my book.'

Many gifted men in this and other lands have written on Shakespeare, labouring towards 'the height of that great argument' in vain. He is, indeed, beyond all praise, as he is 'beyond all Greek, beyond all Roman fame.' In fact, any one who now praises Shakespeare, readily gets the blame of commonplace, or of formally setting forth what every one believes and takes for granted. It is true that such praise is often a mere repetition of phrases that pass current by being taken on authority, for many men can praise and even quote Shakespeare, who have never read him. His phrases are in daily use among those who know not from what source they come. You say, 'Conscience makes cowards of us all.' You speak of one who 'sits like Patience on a monument.' You refer to 'the worm in the bud;' or to a 'custom more honoured in the breach than the observance,' though you do not think of the original author of these expressions. His phrases have, indeed, become largely incorporated into our language, and, oftener than we know it, we think according to the ideas which he originated. Most educated people nowadays would be ashamed to confess ignorance of Shakespeare, yet it is my belief that, even among the readers, there is very little reading of Shakespeare done. Therefore, as my object is to promote the growth of a literary interest, instead of writing a useless eulogy on Shakespeare, I shall first refer to some of the hindrances by which people in our days are kept from studying him, and then go on with some general criticisms.

There are still some religious, but ignorant people among

us, who devoutly abhor Shakespeare as a 'play-book.' There are a great many people who constantly read their Bible without taking any proper pains to understand it, and such good folks will be surprised to hear that the Bible itself contains a sacred drama, namely, 'Job.' That fact should warn them of their mistake in indiscriminately decrying all 'play books.' Are we to consider all plays bad when found in their original English, but excellent when translated from the Hebrew or Greek? There are few who would venture to consign Sophocles to oblivion because his works happen to take the form of plays; yet the reader of Sophocles who afterwards comes to Shakespeare, feels like one inhaling the free open breath of heaven after the heavy atmosphere of a close chamber. It is admitted that many plays have an immoral tendency; but who can create loathing of vice and admiring love of virtue as Shakespeare does? No doubt he has objectionable things caused by the conditions of his work, the requirements of a theatre; but we should remember that the best work which man can do has to be done under conditions in some respects objectionable. We behold the laws of eminent statesmen enacted under pressure from party influences which always somewhat mar the work. There is no theological treatise, however broad or Catholic, that does not bear some offensive trace of the peculiarities of the Church which produced it. After all, the conditions under which we do our work are of little consequence, if only we earnestly aim at doing it well. It was Shakespeare's lot to be bound to his life-work by the conditions of a theatre; if the conditions of your life-work, or mine, are better, it will be the more shame for us if it turns out a poor trifling matter in the end. Shakespeare did his best to ennoble his work, to elevate the stage; and thus he not only ennobled himself, but became the fountain of culture to a large portion of the human race.

'Honour and shame from no conditions rise,
Act well your part, there all the honour lies.'

We know, indeed, that in Shakespeare's noble soul the conditions under which he did his work were at times felt to be both cramping and unpleasant. Nevertheless, he continued earnestly, industriously, powerfully struggling to realize what seemed the best possible to *him*. 'Play-houses' and 'play-books' were far more generally odious then than they are now; there are indications that even in the home to which he retired in Stratford he was made to feel the ignominy which the popular mind attached to his profession. Here are some of his own sad reflections on this subject addressed to a friend :

> ' O for my sake do you with Fortune chide,
> The guilty goddess of my harmful deeds,
> That did not better for my life provide
> Than public means which public manners breeds ;
> Thence comes it that my name receives a brand,
> And almost thence my nature is subdued
> To what it works in, like a dyer's hand :
> Pity me then, and wish I were renewed !'

There is no more interesting spectacle than that of a fellow creature of essentially noble nature battling amid evil elements that threaten to overwhelm him, but are used by him as helps in a progress which is constantly upward. Men who make even their misdeeds steps of the ladder on which they rise to the summits of virtue, who thus

> ' Rise on stepping stones
> Of their dead selves to higher things,'

are the true heroes of history. They are not failing, though they may now and then utter ' a cry '

> ' Like a strong swimmer in his agony '—

a cry such as we hear in more than one of Shakespeare's sonnets :

> ' Alas, 'tis true, I have gone here and there,
> And made myself a motley to the view,
> Gored mine own thoughts, sold cheap what is most dear,
> Made old offences of affections new.
> Most true it is that I have looked on truth
> Askance and strangely : but by all above
> These blenches gave my heart another youth,
> And worse essays proved thee my best of love.
> Now all is done ! have what shall have no end !
> Mine appetite I never more will grind
> On newer proof, to try an older friend,
> A god in love, to whom I am confined :

> Then give me welcome, next to heaven the best,
> Even to thy pure and most, most loving breast.'

Shakespeare, indeed, regretted some of the conditions under which his earthly life were passed; he was ashamed of some things connected with the play-house; but did he ever regret that he had written 'Othello?' was he ever ashamed of being the author of 'Lear?' Did he ever regret having warned the world in that sublime and most powerful way of the danger which may arise from a groundless suspicion if permitted to enter a great creative mind and to work there, even when the subject of this incurable plague is otherwise eminently brave, and wise, and good, as Othello was? Was he ever ashamed of illustrating in the magnificent manner we see in 'Lear,' the foul deformity of filial ingratitude, and the mad obstinacy of parental prejudice? Surely not. Narrow views like those to which I have alluded belong to an age that is passing, or past. One who treats Shakespeare ignominiously as a common 'play-book,' may sometimes yet be applauded by the rudest and rawest portion of the religious public, but he will not less effectually receive the disgraceful brand of Gothic ignorance, or run a risk of being expelled beyond the utmost verge of civilization. But people generally, even where they are mostly Puritan, have intelligence enough to know that Shakespeare is not one of your unscrupulous vagabond players. He never wrote a play, like one of Byron's, whose object is to sophisticate, and make the worse appear the better cause; he never dresses up vice to make it an attractive decoy for the young. In him you find no blatant blasphemy, or sneers at religion. A great mind knows a great subject, and can treat it with respect.

Objectors more reasonable than those to whom we have been referring have spoken of Shakespeare's greatest works as wanting in a moral purpose: the tendency of the play, they complain, is not towards some important moral lesson. Now, we admit that he does not put his moral purpose obviously forward; but this is a merit in Shakespeare, not a fault. If the moral purpose is hidden, it is only that it may be more surely accomplished. And herein lies much of his consummate power as a dramatist. When he seems to be only amusing, he is always instructing and warning us. Such lessons he gives as you can only get amid the stern realities of life, and by a dear-bought experience. Neither in this mysterious world, this great school of Providence to which we have all been put, do we find the lesson in large capitals posted on the walls. Shakespeare does teach virtue, but not by the bare enunciation of potent principles and proverbs—he leaves that to pedants like Polonius. His aim is to make men virtuous ere they are aware, by arousing within them some powerful enthusiasm, even as Prince Hal is reformed, and made a noble king by his passion for military glory. What Shakespeare understands by virtue was not the cheap, easily-gotten article possessed by respectable people, whose circumstances have always kept them aloof from temptation. The only virtue valuable in his eyes is that which has stood the most terrible test, as in the case of an Isabella or a Marina.

The ordinary preacher of virtue must be often dry, and tedious, and weak; Shakespeare is always delightful, always attractive, and therefore always efficient. With what almost superhuman power he depicts the horrors of crime, when Macbeth's imagination, working fearfully before the deed, calls up the 'air-drawn dagger,' and when after trying to clutch it, he cries:

> 'I see thee still,
> And on thy blade and dudgeon gouts of blood,
> Which was not so before:—there's no such thing !
> It is the bloody business that informs
> Thus to my eyes.'

And after having done the deed, when he tells his wife-accomplice he had heard one on the corridor praying 'God bless us,' and that he (her husband) could not say 'Amen'—it 'stuck in his throat'—and when he adds:

> 'Methought I heard a voice cry "Sleep no more !
> Macbeth doth murder Sleep"—the innocent Sleep !'

all must feel that crime is an infinitely and unspeakably dreadful thing.

Or when he brings before us that piteous, terrible scene, in which Macbeth's wife, whose hard brain has reeled at length, goes about with her taper at midnight fast asleep, ever and anon putting forth her utmost energy to wash the blood-stain from her hand—do we not feel that one might write many essays on murder without producing in the minds of his readers one-tenth of the moving effect of that single scene ?—or of another, surely the most powerful of all, in which Macbeth, after his second murder, fancies he sees the ghost of Banquo come into the banquet-hall, and take the vacant seat at the royal feast; where the guests, first horrified by the expression of the king's countenance, which proclaims a portentous inward agony, are then startled by the usurper's abrupt earnest words addressed to no visible form :

> 'Thou canst not say I did it : never shake
> Thy gory locks at me.'

It should be remembered that Shakespeare's vocation is that of an artist, not that of a preacher; yet in this awfully efficient manner he preaches against crime, and in a manner equally powerful he excites love for every virtue. It is his to teach virtue not in cold didactic lines or frigid moral saws. He makes men pure by a quickening process within, rousing the best and highest part of their nature with its strongest activities; giving not merely a correct knowledge of what is right, but a passionate love for the more excellent way.

We certainly cannot defend the moral tendency of all that Shakespeare has written; but respecting a large portion of his writings what we have said is only fair and right. The moral teaching is, however, only one of the elements embraced in that manifold composite product, which we may designate Shakespeare's art. He is the revealing genius or law-giver of dramatic, as Homer is of heroic, poetry. His characters are therefore his greatest glory. On account of them he has received the title of 'supreme anatomist of the human heart.' His characters are so true to nature, so numerous, so perfectly consistent throughout all the scenes, that Goëthe describes himself as 'despairing before his versatility in which he had exhausted the whole of human nature in all directions.' Such perfection and variety of representation must appear to ordinary minds little short of miraculous. Though the recorded incidents of his outward career are so few and trifling,' says Whipple, 'yet he lived a more various life—a life more crowded with ideas, passions, volitions, and events—than any potentate that the world has ever seen. Compared with his experience, the experience of Alexander and Hannibal, of Cæsar or Napoleon, was narrow and one-sided. He had projected himself into almost all varieties of human character, and in imagination had intensely realized and lived the life of each. From the throne of the monarch to the bench of the village ale-house there were few positions in which he had not placed himself, and which he had not for a time identified with his own. No man had ever seen nature and human life in so many points of view, for he had looked upon them through the eyes of Master Slender and Hamlet, of Caliban and Othello, of Dogberry and Mark Antony, of ancient Pistol and Julius Cæsar, of Mistress Tearsheet and Imogen, of Dame Quickly and Macbeth's wife, of Robin Goodfellow and Titania, of Hecate and Ariel. No king or queen of his time had so completely felt the cares and enjoyed the dignity of the regal state, as this playwright, who usurped it by his thought alone; and the freshest and simplest maiden in Europe had no innocent heart-experience which this man could not share—escaping in an instant from the shattered brain of Lear or the hag-haunted imagination of Macbeth, in order to feel the tender flutter of her soul in his own. And none of these forms, though mightier or more exquisite than the ordinary forms of humanity, could hold or imprison him a moment longer than he chose to abide in it. He was on an excursion through the world of thought and action, to seize the essence of all the excitements of human nature—terrible, painful, criminal, rapturous, or humorous; and to do this in a short, earthly career, he was compelled to condense ages into days, and lives into minutes. He exhausts in a short time all the glory and all the agony there is on the throne or on the couch of Henry IV., and then, wearied with royalty, is off to the Boar's Head to have a rouse with Sir John. He feels all the flaming pride and scorn of the aristocrat Coriolanus; his brain widens with the imperial ideas, and his heart beats with the measureless ambition of the autocrat Cæsar; and anon he has donned a greasy apron, plunged into the roaring Roman mob, and is yelling against aristocrat and autocrat with all the gusto of democratic rage. He is now a prattling child, and in a second he is a murderer with a knife at its throat. He is capable of *being* all that he imaginatively *sees*.'

It is truly astonishing to consider how vastly numerous and how varied were the impressions and ideas which his intellect had received and stored up; but it is even more astonishing to witness the displays of that indomitable mental energy which could make all these ideas and impressions its servants, the mind preserving itself independent and superior lord of them all. 'What the blue dome of air is to the tempest raging beneath it'—such (says one) is Shakespeare's mighty intellect to the scenes of his poetry.

In nothing do we see his greatness better manifested than in his large tolerance. Many men are uncharitable by defect of sympathy and defect of insight. 'This toleration' (says Whipple), 'without which an intimate knowledge of other natures is impossible, Shakespeare possessed beyond any other man recorded in literature or history. It is a moral as well as a mental trait, and belongs to the highest class of virtues. It is a virtue which, if generally exercised, would remove mutual hostility by enlightening mutual ignorance. And in Shakespeare we have for once a man great enough to be modest and charitable; who has got the giant's power, but far from using it like a giant, trampling on weaker creatures, prefers to feel them in his arms rather than feel them under his feet; and whose toleration of others is the exercise of humility, veracity, beneficence, and justice, as well as the exercise of reason, imagination, and humour. We shall never appreciate Shakespeare's genius till we recognise in him the exercise of the most difficult virtues as well as the exercise of the most wide-reaching intelligence.' His beautiful and noble characters are indeed wonderful effects of genius; 'but the marvel of his comprehensiveness is his mode of dealing with the vulgar, the vicious, and the low—with persons who are commonly spurned as dolts or knaves. His serene benevolence did not pause at what are called "deserving objects of charity," but extended to the undeserving, who are, in truth, the proper objects of charity . . . . Milton can do justice to the Devil, but not, like Shakespeare, to "poor devils." But it may be doubted if the wise and good have the right to cut the providential bond which connects them with the foolish and the bad, and set up an aristocratic humanity of their own ten times more supercilious than the aristocracy of blood. Divorce the loftiest qualities from humility and geniality, and they quickly contract a Pharisaic taint . . . . but Shakespeare had none of this pride of superiority, either in its noble or ignoble form. How humanely he clings to the most unpromising forms of human nature, insists on their right to speak for themselves as much as if they were passionate Romeos and high-aspiring Buckinghams, and does for them what he might have desired should be done for himself had he been Dogberry, or Bottom, or Abhorson, or Bardolph, or any of the rest. The low characters of Ben Jonson's plays excite only contempt or disgust. Shakespeare takes the same materials as Ben, passes them through the medium of his imaginative humour, and changes them into subjects of the most soul-enriching mirth.'

All Shakespeare's characters bear to be treated like real men and women, who are understood by accurate observation of their manner as well as their words and actions. To make his readers acquainted with one of his characters this poet does not depend on a description or analysis put into the mouth of another character; each character by his action and manner creates an impression for himself as in actual life. And it must not be forgotten that, while all his characters are original, his women are specially and peculiarly so. The appearance in our literature of such women as Cordelia, Miranda, Desdemona, Imogen, 'was the signal of a new age and a new life for the world.' There are few, if any, really fine women in our literature before Shakespeare's ; and one critic pronounces them the most exquisite creations in all literature. 'Literature boasts many eminent female poets and novelists; but not one has ever approached Shakespeare in the purity, the sweetness, the refinement, the elevation of his perceptions of feminine character —much less approached him in the power of embodying those perceptions in persons. These characters are so thoroughly domesticated on earth, that we are tempted to forget the "heaven of invention" from which he brought them. The most beautiful of spirits, they are the most tender of daughters, lovers, and wives. They are "airy shapes," but they "syllable men's names."'

They are women whose purity is evidently inborn, whose high and beautiful morality is an instinct rather than a definite rule of life—the perfect whiteness of whose souls, shining through them, strikes us as the fabled brilliance of the Holy Grail, descending on a beam of celestial light, struck the eyes of unholy knights. They are women to whom we rapturously accord perfection, as we hardly ever do to the best of men— women in whom antagonistic powers of wisdom and love, action and thought, are united, making them fit to be rulers, and making us feel as if every other sovereignty was unlawful compared with theirs. Whoever has seen the indescribable excellence that resides in Isabella, or in the beautiful unfortunate Desdemona—whoever has seen but *that*, is infinitely debtor to Shakespeare.

Though this great writer instructs and elevates us, yet his permanent power greatly depends on the fact that he is an exhaustless source of pleasure. Every page is delightfully readable, and always fresh. Without referring to other elements of pleasure, his *humour* alone would authorize the assertion of De Quincey that Shakespeare is to be included in the most important luxuries of civilization. How often, and for how many, the weary hour has been brightened by means of the pages in which Mrs. Quickly, or Launce, or Holofernes, or Jaques, or, above all, the 'fat knight' appears! We have a delicious sense of touching the very sublime of the ridiculous in scenes like that in which the whimsical, indignant Welshman makes Pistol 'eat the leek'—that wherein Falstaff pours out his ludicrous description of his experience in the clothes-basket, or the bewitching braggadocio of how he 'peppered' the eleven knights in buckram suits—that in which Costard exposes Holofernes at the games, when the latter cries out:

'Dost thou infamonize me among the potentates?
Thou shalt die'—

or that in which Mrs. Quickly gives an account of old Jack's death, how 'a' babbled o' the green fields,' the poor old soul! It is pleasant laughter—hearty, healthy, and good-humoured, that you get from Shakespeare's scenes—laughter that a villain could neither give nor receive.

I resist the solicitations of an agreeable subject, and conclude with one or two general remarks—scintillations which may give you a momentary perception of its greatness. It has been remarked of Thomas Carlyle that, though he devoted himself to literature, he thought the best writing a poor performance in comparison with action right and strong. And Shakespeare strongly indicates the same preference. Not the irresolute Hamlet, but bold 'Prince Harry, with his beaver on,' is the man in whom he fully delights. His hero is the man who meets danger and misfortune with a lion front; he who lets slip the helm in a storm is left to the scornful irony of events. Heaven does not help the pious, but indolent and hesitating Henry VI., but the pious and pure Isabella, who helps herself, is successful. How awfully in Antony the waste through indolence of distinguished powers is punished; even Hamlet, with all his intellectual brilliance, must perish because of his over-sensibility and proneness to speculate at the moment of action. This is another evidence that Shakespeare possessed not only imagination, but also sagacity of the highest order. Indeed, it is now fully admitted that in the conduct of his plays his judgment is as conspicuous as his genius. He has been even hailed as the pioneer and guide of true philosophy; and Buckle, in an eloquent passage, shows how much the spirit of Shakespeare had to do with the rise and progress of science. Moralists and practical men acknowledge him to be the rarest judge of human character and human affairs, and therefore a guide for this world of unquestionable authority. And the greatest genius of Germany confesses that he 'has stood lost before his power and repose, and felt wholly discouraged by his unfathomable and unattainable excellences.' Many other great poets have acknowledged Shakespeare their master; they have styled him the 'myriad-minded.' Apart from his dramatic power, they have called him most poetical of poets. The highest heaven of invention which other poets *sometimes* reach, is his familiar home. Shall we give him higher praise? Then we shall say he shows that the highest genius is inconsistent with anything but the noblest virtue and the purest religion. Let any one who wishes a good illustration of his transcendent powers just make a study of this one subject—his treatment of the supernatural. A most interesting little treatise might be written on that alone. We have spoken of the way in which other poets—we might say all other poets—have looked up to him. We conclude in the language of *one* of these, the most cultured, the most virtuous, and the sublimest of them all. Anything like a just appreciation Shakespeare requires no less than Miltonic words:

> 'What needs my Shakespeare for his honour'd bones
> The labour of an age in pilèd stones,
> Or that his hallow'd reliques should be hid
> Under a star-y-pointing pyramid?
> Dear son of memory, great heir of fame,
> What need'st thou such weak witness of thy fame?
> Thou in our wonder and astonishment
> Hast built thyself a live-long monument;
> For whilst to the shame of slow-endeavouring art
> Thy easy numbers flow, and that each heart
> Hath from the leaves of that unvalued book
> Those Delphic lines with deep impression took,
> Then thou our fancy of itself bereaving,
> Dost make us marble with too much conceiving,
> And so sepulchrèd, in such pomp dost lie,
> That kings for such a tomb would wish to die.'

HAMLET.*

WHO has not sometimes reflected with remorse and shame on the difference between his will and his deed—his resolve and his performance—his sense of duty and its fulfilment? Intentions conceived in a moment of deep feeling in solitude, have appeared to possess immense energy, yet afterwards, just when they are required, when they should take practical effect and shape, they disappear like a deceitful brook in desert sands. We have heard the painful cry of an earnest thinker, who was also an earnest worker—'What I would, that I do not!'—and we have a striking proof that great minds travelling in different ways arrive at the same high spiritual truth, in the fact that this thought of St. Paul's is the central idea of the great tragedy 'Hamlet.'

> 'Thus conscience does make cowards of us all,
> And thus the native hue of resolution
> Is sicklied o'er with the pale cast of thought,
> And enterprises of great pith and moment
> With this regard their currents turn arwy,
> And lose the name of action.'

Observe—Hamlet's irresolution is not wholly a fault. It is not simply weakness, or timidity, or cowardice. Nor is it the inborn tendency to evil, or the innate aversion to duty, to which the preacher so often directs attention. Hamlet's irresolution, strange to say, is caused by some of the noblest faculties and divinest endowments of his nature. His *conscience* makes

* Additional illustration of the genius of Shakespeare.

him a coward. His resolution is sicklied o'er with the pale cast of *thought.* He is weakened by the endless and infinite play of his 'noble and most sovereign reason.' Above all, his powerful *imagination* magnifies his burden a thousandfold, and makes him stagger under it. Even the blaze of feeling which accompanies the formation of his resolution diminishes his practical power in dealing with men and things—as if in this precocious heat the strength of his will was self-consumed.

While we praise culture in opposition to Philistinism, let us admit the defects and deficiencies of the man of culture. He may be deficient in what men call stamina. He may be inefficient by the very impartiality and many-sidedness of his mind. 'By thinking too precisely on the event' he may delay action till action becomes useless. He may want that estimable quality 'decision of character'—a want that may cause infinite distress to himself and others. So it was with Hamlet. Let us, therefore, attend to the high lesson which this mighty moralist Shakespeare, living three centuries beyond his time, seems to have specially designed for our day. For *when* has the world ever had so many inefficient dreamers—so many restless, unsatisfied sceptics—so many good reasoners unprepared for action—or so many men of general ability without an object, or a fulcrum, as appear in this nineteenth century of grace?

I hold it is no disparagement to this highly interesting philosophical drama, that its kernel or core (so to speak) is a noble and eminently useful moral. Nor is it inconsistent with this object that Shakespeare should have chosen for his purpose a story of revenge. The fact that the principal action of the play consists, not in returning good for evil but in returning evil for evil, does not, in the circumstances, hinder the drama from having a highly moral or even Christian tendency. That a son should seek to bring punishment on his father's murderer is not necessarily a bad revenge, but such as may spring from a sense of duty and the fear of God. The irrepressible horror of murder which even inanimate nature seems to express, is sanctioned by conscience and by our highest ideas of morality; nor was the Divine law of returning good for evil intended to stop the crying of a brother's blood uttered from the ground. Hence Shakespeare gives to Hamlet's revenge those great and mysterious supernatural sanctions implied in the solemn denunciations of the Ghost. Having discovered his uncle to be a usurper, Hamlet must consider himself king in right, and since murder pollutes the very seat of justice, it is Hamlet's duty, acting as chief magistrate, to doom the great offender, and take away the national reproach. The message borne to guilty kings by Hebrew prophets often was—'Zion shall be redeemed with judgment;' nor shall any nation be redeemed without it. The high and noble task of visiting with punishment a powerful, wicked ruler, has often been celebrated by prophets and poets. Milton has endorsed what Seneca uttered :

> 'There can be slain
> No sacrifice to God more acceptable
> Than an unjust and wicked king.'

And the son who would not seek to punish the murderer of his father is one who rather displays his want of affection than manifests a Christian spirit.

Whatever doctrines be afloat, a nation, as a whole, never fails to manifest its horror of a capital crime openly committed. And it is a significant fact, accounting somewhat for the marked manner in which the play was received from the first, that there had occurred not many years before a royal crime bearing a striking resemblance to that which is the subject of the drama. The awful murder of Darnley, and the subsequent marriage of his Queen and his murderer, had convulsed two nations; and if Shakespeare really intended to veil this terrible tragedy under the name of Hamlet, his historical fidelity respecting the character of the Queen is striking enough. It is still a disputed point among historians whether

Mary Queen of Scots was accessory to her husband's murder; and Shakespeare in the play has contrived to give a like dubiety to the character of Queen Gertrude. Should we carry the parallel further, and say that Shakespeare intended to flatter Mary's *son*, the reigning King, James I., by the character of Hamlet, we should verge on something not quite worthy of our great poet. . Yet even this *may* be so; for with the most exalted genius, the *man* Shakespeare had often to succumb to the poor conditions of his earthly life: and the despicable hesitancy of a weakling monarch may have been flattered by the high-minded and noble irresolution of Hamlet.

1. Let us try to draw together from various parts of the play a picture of Hamlet as complete as possible. Our first knowledge of him is of a young prince who has been receiving a liberal education at a famous university, and is suddenly brought home by the astounding intelligence that his royal father is dead. We look upon him first clad in a suit of mourning—wrapped in his 'inky cloak'—and filled with a deeper melancholy than can be expressed by the 'trappings and the suits of woe.' Within the brief moment in which he realized his bereavement, the whole aspect of his life has changed. To the tidings of his father's death is immediately added the news that his uncle has been elected King. Hamlet, through the artifice of his astute uncle, or by some unaccountable fluctuation of popular feeling, is passed over. By some means or other his uncle had 'popp'd between the election and his hopes,' and this young man of gentle nature, of great thoughtfulness, of noble intentions, is made to feel as a stranger, a poor dependent, in the house which he had thought would receive him as master.

While affable and free in his manners, he had preserved a high sense of his princely dignity, and of the duties of the great office to which he looked forward. Those who knew him before the great cloud fell over his life, noted his kingly qualities; even the crafty and cruel Claudius, at the moment when he hates and fears him most, speaks of him as 'being remiss, most generous, and 'free from all contriving;' and Ophelia only spoke the common sentiment when she called him

> ' The expectancy and rose of the fair state,
> The glass of fashion and the mould of form,
> The observed of all observers.'

It was the verdict of Fortinbras that Hamlet 'was likely, had he been put on, to have proved most royally.' To his other distinguished qualities there is added that perilous endowment, a highly poetic imagination. Hamlet has a decided habit of introspection or self-review; he has more than the ordinary portion of sensibility and soul; and, as we might therefore expect, he has a constitutional disposition to melancholy.

We are first to fancy his state of mind when, to the dejection caused by the loss of his noble father and his kingdom at one blow, were added the sorrow and shame of the news of his mother's hasty marriage with his uncle. Then for the first time, and before he comes to a darker hour, in which he utters the sublime soliloquy 'To be or not to be,' his thoughts turn to suicide: he wishes that ' the Everlasting had not fixed his canon 'gainst self-slaughter.' 'Oh God!' cries the solitary orphaned youth, whose desolation repeated blows of Fortune have so speedily accomplished,

> ' O God !
> How weary, stale, flat, and unprofitable
> Seem to me all the uses of this world !'

Not only has he lost the best of earthly friends and the hope of reigning, not only does he feel himself a stranger and dependent in his princely home; he has, in a sense, lost his mother, to whose society he looked for his last consolation, to whose bosom he thought he could betake himself when every refuge failed; and his high moral nature is shocked and outraged by the unseemly slight put upon his father's memory by her to whom he had been accustomed to look for the very highest example of goodness and purity:

> 'And yet, within a month—
> Let me not think on't ! . . . Frailty, thy name is woman !—
> A little month ; or ere those shoes were old
> With which she followed my poor father's body . . .
> . She married with my uncle, my father's brother !'

Can Hamlet suffer more ? Can aught worse than this be inflicted on his sensitive, aspiring, imaginative soul ? ' Yes : the cruel Erinys, the author of human tragedy, has reserved one blow, the merciless infliction of which makes his reason stagger, and for ever closes upon him the door of hope. It is the knowledge of his father's MURDER, involving his mother's and his uncle's guilt. After this revelation, made with every circumstance of solemnity and horror by the Ghost, Hamlet is no more the same man that he was. It is asked, was Hamlet really mad ? Certainly his state of mind was such as made the assumption of madness easy; and what mind hemmed in so completely by misery so awful, so hopeless, *could* be perfectly sane ?

After that horrible revelation, how can he live in the presence of the guilty pair ? How can he raise an unnatural hand with the weapon of justice against them ? Can he slay *him*, and live henceforth in the frightful shame which an explanation of that deed would involve ? Can he spare his mother's life, and tell the world she is an adulteress, perhaps an accomplice in the murder ? In any case, life with such recollections and such dishonour must be a burden to him. He could not enjoy the crown, even if he were able to snatch it from his uncle. His bright hope of happiness with the fair Ophelia is also suddenly extinguished : what heart can he have for revenge which will make that gentle, beautiful girl the partner of his splendour and disgrace ? To his sensitive, refined, honourable soul the idea is insupportable. And no less insupportable is the thought of living unrevenged either at home or in exile. This the voice of his father's blood crying from the ground sternly forbids. The foul, unnatural deed demands an expiation, and as if by a superior power, he feels himself sternly grasped as the instrument of vengeance. This is what Shakespeare means by the commanding Ghost: to a mind like Hamlet's it was Ghost enough.

It is a mind delighting in speculation, but too often unready for action. Subtle and penetrating, it pursues this dreadful subject constantly, in all its bearings: and so keen is Hamlet's nature that he may almost be said to experience the effect which he imagines. And, turn what way he will, he must face a dreadful consequence: to slay his uncle and live thereafter in his mother's shame, *or* to spare his uncle and fall in with *such* a family life, with dread reproaches from his father's spirit sounding in his ears! Is it wonderful he thinks of suicide to avoid the excruciating alternative? that to his seething imagination the spirit world is open, and he sees such sights as make

'Each particular hair to stand on end,
Like quills upon the fretful porpentine'?

Is it strange that he falls into sudden abstracted moods—

'Bending the eye on vacancy,
And with the incorporal air holding discourse'?—

or that he sometimes hints to his friends that he is 'dreadfully attended?'

At first we are displeased with the play. We wonder why the principal action is so much delayed. We cannot see what hinders the execution of this much-talked-of revenge. Surely the thing was in Hamlet's power. He is the son of a most popular king—a man whose memory lives in the affections of his people so much that they are strongly prejudiced in favour of his son. Surely it is in the power of young Hamlet, a favourite with the people, both on his own and on his father's account, a person of much address and richly endowed by nature and by culture, to rouse the people against a usurper who is of comparatively mean endowments—no more to be compared to his brother 'than Hyperion to a satyr!' The play itself shows us, as if in self-condemnation, how easily Laertes (a man greatly inferior to Hamlet in position and endowments), when *his* father was accidentally slain, could raise a dangerous commotion which seemed to imperil the throne. But Hamlet shows no such vigour, makes no public outcry, is even anxious to keep secret the revelation of the Ghost, and instead of directly appealing to his country for justice, he adopts roundabout methods, feigning madness, using a play to 'catch the conscience of the King,' and continually debating the matter with himself in long soliloquies.

But when we have learnt to regard the play as mainly an exhibition of Hamlet's remarkable nature, it no longer displeases. We study it with keener interest for something better than the action. When we become aware that it is Shakespeare's design to show us a man of the highest intellectual and moral endowments in a position requiring promptitude of action, we become intensely interested. As we know the danger there is in an over-balance of intellect or feeling, as we are aware that to one who waits to scrutinize every possible consequence and relation of his deed, action becomes impossible, we see that the slowness of the main action in the play, instead of being a fault, must be attributed to the deep philosophy of the poet.

Hamlet, while hearing the horrible relation of the Ghost, is full of promptitude, is absolutely decided. Before the Ghost has done, he cries out:

> 'Haste me to know't, that I with wings as swift
> As meditation, or the thoughts of love,
> May sweep to my revenge.'

But he has to learn the difference between the state of the will in warm moments when passion reigns, and its ordinary state when doubts begin and difficulties arise. Then to his imaginative mind the difficulties become tremendous, for to him difficulties occur that would occur to no one else. He begins to think this Ghost may be a devil, sent to ruin his soul by deceiving him. He must have this doubt resolved by means of some test before he can determine to act. Meantime, his will is enfeebled by delay. But after he has obtained confirmation of the Ghost's story by watching the King's countenance during the acting of 'Gonsago's murder,' he is no better prepared for action than before. Quite passively he allows the King to pack him off for England, and had he arrived there, the world would have heard no more of his revenge. An accident—the ship meeting with a pirate—casts him again on Danish soil—full of resentment, one would imagine, at the discovery of the King's plot against his own life. But no! he is only sick at heart because action seems inevitable. *Even to the last* he is without a plan. He chances to engage in a fencing bout with Laertes; finds himself mortally wounded, and his mother poisoned by the King's device; kills the King in a rage; and dies. The King's death seems rather accidental than the effect of Hamlet's purpose. Hamlet seems to be an instrument rather than an agent all through.

Hamlet is not a hero. He wants something needful to complete a character truly heroic; but he is perhaps more deeply interesting than if he were a victor always strong and secure. He is not one of those firm, positive minds who never doubt, who carry a fixed idea through all storms, through all mists and darkness, unchangeable as the star, and successful as fate. The mind of Hamlet was cast in a different mould; its fine elements were somewhat loosely thrown together. He has the incurable trick of endless speculation. He dwells so much in an imaginary and so little in a real world, he holds 'there is nothing either good or bad, but thinking makes it so'—a saying which indicates a strong poetic imagination, and a sort of self-abuse which results from thinking to excess. He has not been accustomed to restrain his thinking within prescribed limits, nor to make it travel by ordinary routes. A definite course of action would have resulted from the adoption of any intellectual system, but he had discovered none which he could honestly adopt. Once a remark drops from him indicating that with the orthodoxy of the time he was far from fully satisfied :

> 'There are more things in heaven and earth, Horatio,
> Than are dreamt of in your philosophy.'

Now, though Shakespeare deeply sympathizes with this sort of mind, it is not his ideal of perfection, he does not fully approve of it, nay, he seriously disapproves, and hence Hamlet in the play is a failure. While the definite vigour of Laertes would have produced but one death, Hamlet's hesitating, clumsy revenge causes eight deaths instead of one. He is so genial, thoughtful, humorous, pathetic, sarcastic, that he cannot fail to be attractive, but with all his fine ideas and superior knowledge he stumbles, like poor Burns, who every day transgressed his favourite maxim:

> 'On reason build resolve,
> The column of true majesty in man.'

Yet while in one sense Hamlet's life is a failure, in another and perhaps higher sense it is a success. Though he may at times envy, like Burns, the 'sons of busy life,' the men of practical talent, yet on the whole he would not exchange cases with any of them. Horatio is the finest character in the play after Hamlet, yet how small beside Hamlet we feel Horatio to be! Hamlet saw in Horatio the qualities in which he felt himself deficient, and reposed a confidence in him which he gave to no one else:

> 'For thou hast been
> As one in suffering all that suffers nothing,
> A man that fortune's buffets and rewards
> Has ta'en with equal thanks.'

'O for stability and calmness like thine, Horatio!' Hamlet is often ready to exclaim, when after one of his fits of excitement or one of his dark melancholy moods, he meets his self-possessed, prudent, clear-sighted, cool, somewhat stoical friend —'O for calmness like thine!'

> 'And bless'd are those
> Whose blood and judgment are so well commingled,
> That they are not a pipe for fortune's finger
> To sound what stop she please. Give me the man
> That is not passion's slave and I will wear him
> In my heart's core, ay, in my heart of heart,
> As I do thee.'

Those admirable endowments of imagination and feeling are felt to be perilous, and, like Scott and Burns, Hamlet sometimes thinks the man happy who is without them. A moment of confidence succeeded by doubt, a moment of violent energy succeeded by irresolution, a moment of keen, bright hope blotted out at once by the blackest despair—this is what Hamlet knew—what all poetic natures know; and this why a friend 'who is not passion's slave' is so precious to them.

Shakespeare brings out the character of Hamlet by contrast not only with this 'antique Roman' Horatio, but with Fortinbras, Osric, Laertes, and others in the play, who may be regarded as foils by means of which every side of Hamlet's character can be seen. Meeting Hamlet accidentally, Fortinbras awakes some of his most remarkable self-condemning reflection. He sees Fortinbras 'with divine ambition puff'd,' leading an army 'to gain a little patch of ground not worth five ducats,'

'Exposing what is mortal and unsure
To all that fortune death and danger dare
Even for an egg-shell,'

while *he*, who has cause grave enough to give countenance to the most dangerous enterprise, is inactive; and he exclaims,

'Whether it be
Bestial oblivion, or some craven scruple
Of thinking too precisely on the event—
A thought which, quartered, hath but one part wisdom
And ever three parts coward,—I do not know
Why yet I live to say "This thing's to do,"
Sith I have cause and will and strength and means
To do't.'

And even while engaged in these self-accusing thoughts Hamlet is on his way to England, to end by landing there all possibility that 'the thing' ever will be done!

And as already noticed, how marked the contrast between Laertes, when *his* father is killed, and Hamlet hesitating over thoughts of vengeance! Laertes' father is not indeed to be compared with Hamlet's, being no better than an old formal time-serving courtier, with a good memory for wise sayings, called by Hamlet a 'tedious old fool,' 'a foolish prating knave,' and treated by him as a conceited pedant, and one to be made game of; yet see the promptitude, the determination, the passion with which *his* son seeks vengeance! Rousing the populace, and rushing into the King's presence at the head of a mob, his words are brief but pointed: 'O thou vile King, give me my father!' He curses the drop of blood that is calm within him—sends allegiance to hell, dares damnation—while Hamlet, having far deeper injuries, is perhaps hesitating whether he should kill *himself* or the King, puzzling as to whether the 'sleep' of death may be disturbed by 'dreams,' and whether he should have any

> 'dread of something after death,
> That undiscovered country from whose bourn
> No traveller returns.'

Yet there are other views in which Hamlet contrasts more favourably with men like Laertes. O how delightfully different he is from them all! They want all his delicacy and depth of feeling, all his splendid intellectuality, all his beautiful and profound thoughts. Compared with him, how coarse and commonplace other men appear. They are unscrupulous, heartless, and heedless in pursuit of their purposes, he just the opposite of all this in pursuing his; they are uninteresting, he always interesting; they are conventional, he original. Some of them, like the courtier Osric, having got but the 'tune o' the time and outward habit of encounter,' can only say what has been already said; but Hamlet brings a fresh mind to every subject, and if he hesitates, it is because he makes his own opinions instead of adopting those ready-made, and because there is an earnestness and a conscientiousness in his thinking which ordinary minds know nothing of. Like all who have possessed the greatest spiritual gifts, Hamlet is simple and childlike, and so 'free from all contriving,' that men of the world consider him an easy prey. He chooses for his bosom friend, not some noble of his own rank, but the simple scholar Horatio, whose nature draws him like a magnet. Through all his scepticism he has struggled up to belief in God, and he affirms

> 'There's a Divinity that shapes our ends,
> Rough-hew them as we will.'

No one perceives better or blames more severely than himself the sad waverings of his nature, his alternate inertness and passion, indolence and excitement, with all the torments and faults resulting; yet he knows there is a virtuous and wise irresolution as well as one of weakness : and he may sometimes justly think that if he had less conscience, less tenderness, less sense of honour, or even less sensitiveness of organization, he could be more decided. When the signal of the 'Danish rouse,' which he pronounces a 'custom more honour'd in the breach than the observance,' leads him to think of the weakness of the drunkard, we know that he feels his own infirmity in speaking to all hearts thus :

> 'So oft it chances with particular men,
> That for some vicious mole of nature in them,
> As in their birth—wherein they are not guilty,
> Since nature cannot choose its origin—
> By the o'ergrowth of some complexion
> Oft breaking down the pales and forts of reason,
> Or by some habit that too much o'er-leavens
> The form of plausive manners, that these men,
> Carrying, I say, the stamp of one defect,
> Being nature's livery or fortune's star—
> Their virtues else, be they as pure as grace,
> As infinite as man may undergo—
> Shall in the general censure take corruption
> From that particular fault : the dram of evil
> Doth all the noble substance oft debase
> To its own scandal.'

Hamlet doubtless felt 'the dram of evil' in his own case was his weakness of will; and whether this defect was born with him or was the result of peculiar trials—whether it was 'nature's livery or fortune's star'—it certainly 'debased all the noble substance' in which it dwelt. It is the fairest rose that may have the canker. Most of us may have noticed once in our lifetime some man of fine talents who was hindered from rising to his natural zenith by some slight circumstance—as the giant Gulliver was kept stretched on the ground by the pins of the Lilliputians.

Perhaps, indeed, we should not see in Hamlet any inherent defect of will, but rather that indifference to the ordinary objects and prizes of life produced by the 'glance of melancholy' or genius :

> 'The glance of melancholy is a fearful gift !
> What is it but the telescope of truth,
> That strips the distance of its fantasies,
> And brings life near in utter nakedness,
> Making the sad reality too real.'*

The earnest glance of genius, peering into all earthly excellences, sees in them all a taint of dissatisfaction and decay.

> 'There lives within the very flame of love
> A kind of wick or snuff that will abate it,
> And nothing is at a like goodness still,
> For goodness growing to a pleurisy
> Dies of its own too much.'

Even that oft-quoted speech of Hamlet on the dignity of man includes the same sad reflection ; and when we leave out the concluding lines, as is frequently done, it loses its original purport in our mouths : 'What a piece of work is man ! how noble in reason ! how infinite in faculty ! in form and moving how express and admirable ! in action how like an angel ! in apprehension how like a God ! the beauty of the world ! the paragon of animals !' We like to stop here. We even feel repelled by the concluding words : 'And yet, to me, what is this quintessence of dust ? Man delights not me.' Yes ! genius with its earnest eye, piercing the 'centre and the sum of things,' cries 'All is vanity !' Some of the greatest minds have doubted whether on the whole life be worth living; some, like Hugh Miller, have deliberately thrown the gift away ; and Hamlet once asks, 'What should such fellows as I do crawling between earth and heaven?' Even in his most ordinary tone of conversation this undervaluing of life is discernible, as when dismissing Horatio and the soldiers on the platform :

* Byron.

> 'And so, without more circumstance at all,
> I hold it fit that we shake hands and part,
> You, as your business and desire shall point you,
> For every man hath business and desire,
> *Such as it is;* and for my own poor part,
> Look you, I'll go pray.'

Indifference to the objects of life—even disgust of life—has something to do with Hamlet's irresolution.

Hamlet, as has been said, is not Shakespeare's hero, though perhaps he most perfectly represents Shakespeare's *self.* Shakespeare's fullest approval is not bestowed on a man so like himself; it is with Prince Harry in his splendid martial success rather than with Hamlet in deep soliloquies. It has been said that Hamlet is even a eulogy of the active nature by a picture of the contrary, our poet being strongly of opinion that all cultivation of intellect and heart, without discipline of the will and exercise of the active powers, is fruitless. There is so much mockery of the world, subtle sarcasm, and ironical levity in Hamlet—or, again, such dreamy speculation—that we are seldom sure whether he is altogether in earnest. There is, however, one scene in which he rises to the full dignity of serious and powerful action; and if we would see Hamlet as he *might* have been but for the terrible contradictions of his fate—if we would see his commanding powers in full exercise, and see him towering above ordinary men in all the majesty of his powerful nature—we should study that scene in which he deals with his mother alone. We think a messenger from heaven could scarce deal with the erring soul at once more mildly, faithfully, and effectually than Hamlet, whose bearing can be compared only to the holy boldness of the Hebrew prophet, who looked into the eyes of the guilty King, while darting into his conscience the words terrible and brief, 'Thou art the man!'

There is one side of Hamlet's character, very prominent in the play, to which I have not done justice here. I refer to the humorous or satirical element. By this he has such a triumph as nature allows to the man of feeling over the steady, plodding, prudent people whom he usually finds in worldly circumstances superior to his own. In Jaques, who is an inferior Hamlet, Shakespeare had already vindicated the position of a public censor who kept in check evils which the law could not deal with. It cannot be said that the consequences of bad taste, or the stupid preferences of commonplace minds, are unimportant, yet even the all-powerful British Government cannot prevent their occurrence. It is for Shakespeare, and such as he, by the mouths of their Hamlets and otherwise, to check such evils. When, for example, Polonius interrupts the player while uttering his splendid speech on the death of Priam, saying, with the inane indifference of one that fails to comprehend, 'This is too long;' Hamlet answers: 'It shall to the barber's with your beard—Prithee, say on—he's for a jig or tale of bawdry, or he sleeps.'

And it speaks ill for our boasted civilization that there are *still* large numbers of respectable people who are incapable of taking so much interest in fine poetry as to keep them awake during its recital. But, like all such people, Polonius wants to have the credit of something better, and boasts that he once acted Julius Cæsar at the university in his youth, and was killed in the Capitol by Brutus. 'It was a brute part of him to kill so capital a calf there,' rejoins the sarcastic Hamlet, who proceeds to worse mockery of the servile old courtier when, pointing to the cloud, he gets him to say first that it is like a camel, then that it is like a weasel, and finally that it is 'very like a whale.' [In scorn of similar time-serving, he takes off the 'water-fly' Osric, making him say the weather is very cold after he had said, ''Tis very hot;' and then again: 'Exceedingly, my lord; it is very sultry—as 'twere—I cannot tell how.'

In another passage Hamlet's melancholy is finely mingled with this satire, while the appearance of madness is well sustained. After a few of Hamlet's pungent speeches, Polonius says, 'My honourable lord, I will most humbly take my leave of you;' and Hamlet answers: 'You cannot, sir, take from me anything that I will more willingly part withal!—except my life, except my life, except my life!',

To the view which we have taken of Hamlet's character we are aware that objections may be made. We will now briefly consider some of these, leading as they do to the chief moot-points of the play—to the battlefields of critics. If Hamlet's nature was so truly gentle and noble as it has been represented, what about his rudeness, almost brutality, to Ophelia? If he be so highly conscientious, what about his stratagem causing the death of the King's messengers, Rosencrantz and Guildenstern? If he is so guileless and straightforward, why is he 'mad in craft?' Above all, what shall we say of the man who refuses to kill his uncle only because he is praying, and resolves to wait for an opportunity to kill him when he is drunk, that thus he may secure his damnation? Is this, it is asked, is this the deeply moral nature that not only hates evil in itself, but even feels outraged by the guilt of others? Such questions have been asked by critics, from Dr. Johnson and Steevens downwards, and have even led some so far as to accuse our great Shakespeare of something like literary bungling.

Now we at once admit that Hamlet is not an *even* character. He is too much a man of feeling not to be impulsive and somewhat inconsistent. We find him expressing sincere repentance for his outrageous conduct at Ophelia's grave; also for the rash plunge into the arras by which he unwittingly slew her father. And it is to be noted that Hamlet's character necessarily alters during the course of the play. After he becomes aware of his uncle's and his mother's guilt, he is a changed man. His belief in human nature is destroyed. Henceforth he sees human nature as something incurably bad. Though not a misanthrope of the type of Timon, his usual tone in company is that of sarcasm and satire. Since he has found his own mother guilty, even his fair Ophelia can be loved—can be trusted—no more. He now dislikes the thought of marriage, and therefore presents to her an exaggerated picture of his own depravity, and rudely accuses her of being capable of the like. His rudeness and severity to her were assumed; he believed his duty to her required the proposed match to be broken off, and he therefore wished her to dislike him; besides, his own overwhelming sorrow may have made him forgetful of her feelings. Yet we observe more than one lingering token of tenderness in the midst of his despair—as when he advises her to 'go to a nunnery,' unwilling she should be another's, though she cannot be his. Shakespeare knew well the infirmity of the man of genius in this matter, and doubtless intended it should be seen in Hamlet. The history of men of genius seems to show that their love is more intense, and also more uncertain, than other men's. Because they have an ideal of love far beyond anything attainable in actual life, they at times despise their own best joy. Thus Hamlet, in the last scene between him and Ophelia, declares, 'I did love you once,' and then, in the very next sentence, 'I loved you not.' Like all such men he sees imperfection in his love, and even doubts at times whether it be love at all. Thus Tennyson, after saying many touching and beautiful things of Arthur, exclaims once:

'I cannot love thee as I ought!'

and again:

'What keeps a spirit always true
To that ideal which he bears?
What record? Not the sinless years
That breathed beneath the Syrian blue.'

In Hamlet Shakespeare has given us the man of genius encumbered as he is in actual life by the difficulties of action—difficulties which could be more easily dealt with by a man of less refined and less imaginative temperament, as a blunt knife cuts your paper better than a sharp one. It is his nature to form an ideal of conduct extreme and impossible in its perfection. This tendency not only explains his contemptuous treatment of his love, but also the somewhat shocking reason which he gives for delaying to kill his uncle when he found him engaged in prayer. When he says he will wait till he finds him engaged in some act 'that has no relish of salvation in't,' he speaks like the man of feeling who is extreme in his imaginary, but very moderate in his actual, deeds. He thinks he must have a perfect revenge or none, and while engrossed with this thought, he does not realize what his perfect revenge, if reduced to literal fact, would be. The Ghost had by fearful allusions impressed on his mind the fact that his father had been taken unprepared, therefore he feels that a corresponding revenge requires that the murderer should *also* be taken unprepared. It is only his way of elevating practical matters into speculations—his mental striving after an ideal harmony, while forgetful of material limitations. And it may be even questioned whether Hamlet's strange mind were not at this moment practising a kind of self-deception, and by means of this horrible theory of revenge indulging his reluctance to act. The more we meditate on the scene referred to, the more we are struck with this. Here at length he has the amplest opportunity of performing what with the most awful solemnity he had vowed to do; and it is just *now*, for the first time, he feels how vast the gulf is between his resolution and his deed. From crossing that awful gulf his soul is shrinking back, but he does not observe her alarm. He deceives himself with a *reason* for delay which his fine imagination readily furnishes. 'This is not the *moment* for the fatal stroke,' his evil genius whispers; and we know that to the irresolute man *every* opportunity is in some respect objectionable. 'This is not the moment for your perfect revenge; see, he is praying.' The circumstance which would have provoked another instantly to commit the deed, is by his ingenuity and repugnance to action turned to a reason against it. This therefore is *not* the diabolical wickedness some have imagined it to be; rather it is the extreme exhibition of Hamlet's indecision.

Perhaps his inserting the names of the King's messengers in the commission instead of his own, and thus procuring their death, is not quite defensible. It was not Shakespeare's intention to present Hamlet as anything better than a 'natural' man. His carnal satisfaction at the destruction of his enemies is undisguised. Like most modern Christians, he lacks sufficient grace to return good for evil. And judging from what we daily see, even 'conversion,' were it repeated some half dozen times, would scarce bring him to *that*. Rosencrantz and Guildenstern are not indeed persons deserving of high consideration. They are the usurper's tools and flunkeys. They have been set to watch Hamlet, and are ready to pick up his unguarded expressions and bring them in evidence to ruin him. To their face he accuses them of 'going about to recover the wind of him, as if they would drive him into a toil.' He speaks to his mother of 'my two school-fellows whom I will trust as I will adders fang'd,' and adds :

> 'It shall go hard
> But I will delve one yard below their mines,
> And blow them at the moon.'

And when at length the actual fact is before his eyes, and he reads his own name in the murderous commission which they carry, enraged, and in haste, and doubtless with a touch of that wit that never entirely forsakes him, he inserts their names, and makes them the bearers of their own death warrant. If they did not know all the wickedness of the King's plot, they had at any rate willingly lent themselves to his nefarious designs against Hamlet. 'They did make love to this employment,' says Hamlet, in explaining to Horatio, and adds :

> 'They are not near my conscience ; their defeat
> Does by their own insinuation grow :
> 'Tis dangerous when the baser nature comes
> Between the pass and fell incensed points
> Of mighty opposites '—.

such as he and the usurper were. It was near the end, when Hamlet had been driven to the verge of desperation by repeated ills ; and we know that gentlest natures when pushed to extreme (like the mother bird defending her young), attack their foes with peculiar intensity of bitterness. He had one morning awaked from his dreams, and found that by the wicked deeds of others all his earthly hopes were blasted. Fresh injuries are heaped on the crushed heart which can get no revenge, till in gloomy moments he calls himself a 'tame snake,' and one that 'lacks gall to make oppression bitter.' Can we wonder, when he manifests, after all, that he has 'something in him dangerous?' A trifle of vindictiveness does not make him lose our sympathy, and certainly does not make his character seem inconsistent.

He makes in the last scene a deep expiation. Evils in others—complicated mistakes and faults—combine with his one great infirmity, irresolution, and draw on a general ruin, which is too like scenes that unhappy men have witnessed, not to enlist our deepest sympathy. We almost fancy we are more than spectators of this unfortunate concurrence of causes; so skilfully does the magician work, that we are almost persuaded that we have ourselves assisted at the dread *dénouement*.

How different, under different circumstances, this strange and always interesting Hamlet would have been! By his powerful, penetrating intellect, by his deep and sound reflection on men and things, by his exquisite wit and delightful humour, he would have adorned, had he been permitted to occupy, the great position to which he was born. But it was his lot to fall upon an iron time; and the heavy weight of the dreadful task laid upon him was ill suited to his mild and humourful nature. He was (as Goëthe puts it) like a fine porcelain jar in which an oak has been planted; the great roots expand, and the jar is shivered. Thus Hamlet, a lovely, pure, noble, and most moral nature, without the nerve of some inferior men, sinks beneath a burden which he cannot bear and must not cast away. He himself often felt extremely this incongruity between his own delicate nature and the rude requirements of the world, as when, after the Ghost's announcement, and when his passion begins to cool, he exclaims:

'The time is out of joint—O cursèd spite,
That ever I was born to set it right!'

I have endeavoured to illustrate the genius of Shakespeare in what is in some respects his most remarkable creation,

Hamlet. We may triumphantly ask, where in all the literature of the world is there such another? Where is there such dealing with the deeper springs of human nature? Where else is there such a presentation of the modern intellect and heart, with such powerful energies, such noble attributes, such vast and various resources, that it attracts and interests the vulgar and refined, the philosopher and practical man alike? And what a collection of pieces of pure poetry, practical philosophy, shrewd observation, scathing satire, and genuine wit we have in the whole of this great drama! What a rare privilege we have, in those splendid soliloquies of Hamlet, of observing the inner workings of thought and feeling, which in the case of the world's great men are usually concealed by a necessary reserve!

The Germans say 'Hamlet' has influenced their nation more than any other poem except 'Faust.' To one eminent German 'Hamlet' seems a perfect allegorical representation of a nation whose weakness has been its tendency to go to the intellectual extreme. Professor Gervinus says : 'Hamlet is Germany. We Germans have been deeply absorbed with the cultivation of the mind and heart to forgetfulness of the world without. Wittenberg and its bequests lay nearer our hearts than warlike struggles for honour and power. The spirits of our forefathers approached us in those early days of our political elevation from the French yoke, and rejoiced over our quick resolve. But we soon let our ardour drop—we flew from the real to the ideal—losing delight in existence. Too much study injured the sure tact of instinctive life among us. We grew sceptically embittered against the world. Have we not all in the soliloquies of our literature felt proud in the acquisitions of our mind, and found man so like a god, so noble in reason, etc., without delighting in him? .... Each, fancying he must be his country's saviour, forgets the near for the distant—thinks not of his individual present duty. Hamlet should first eform himself. A purely intellectual life has so fostered our egotism, that each person feels he is the champion of the world, while all are incapable of satisfying any demands.' There is, I may add, a country nearer home to which these remarks of the learned German would quite as well apply. Would that our inconstant, irresolute *Irishmen* would begin reforms by each reforming himself! Would that each were less given to 'fancying himself his country's saviour,' and more given to think of 'individual present duty !' Would that there were fewer who desire to pose as 'champions of the world,' consuming in ideal and misleading pictures the strength that ought to be employed in practical efforts—in ordinary common-place *work*. The evils of Ireland are ready to fly at the magic touch of intelligent industry, watchful promptitude, unyielding energy—but our country will, without these, remain incurable as Moore's ' Dismal Swamp,' in spite of the most enlightened statemanship, backed by all the 'resources of civilization.' But the tragic close of the play brings before us not an ideal, but the real world. The blundering revenge which causes four deaths while aiming at one, is intended to characterize the man who, infirm from noble causes, still *is* 'infirm of purpose.' On account of so many deaths, French critics have sneered at 'Hamlet' as a 'barbarous and bloody' tragedy; but what should we expect in connexion with the painful mysteries of the human soul, its contradictions of faith and scepticism, of self-imposed bondage and self-asserting freedom, of lawless desire and legal restraint, but just such dread calamities in the actual world as have in all ages perplexed the wisest, who could only gaze and wonder at the sublime but obscure enigma of life ?

MILTON.

MILTON, who, at the age of twenty-two, sang over Shakespeare's grave as we have seen (p. 60), was eight years old when Shakespeare died. We may, therefore, regard him at that age as the boy-prophet of England; for there was no successor with high spiritual and artistic faculty worthy of Shakespeare till Milton came. Perhaps even more markedly than either Chaucer or Shakespeare, Milton was the product of his age. I have spoken of Chaucer's fourteenth century as an intellectual spring-time for European nations; but what shall I say of this marvellous seventeenth century, in which Milton wrote and Cromwell warred? My aim is to keep on ground strictly literary, avoiding the political as much as possible; but while treating of such authors as Milton we do not profess to be able to keep our nerves wholly free from the thrill of the mighty events amid which they wrote, events which caused these strong pulsations of life still throbbing in their songs. One can hardly characterize the seventeenth century without indicating political or religious bias; but it is safe to say that the key which explains our present religious, political, and social phenomena is to be found in that wonderful era. According to one party, it was a time when England, seething and convulsed with sects which were the hydra-brood of heresy, experienced at length the explosion which made the return of orthodoxy for ever impossible. According to another party, it was the time when Englishmen were fullest of a divine heroic spirit, when in men's hearts faith in God was most real and strong, when the eternal distinctions of right and wrong were most powerfully felt and most grandly vindicated, when time-serving formalism and shams of all sorts were shaken off by men who rose like Titans to consciousness of mighty power which had slumbered in them while they lay beneath the nightmare of religious falsehood and the incubus of political tyranny. By a judicious use of the literature of the time, we may get each of these opinions to modify the other. No man will despise that century with which Thomas Carlyle (no sectarian bigot) sees 'the last glimpse of the godlike vanishing from England;' and if any are tempted to overrate its importance, a perusal of the poem called 'Hudibras' will reduce their enthusiasm to the proper level. If we listen to the loud boom of Milton's cannon :

> 'Cromwell, our chief of men, who through a cloud
> Not of war only, but detractions rude,
> Guided by faith and matchless fortitude,
> To peace and truth thy glorious way hast ploughed!'

we should also hear the sharp-shooting of Butler, who associates the great military genius and his friend the great poetic genius of his time with

> 'A sect whose chief devotion lies
> In odd perverse antipathies,
> In falling out with that or this,
> And finding somewhat still amiss.
> More peevish, cross, and splenetic
> Than dog distract or monkey sick,
> That with more care keep holiday
> The wrong, than others the right way, . . .
> Still so perverse and opposite
> As if they worshipped God for spite.'

Milton, who was born in 1608, was only four years older than Butler, and for upwards of half a century these two great representatives of serious and comic poetry respectively were contemporary and by no means unconcerned spectators of England's varying fortunes in that eventful time. Never did a great political party in any age idolize and rejoice in a poem as the Cavaliers rejoiced in and idolized the brilliant production of Butler's pungent humour and caustic wit, wherein the swarming sects, Presbyterian, Independent, Baptist, Quaker, get such a 'smoking' as would have fully satisfied Laud himself. But while Butler was thus gloried in by one party, Milton was to an equal or superior degree the glory of the other. The erudition of Butler was great, that of Milton was greater, and surely his art was of a higher order, as his muse was more refined. Milton could not contend with Butler's shafts of wit; Butler could not rise to Milton's lofty argument or bold sublimity. If the Cavaliers were proud that the best satirical poem had proceeded from their party, the Roundheads were equally proud that from *them* had proceeded England's great epic. Both poems are highly distinguished for the amount of clear thinking and valuable instruction which they contain. And such is the triumph of literary genius, that now both parties can heartily join in applauding both great poems, and English-speaking men everywhere over the globe, whatever their politics and whatever their creed, are equally ready to honour and applaud the satiric genius of Butler and the sublime genius of Milton.

My experience of readers compels me to place Milton in the class of authors that are much praised and little read. To the common mind he seems less accessible, or less attractive, than some other great writers. What Wordsworth has said of Milton's soul— it 'dwelt apart'—is too true of Milton's works; along with some few other authors of the first rank, he is not meddled with by the ' ordinary reader.' In many people there exists a salutary dread of Milton; and they would as soon take up a book of sermons, if they wanted amusement, as 'Paradise Lost.' Some of us have had to *parse* that terrible blank verse at school, and rueful scenes in that connexion may be supplied by memory. To many minds there is an awful severity, almost a religious rigour, about Milton, which hinders them from associating him with pleasant books of poetry to which men go for instructive amusement.

Let the young reader believe me when I assure him that much of this is prejudice and misconception; let him take my advice to be better acquainted with the author, and he will soon see that he is neither a rigid ascetic nor a hard, dry writer, difficult to understand. I have seen a portrait by the celebrated Janssens of the boy Milton; a sweet and beautiful child's face it was; and the painting, even at the time when Milton's father first showed it to his friends in Bread Street, London, must have seemed to warrant the expense incurred by the fond parent. An engraving of this picture, and also an engraving of one taken at the age of twenty-one, are given in Professor Masson's great work on the 'Life of Milton and History of his Times.' One has only to look at these two portraits to get rid of the idea of rigid unsightly Puritanic severity and hard heavy scholarship sometimes associated with Milton. There surely never was a pleasanter little boy than John Milton at the age of ten. Evidently a gentle, lovable child, with a delightful solidity in one so young. There is, no doubt, a certain seriousness in him which, however, is not inconsistent with the cheerful beauty which nature bestows on her most favoured flowers. Or, looking at the portrait taken at twenty-one, where would one see a handsomer, more amiable-looking, or more interesting youth than this, with his long flowing auburn locks parted in front, his pure white and red complexion, his large full forehead, and deep grey eyes? It is somewhat difficult to, imagine the presence of such a young man, of middle height, of erect and manly bearing, being disagreeable to any young lady; yet it is an historical fact, that after a short stay under his roof, his young wife left him and refused to return. And I fear there are young ladies who, under misconceptions as strange, shrink from Milton even now! Let them remember that Milton's bride soon repented the rash step which she had taken; as, we hope, some other young pleasure-seekers, who have been repelled by the apparent difficulty of Milton, will repent and return. Many a young truant of good natural intelligence has become a constant and loving student from the moment when he allowed the real nature of his studies to flash upon his understanding and be felt within him; and then, pitying his former self, he may have the Miltonic feeling, though not the Miltonic power of expression of that well-known passage in 'Comus:'

> 'How charming is divine philosophy ¡
> Not harsh and crabbèd, as dull fools suppose,
> But musical as is Apollo's lute,
> And a perpetual feast of nectar'd sweets,
> Where no crude surfeit reigns.'

Milton's father did not always live in that Bread Street, London, where our great epic poet was born, and where the father amassed a considerable fortune by his own industry as a scrivener, or writer of legal documents. John Milton, senior, was born of gentle blood in Oxfordshire, but was disinherited by his father because he saw fit to embrace Protestant opinions. Coming to London to push his fortune, he learnt the scrivener business with some relatives, and prospered in that way of living. His leading taste was for music—he was a good organist and a clever composer; besides, he was a man of independent and cultured mind, who, after business hours, made the evenings in Bread Street very pleasant to his wife and his three children, Anne, John, and Christopher. Besides his music, he would give them readings from good religious books of the right old Puritan ring which he liked, also some poetry, perhaps the 'Faërie Queen,' or Sylvester's 'Du Bartas' (poem on the Creation), two books which had an important influence on the mind of his eldest son, who was his favourite, and to whose training he devoted himself with all his wisdom and zeal. The boy, inheriting his father's musical passion, could play beautifully when a mere child, and gave even then intellectual promise so distinct, that his father felt no care or expense too great to be employed on his education. And we should note that Milton's musical taste, developed thus amid the sweetest and happiest of home influences, was an important element in the formation of the future poet. Coleridge calls Milton a musical rather than a picturesque poet, and though we cannot think Milton's poetry wanting in picturesqueness (witness 'Allegro' and 'Penseroso'), it is true that those who have the finest ear for music are (other things being equal) most capable of enjoying the charm of Milton's verse.

St. Paul's Grammar School, one of the best in London, had the honour of receiving young Milton as a pupil, and besides daily instruction there, he had the aid of masters at home. His application was wonderful; the fire in his soul was early lighted, and blazed long. Even when a boy, he often sat up half the night with his books, and thus, as he thought, laid the foundation of that sad injury to his eyes which ultimately left him to sing his sublime song of the wars of the angels and the glories of the heavenly places, while to his outward vision the earth and sky, and the sun itself, were blank. Fortunately for the world, this did not happen till Milton was forty-six years of age; otherwise we should not have those vivid and exquisite delineations of nature which he drew from memory and embodied in his latest poems. The boy was ripe for college at fifteen, and the following year he entered Cambridge, his father having designed him for the Church.

Shakespeare was then dead but eight years. Had he ever seen, as he passed through Bread Street on his way to his favourite haunt the Mermaid Tavern, close at hand, going to meet Ben Jonson and other wits—had the great dramatist ever noticed on the doorstep under the sign of the Spread Eagle a sunny-faced, serious-eyed, auburn-haired, handsome boy named John Milton? It is quite possible, and even likely; but there is no record of the fact. As London was not a large city then, and everyone knew Shakespeare's appearance on the street, it is very probable he had at least been pointed out to the boy Milton by his father.

Milton at college was no idler, tasting only the easily accessible sweets of literature and avoiding hard work. With his fine taste and steady industry he soon became an accomplished linguist, so that when he afterwards travelled on the Continent he was able to write Italian poems which the Italians themselves admired. He wrote Latin more elegantly than any scholar in Europe. Though a hard student, and given to late hours, he did not neglect, but was extremely fond of manly exercises; and though, on account of his beauty, his fellow-students nicknamed him 'The Lady,' he would have been a troublesome lady to any who crossed him, for he was an expert and skilful swordsman. We need hardly be surprised that a young man of his bold original type found the formal ways of college life irksome at times, that he quarrelled once with the authorities, and suffered what is called rustication. Even at the present day the learned professors of Cambridge, should a young Milton come to study under them, might fail to discern his presence. Though ultimately Milton's superior merit was recognised, it is a fact that his young friend Edward King, five years his junior, whom he afterwards mourned as 'Lycidas,' was promoted to a fellowship over his head. Also, when a book of poems was collected from the students and presented to the King, it contained none of Milton's verses.

His first original poetry was written at college at the age of seventeen, the lines 'On the Death of a Fair Infant,' his sister's daughter. They contain a reference to the Great Plague then wasting London.

> 'But oh, why did'st thou not stay here below
> To bless us with thy heaven-loved innocence,
> To slake His wrath whom sin hath made our foe,
> To turn swift-rushing black Perdition hence,
> Or drive away the slaughtering Pestilence,
> To stand 'twixt us and our deserved smart?
> But thou can'st best perform that office were thou art.'

Reading this, we are struck by the fact that Milton thus early adopted (with a slight modification) Chaucer's beautiful stanza, showing he had already found a kindred spirit in that first great English man of letters. And as to the sentiment, how different it is here, from that of the severe, strict Puritan which Milton afterwards became! The idea of the child's soul in heaven acting the part of a guardian angel to save its friends from the Plague does not savour much of Puritanism.

One fancies the Cambridge professors might have read with no ordinary feelings of respect the college exercises sent in by the young student from Bread Street, London; for even from his class exercises *we* think they might have known the fact that one of the world's greatest bards had arisen in England. Some hold the opinion that much learning and thorough universal culture are unfavourable to the growth of original genius. Poetry made behind a plough is therefore sometimes received with more confidence than that composed in college halls. This idea receives no support from the case of Milton. He at least was not afraid his genius could be smothered under stores of learning, or could be cultivated down to insignificance. Natural genius, when it is real, will overcome all difficulties— the difficulty of too little education, or too much; but we can hardly think there is any force in the notion that the less learning a man has the brighter will his genius burn. As a short specimen of Milton's college poetry, take the following extract from one of his class exercises, written at nineteen, which is remarkable as setting forth at this early date his desire for a theme like that of the sublime epic which occupied the close of his life—a 'subject'

> 'Such where the deep transported mind may soar
> Above the wheeling poles, and at Heaven's door
> Look in, and see each blissful deity
> How he before the thunderous throne doth lie,
> Listening to what unshorn Apollo sings
> To the touch of golden wires, while Hebe brings
> Immortal nectar to her kingly sire;
> Then passing through the spheres of watchful fire,
> And misty regions of wide air next under,
> And hills of snow, and lofts of pilèd thunder,
> May tell at length how green-eyed Neptune raves,
> In heaven's defiance mustering all his waves.'

Though Milton was probably looking forward to the Church, in obedience to his father's wishes, it was not, we presume, in the spirit of the Puritan party, which is so little visible in these verses, or even in the spirit in which he afterwards wrote those terrible controversial pamphlets on Church government, divorce, and other theological questions of the day. The fact is, Milton as a student shows little or nothing of the Puritan, having signed at least twice the articles and formularies of the Church of England; and after taking his bachelor's and master's degree, he would probably have gone on to take orders, had he not just then been stirred too profoundly in his sensitive poet-nature by the beginnings of that mighty shaking of the nation which ended in its severance into two great parties, and the dread commotion with which they rushed together in the Civil War. Nor was it on account of Puritanic scruples that Milton at last turned away from the ministerial office. He took a higher stand than those who were offended at surplices, kneeling, forms of prayer, and Arminian doctrine. It was not so much the ritualism of the Church as the tyranny exercised by its rulers that disgusted Milton. Here are his own words:

'The Church to whose service, by the intentions of my parents and friends, I was destined of a child and in mine own resolutions, till, coming to some maturity of years, and perceiving what tyranny had invaded in the Church—that he who would take orders must subscribe slave, and take an oath withal, which unless he took with a conscience that would retch, he must either straight perjure or split his faith—I thought it better to prefer a blameless silence before the sacred office of speaking, bought and begun with servitude and forswearing.'

We can hardly regret that Milton did not become a clergyman. Had he entered the Church he might not have become the glorious poet of whom all England and the world is proud. Would his genius not have dwindled in the ecclesiastical gown? We cannot tell; but we are sure he did right in obeying his conscience, even when it led him away from the Church. His wisdom is vindicated by the result. It was not for *him* to preach ephemeral sermons, and be saddled with routine parochial duties; for him was spacious leisure, scope, and freedom, that in the exercise of his sublime gift his preaching might form a 'fountain of immortal drink' to all ages and all lands.

Even before leaving college, and before his quiet retirement to his father's country residence at Horton, he had written at the age of twenty-one an Ode, which no less a judge than Hallam pronounces to be 'perhaps the best in the English language.' It was in the Christmas vacation of 1629 he wrote the splendid 'Ode on the Morning of Christ's Nativity.' This I shall not quote, as it is, or ought to be, on the tongue and heart of every school boy who reads English; but a simple reference to one or two of its beauties may be agreeable. The occurrence of the Nativity in winter is poetically explained by saying that Nature, in sympathy with her great Master in his lowly condition, 'had doft her gaudy trim,' and at the same time, conscious of the polluting presence of sin, had wooed the gentle air 'to hide her guilty front with innocent snow.' Then we have the descent of the angel Peace, 'with turtle wing the amorous clouds dividing, and waving wide her myrtle wand' that had such wondrous effects. The effect of Christ's birth on the pagan gods and oracles is described in exquisite words:

'The oracles are dumb, no voice or hideous hum
Runs through the archèd roofs in words deceiving;
Apollo from his shrine can no more divine,
With hollow shriek the steep of Delphos leaving;
No nightly trance or breathèd spell
Inspires the pale-eyed priest from the prophetic cell.'

And he sums up the entire discomfiture of the whole host of national gods in the following splendid simile:

'As when the sun in bed, curtain'd with cloudy red,
Pillows his chin upon an orient wave,
The flocking shadows pale troop to th' infernal jail,
Each fetter'd ghost slips to his several grave,
And the yellow-skirted fays
Fly after the night-steeds leaving their moon-loved maze.'

How elevating and pure—I had almost said sacred—is Milton's poetry from first to last! No stain of grossness or license sullies the strains of his youth or of his age. How seldom poets, lovers of nature, susceptible of tenderest feelings, and swayed by strongest passions, have been able to keep their verse immaculate, as Milton has done. It was not that he had a less sensitive nature—his nature was exquisitely sensitive; or that he had less temptations; there were habits among the students of Cambridge in those days which are surprising to read of. The secret of Milton's purity lay in his firm self-government, in the control of an iron will which was upheld by principles learned first in his blameless home, and grasped with the hearty assent of one who sees in their rejection or adoption the difference between death and life. The fixed principle on which his whole character from first to last was built was that of moral integrity. He dreaded sensuality as the cause of spiritual incapacity; he dreaded it as other men dread loss of fortune; moral pollution was feared by him as loss of reason is feared by others.

We are not to understand from this that he affected what is called puritanical strictness; he mixed freely with the world and read books of all kinds, not believing in a secluded or 'cloistered virtue,' but in one more able to face and withstand the rude shocks of evil. Though a hard student, he was no mere bookworm. The natural gaiety and romance of youth were in him not less but greater than in others. Yet there is every reason to believe he kept himself pure. A phase of Milton's character not commonly thought of may be seen in his Latin epistles written to his bosom friend Charles Diodati of Florence. He tells in one of these how up to that date he had been 'fancy free,' even laughing love to scorn, till one day a change took place. In one of his walks through the city he chanced to pass through a crowd of fine ladies. We finish the account in his own words: 'In appearance,' says he, 'it might seem a crowd of goddesses going and coming splendidly along the middle of the ways; the growing day shines with two-fold brightness. I do not austerely shun those agreeable sights, but am whirled along wherever my youthful impulse carries me. Too imprudent, I let my eyes meet theirs, and am unable to master them. One by chance I beheld pre-eminent over the rest, and that glance was the beginning of my malady. Such as she would Venus wish herself to be seen by mortals. . . . Immediately unaccustomed pains were felt in my heart. Being in love, I inly burn, I am all one flame. Meanwhile she who alone pleased me was snatched away from my eyes, never to return. . . . Overcome with grief, I can neither desist from love begun, nor follow it out. . . .' Believe me, no one ever burned so unhappily. I may be set up as the first and only instance of a chance so hard.' Then in the old classic tongue which he has adopted, he prays the winged god of love to spare him: 'Take away at length—and yet take not away my pains! I know not why, but every lover is sweetly miserable. But do thou kindly grant that if ever hereafter I and my love meet, one arrow may transfix the two, and make us lovers.'

From passages like this in Milton's youthful writings, we see that it was not a constitutional coldness that made him tread so successfully the path of virtue; and we may profitably reflect on the power of will that was needed to control so completely a nature so susceptible as his.

Milton's great epic has doubtless sometimes overshadowed his other poems, and hindered the young from taking kindly to him as they do to other poets. If he had not written 'Paradise Lost,' it is possible he might have been by his earlier writings a more general favourite. At any rate, by thinking of Milton too exclusively in connexion with the larger poem, some may have escaped the charm, the exquisite ease and geniality of the delightful minor pieces which he wrote after leaving college at Horton, his father's country residence. Here he conscientiously pursued his studies, and though he had relinquished the idea of a profession, he began consciously to set before him an ideal life-work which was more perfectly in accordance with the endowments of his noble nature. To him poetry was no mere bagatelle or youthful frivolity. It was the serious business, the great and high undertaking of his life. It was the channel through which could be exercised the highest functions which it is given to a human being to perform. Labour and study, he nobly says, he 'accepted as his portion in this life.' And already he felt growing upon him an inward prompting—a strong propensity of nature—to leave something to after times, 'so written as they should not willingly let it die.' His ambition was, he says, to be 'an interpreter and relater of the best and sagest things among mine own citizens throughout the island, in the mother-dialect—that what the greatest and choicest wits of Athens, Rome, or modern Italy, and those Hebrews of old, did for their country, I, in my proportion, with this over and above of being a Christian, might do for mine, not caring to be once named abroad, though perhaps I could attain to that, but content with these British islands as my world.'

The nature, the capacities, and powers of Milton's soul were to him, when he became fully conscious of them, equivalent to a distinct prophecy of the great epic which crowned the close of his life, and raised him to equality with Dante and Homer. It was not unwittingly or by chance that he accomplished that great work; his whole previous life had consisted of preparation and looking forward to it. Engaged as a young man in the exciting and bitter theologic controversies of the age, the vision of his highest work kept floating in his view; and even then, in the midst of some stiff Puritanic reasoning, he inserted a passage whose noble words deserve to be framed and hung up in the chamber of every student:

'I was confirmed in this opinion, that he who would not be frustrate of his hope to write well hereafter in laudable things, ought himself to be a true poem; that is, a composition and pattern of the best and honourablest things; not presuming to sing the high praises of heroic men or famous cities, unless he have in himself the experience and the practice of all that is praiseworthy.'

Elsewhere, alluding to the great design 'of highest hope and hardest attempting,' he desires for some few years 'to go on trust' with his readers, considering delay regarding it excusable, 'as being a work not to be raised from the heat of youth or the vapours of wine, like that which flows at waste from the pen of some vulgar amourist, or the trencher fury of a rhyming parasite; nor to be obtained by the invocation of Dame Memory and her siren daughters, but by devout prayer to that eternal Spirit, who can enrich with all utterance and knowledge, and sends out His seraphim with the hallowed fire of his altar to touch and purify the lips of whom He pleases. To this must be added industrious and select reading, steady observation, insight into all seemly and generous arts and affairs. Till which in some measure be accomplished, at mine own peril and cost I refuse not to sustain the expectation.'

Milton's literary life has three distinct periods—the beginning, in which most of his minor poems were produced; the end, in which he wrote his two epics and the drama, 'Samson;' and the middle period, wherein originated a huge volume of polemical prose. The middle was by far the longest period, and though we may lament that so large a portion of a life like his should be spent in such discussions as those on Church government, on divorce, or on the conduct of the regicides, we can see even in such work a preparation for that which followed. His lively contact with the great politicians and theologians of the time enabled him to draw those grand portraits and to write those wonderful speeches of the Pandemonium council—the part of his sublime epic in which perhaps he soars highest. But before coming to this, it may be agreeable to dwell a little longer on some poems of the first period.

He is now in the country, at Horton, enjoying a long vacation of five years with his father, delighting in quiet domestic life, delighting in rural scenery, delighting chiefly in the wide range of classic writings, ancient and modern. Leaving college at twenty-three, he commemorated his arrival at that age by a sonnet, in which he mourned his 'late spring,' and the want of 'inward ripeness,' which he thought others of his age possessed. Yet, as a matter of fact, old Ben Jonson was not then in his craft so 'ripe' as this young Milton, for both poets had chanced to write on the same subject, the Death of the Marchioness of Winchester, and a comparison shows at a glance the superiority of the younger poet. Milton's reference to his 'late spring' must therefore be taken as an evidence of that humility which is often conspicuous in the greatest souls, and which is the cause of the immense energy put forth in their onward progress. Therefore, true to a nature distinguished by the utmost tenacity and power at the supreme effort, we find Milton in this sonnet looking forward to the lot—

> 'However mean or high
> To which Time leads me and the will of heaven,'

concluding his meditation with characteristic seriousness:

> 'All is, if I have grace to use it so
> As ever in my great Taskmaster's eye.'

When we have a literary man of this earnest mood, we need not be surprised that the congenial shades of Horton were soon immortalized by inspiring some of the sweetest and most beautiful Arcadian strains possessed by any literature, ancient or modern. We might pause on a sonnet that is vocal with country airs:

> 'O nightingale, that on yon bloomy spray
> Warblest at eve when all the woods are still,
> Thou with fresh hope the lover's heart dost fill,
> While the jolly Hours lead on propitious May '—

did not the twin companions, ever lovely, fresh, and young, 'Allegro' and 'Penseroso,' claim our chief regard. 'While our language lasts,' says Masson, 'these two beautiful compositions will have a place by themselves, safe from the possibility of being ever superseded.' 'These poems,' says Lord Macaulay, 'differ from others as attar of roses differs from ordinary rose-water, the close-packed essence from the thin diluted mixture. They are, indeed, not so much poems as a collection of hints, from each of which the reader is to make out a poem for himself. Every epithet is a text for a stanza.' It is not necessary to produce specimens or draw attention to beauties in poems which most of us have probably committed to memory. But we may observe that there is no inconsistency (as some have thought) in Milton's eulogies, first of the Mirthful and then of the Melancholy man. The Melancholy which he praises is not dulness or mental depression; it is conversant with the highest and purest joys, the most instructive and elevating thoughts. It is not mere gloom and sorrow, but a delightful pensiveness in one who

> 'Hears the Muses in a ring
> Aye round about Jove's altar sing,'

who chooses for his chief companion

> 'Him that yon soars on golden wing,
> Guiding the fiery-wheeled throne,
> The Cherub Contemplation,'

who feels the power of all forms and sounds of beauty in earth and sky, learning their lessons high and sweet,

> 'Till old experience do attain
> To something like prophetic strain.'

Nor has the Mirth which Milton praises any of that levity or folly which would make it inconsistent with the pleasures of Melancholy. The Mirthful (perhaps we should rather say the Cheerful) Man, is one whose enjoyments are such as

> 'To hear the lark begin his flight,
> And singing startle the dull night
> From his watchtower in the skies,
> Till the dappled dawn doth rise.'

This is a kind of mirth to which probably few of us are much accustomed in these degenerate days. The bold and brave, the active and conscientious Milton was astir betimes—'with the earliest bird,' he tells us. The mirth or even cheerfulness which the matin-song of the lark would excite in some of us is rather problematical. It is indeed wonderful how few avail themselves of so classic an occasion for mirth. It is not the less true, however, what our poet says, that the lark's first song is to those who have formed the habit of early rising one of the most exhilarating things in the world. We think, however, we see more of Milton in the 'Penseroso' than in the 'Allegro,' and we believe the former was his favourite. In describing the delights of the Melancholy Man he speaks with his whole soul, as when he speaks of listening to the nightingale at night:

> 'The chauntress oft the woods among
> I woo to hear thy even-song,

> And missing thee I walk unseen
> On the dry smooth-shaven green,
> To behold the wand'ring moon
> Riding near her highest noon,
> Like one that had been led astray
> Through the heaven's wide pathless way.'

The poem is filled with images such as these, which have an air of sadness indeed, but are not less pleasing on that account—nay, in this consists their peculiar charm. One of the delights of the Melancholy (or Contemplative) Man, which is set forth with the utmost beauty of language, indicates how little of the Puritan in spirit Milton at this time was. Indeed, his Puritanism had never anything of the sour Philistine element, but mainly consisted in his hatred of the tyranny of the bishops, and was in fact the native impulse of a free-born soul spurning its unworthy trammels in the Church as in the State. It is curious to find the phrase so characteristic of Ritualism, 'a dim religious light,' can be traced to Milton in the following passage, which sets forth his enjoyment of church architecture, church music, and emblazonry:

> 'But let my due feet never fail
> To walk the studious cloister's pale,
> And love the high embowèd roof,
> With antique pillars massy proof,
> And storied windows richly dight,
> Casting a dim religious light;
> Then let the pealing organ blow
> To the full-voiced choir below,
> In service high and anthems clear
> As may with sweetness, thro' mine ear,
> Dissolve me into ecstasies
> And bring all heaven before my eyes.'

'Comus,' a Masque or short play, also written at Horton, is the story of a great magician of that name, the son of Circe, who dwelt in a deep, dark wood, where he entrapped travellers to drink his liquor, and 'translated them' like Bottom—that is, transformed them into creatures having beasts' heads. The horrible results of unlawful pleasure are thus set forth in allegory; and, on the other hand, the power of virtue is seen in a fair young lady who successfully resists the Enchanter's allurements. Highly characteristic of Milton are his choice and treatment of this subject—the conflicting demands of pleasure and virtue—the difficulty of doing right without going to the extreme of austerity—the difficulty of indulging in pleasure without degrading the higher nature; and Milton's success has been such that 'Comus' has been placed above every other poem of its kind, combining, as it does, pure moral beauty and pure poetic beauty in a way not found elsewhere. Those who object to teaching by fables concerning monsters, and magicians and spells, are answered in the poem itself:

> 'I'll tell ye; 'tis not vain or fabulous,
> Though so esteem'd by shallow ignorance,
> What the sage poets, taught by the heavenly muse,
> Storied of old in high immortal verse,
> Of dire chimæras and enchanted isles,
> And rifted rocks whose entrance leads to Hell:
> For such there are, but unbelief is blind.'

The truth is not less true, or touching, or beautiful, because it is veiled; and the following example from 'Comus' will show that the veil in the case of Milton's allegory is not hard to penetrate. To the young lady overtaken by night in the deep wood, having lost her way and her guides, the great Magician comes with refreshment, offering his cup, and pleading for indulgence thus:

> 'If all the world
> Should in a pet of temperance feed on pulse,
> Drink the clear stream, and nothing wear but frieze,
> The All-giver would be unthank'd, would be unpraised,
> Not half his riches known, and yet despised,
> And we should serve him as a grudging master,
> As a penurious niggard of his wealth,
> And live like nature's bastards, not her sons,
> Who would be quite surcharged with her own weight,
> And strangled with her waste fertility.'

The young lady is by no means deficient in powers of retort, as the following vigorous lines from her speech will show:

> 'Shall I go on?
> Or have I said enough? To him that dares

> Arm his profane tongue with contemptuous words
> Against the sun-clad power of chastity
> Fain would I something say, yet to what end?
> Thou hast no ear nor soul to apprehend
> The sublime notion and high mystery
> That must be utter'd to unfold the sage
> And serious doctrine of Virginity,
> And thou art worthy that thou shouldst not know
> More happiness than is thy present lot.'

This must suffice to indicate the spirit of this fine poem, whose rare beauty is both delightful to the mind and healthful to the soul.

Though I desire to hasten on to the greater poems, I cannot altogether pass over 'Lycidas.' Notwithstanding its condemnation by Dr. Johnson, it still lives and is highly admired. I am not musical, but I can understand a musician's joy in the frequent repetition of a favourite tune. I can never repeat 'Lycidas' too often—the rich ring of the words, and the richer sense, are to me a continual feast. 'Lycidas' (Milton's fellow student, Edward King) was drowned in crossing over to Ireland at the early age of twenty-four, giving occasion to a poem which is to be reckoned with 'In Memoriam' and 'Adonais' among our great elegies. The note appended by Milton tells us that 'in this Monody the Author bewails a learned Friend unfortunately drowned in his passage from Chester on the Irish Seas, 1637; and, by occasion, foretells the ruin of our corrupted Clergy, then in their height.' This refers to the powerful passage in which Milton introduces the Head of the Church, 'The Pilot of the Galilean Lake,' as a mourner, saying:

> 'How well could I have spared for thee, young swain,
> Enow of such as for their bellies' sake
> Creep, and intrude, and climb into the fold !
> Of other care they little reckoning make
> Than how to scramble at the shearer's feast
> And shove away the worthy bidden guest.
> Blind mouths ! that scarce themselves know how to hold
> A sheephook, or have learnt aught else the least
> That to the faithful herdsman's art belongs !
> What recks it them ? What need they ? They are sped ;

> And when they list their lean and flashy songs
> Grate on their scrannel pipes of wretched straw.
> The hungry sheep look up and are not fed,
> But swoln with wind and the rank mist they draw,
> Rot inwardly, and foul contagion spread ;
> Besides what the grim wolf with privy paw
> Daily devours apace and nothing said.
> But that two-handed engine at the door
> Stands ready to smite once, and smite no more.'

When we say that this passage has furnished to Ruskin a text for one of his most brilliant lectures, wherein he expounds it word by word almost, having introduced it as a specimen of a 'true book,' which a man might wish to write with a pen of iron on the rock, as the result of his life and his memorial, other praise is needless.

In the latter part of his life Milton seems to have despised and discarded rhyme as an ornament of poetry, but though his blank verse is matchless for music and rhythm, we are glad he did not adopt this theory till long after he had produced these sweet poems of his youth. In leaving them, we cannot refrain from referring again to the delicacy, the elevation, the sort of virtuous severity they possess, making them remarkable, not indeed beside the modern poetry of Tennyson and others, but beside most of the poetry of the time in which they were written. The purity of the young poet Milton was *sui generis* in its day. We may fitly close our notice of these youthful productions by a sentence from Macaulay, who says: 'The public has long been agreed as to the merit of the most remarkable passages, the incomparable harmony of the numbers, and the excellence of that style, which no rival has been able to equal, and no parodist to degrade, which displays in their highest perfection the idiomatic powers of the English tongue, and to which every ancient and every modern language has contributed something of grace, of energy, or of music.'

In turning to Milton's great work we are to recollect it is the fruit of a strangely eventful time as well as of a mighty genius. Milton was fifty-nine years of age when he succeeded in placing his name upon the same level with that of Homer, Virgil, and Dante, by giving to the world its fourth great epic. By this time, like Homer, he had become blind in the service of his country, and, like Dante, had found his countrymen ungrateful for his service. The enmity of party and his outcast condition (a proclaimed traitor), gave to Milton, as to Dante, leisure to express, in eternal words, the sublime harmonies that dwelt within him. Fallen at last 'on evil days and evil tongues,' poor, old, and blind, yet 'bating not a jot of heart or hope,' Milton is far grander now, when putting forth his mighty energies for a final effort, than he has ever been. Only adversity was needed to make his life sublime—it has come with awful power,—and now the promise of his youth is fulfilled—he is *fit* to write the sublime poem.

Not as an unconcerned spectator, Milton had passed through that magnificent civil conflict caused by the opposing forces of constitutional authority and royal prerogative; when 'awful devout Puritanism' began to face 'decent, dignified Ceremonialism,' he was fully alive to the importance of the issue; and if we catch as we read his great epic its touching undertone of disappointment, why should we wonder? This great soul feels he has outlived the ruin of a noble cause.

Through what awful and glorious, through what wondrous and terrific scenes Milton and his country had passed in those thirty years which divide 'Lycidas' from 'Paradise Lost'! The 'British Solomon,' 'inspired by the Holy Ghost,' had roughly repulsed the Puritan petitioners at Hampton Court. The fires of zeal were thus covered, but not quenched—they smouldered on. The house of Stuart pursued its unwise and imperious course, claiming a divine right to do wrong, favouring ceremonialism, depressing the zealots, granting monopolies, imposing ruinous fines, selling peerages, exacting benevolences, punishing without trial, quartering soldiers. Charles, narrow and obstinate, succeeded James, who was pedantic, but loosely formed, and therefore capable of yielding; and Henrietta of France, with a woman's *élan* towards passionate extremes, helped to steer the realm on the rock. The fearful portent of Strafford's 'Thorough' first horrified the nation, meaning military despotism of the Asiatic kind; then came Laud with *his* 'Thorough'—'uniformity'—a precise system of ecclesiastical drill, to effect which ears began to be cropped, while a New England began to grow up on the other side of the Atlantic. The Philistine 'black-mouths' of the North would not swallow Episcopacy as fast as Laud wanted. They came out in open rebellion—signed their 'Covenant,' and crossed the Border. Then that dreadful 'engine,' the Long Parliament, began its workings in the nation—Strafford and Laud are beheaded, and the Petition of Right framed. It is signed by Charles and—violated! The last stern arbiter, the SWORD, must now decide! Edgehill, Marston Moor, and Naseby, were bloody whirlwinds, in which this political storm was spent. The unconquerable Oliver gained the people's cause; and then—the greatest military genius of the age chose the greatest literary genius for his secretary. Happy age, that saw Cromwell wielding the sword and Milton the pen in defence of England!

Milton had to meet the famous royalist champion Salmasius, who, from his high chair of learning (supposed to be the highest in Europe) attacked the English Republic, fulminating his great Latin book against the barbarous regicide Britons! The eyes of all Europe were on the contest, and Milton, both in logic and Latinity, showed himself superior to his erudite opponent. When writing his *second* reply, the physicians warned him the work would, if persevered in, cost him his eyesight. 'I did not long balance whether my duty should be preferred to my eyes,' said this gallant soldier of liberty afterwards; and when all was darkness, he composed a sonnet addressed to his friend Cyriac Skinner, in which, alluding to his blind eyes, he says:

> 'What supports me, dost thou ask?
> The conscience, Friend, to have lost them overplied
> In liberty's defence, my noble task,
> Of which all Europe talks from side to side.'

But he was soon occupied with something greater than a sonnet

—that great work wherein we now read with all the world the most touching and sublime of complaints :

> 'Thus with the year
> Seasons return ; but not to me returns
> Day or the sweet approach of even or morn,
> Or sight of vernal bloom, or summer's rose,
> Or flocks, or herds, or human face divine. . . .
> So much the rather thou, Celestial Light,
> Shine inward, and the mind through all her powers
> Irradiate : there plant eyes ; all mist from thence
> Purge and disperse, that I may see and tell
> Of things invisible to mortal sight.'

In this spirit 'Paradise Lost' was written, the work foreseen in youth as one 'not to be obtained by invocation' of heathen muses ; therefore, preferring the example of some holy Hebrew prophet to that of Homer, he invokes the

> 'Heavenly Muse that on the secret top
> Or Oreb or of Sinai didst inspire
> That Shepherd who first taught the chosen seed
> In the beginning how the heavens and earth
> Rose out of Chaos.'

Having deliberately raised the Hebrew prophet above the Greek classic, he has the magnanimity to confess his religion in strains worthy of the best Greek artist :

> 'And chiefly thou, O SPIRIT, that dost prefer
> Before all temples the upright heart and pure,
> Instruct me, for thou know'st . . . what in me is dark
> Illumine, what is low raise and support,
> That to the height of this great argument
> I may assert eternal Providence,
> And justify the ways of God to man.'

With such preluding lines he enters on the wide sweep of his great epic—a poem containing in its twelve books the treasured experience of a long life of active thought and thoughtful action, the elevating philosophy of a profound and original thinker, the pure religion of a devout and severely upright soul, and the sublimest poetry ever written by man.

Homer was doubtless personally acquainted with the heroes of the Iliad, had sat in their tents, and mingled with the guests in their feasting-halls. Dante made his epic a solemn satire on his enemies and a solemn eulogy of his friends, in the degrees of punishment he gave to the former and of glory to the latter. Though more disguised, Milton's poem will be found on examination to be no less founded on his personal experience. He had seen the Vanes, and Eliots, and Hampdens of the Long Parliament, the greatest statesmen England had ever seen, or is ever likely to see, else even with *his* poetic genius he could not have drawn the leading senator of Pandemonium thus :

> 'With grave
> Aspect he rose, and in his rising seem'd
> A pillar of state ; deep on his front engraven
> Deliberation sat and public care ;
> And princely counsel in his face yet shone
> Majestic, though in ruin ; sage he stood,
> With Atlantean shoulders fit to bear
> The weight of mightiest monarchies ; his look
> Drew audience and attention still as night,
> Or summer's noontide air, while thus he spake.'

Milton had witnessed the demoniac energy with which a highly gifted man will sometimes seek the phantom called pre-eminence, therefore he was able to draw Satan thus :

> 'Yet not for those,
> Nor what the potent victor in his rage
> Can else inflict, do I repent or change,
> Though changed in outward lustre, that fix'd mind
> And high disdain from sense of injured merit,
> That with the Mightiest raised me to contend . . .
> What though the field be lost,
> All is not lost : the unconquerable will,
> And study of revenge, immortal hate,
> And courage never to submit or yield,
> And what is else not to be overcome ;
> *That* glory never shall his wrath or might
> Extort from me : to bow and sue for grace
> With suppliant knee, and deify his power.'

Milton could not have written the brilliant speeches of the Pandemonium Council if he had never listened to the debates of another Parliament. It was doubtless the theologic section of the Long Parliament he had before his mind, or perhaps the Westminster Assembly created by the Long Parliament and containing some of its members, when he wrote of what happened on the breaking up of the infernal council:

> 'Others apart sat on a hill retired,
> In thoughts more elevate, and reason'd high
> Of providence, foreknowledge, will, and fate,
> Fixed fate, free will, foreknowledge absolute,
> And found no end in wandr'ing mazes lost.'

To some this may seem a satire on the Puritans, but others will see in it something deeper than satire. In a great theologic age such questions were not so contemptible as they have become among our scientists and their followers, and Milton was not ashamed of them, any more than he was ashamed of taking a religious subject for his great epic. In doing so he doubtless diminished its attractiveness to some; but Hallam thinks the Fall of man the finest subject ever chosen for an epic, though he admits that it labours under disadvantages. Some may not like to find such extensive tracts of divinity in the poem, but the supernatural action is not necessarily dull. There is no page in Shakespeare more attractive than that in which we are introduced to the supernatural, as in the Ghost scenes in 'Hamlet,' or those of the weird sisters in 'Macbeth.' Why should we feel less interest in the majestic, powerful, and passionate beings created by Milton than in Shakespeare's spirits? No doubt Shakespeare's dramatic power is superior, and there is something in the form of the epic poem which makes the vividness of the drama not altogether possible in it. Yet I think we must admit that Milton has been successful in one of his characters to a degree that rivals Shakespeare himself. Some have called Satan Milton's hero, and certainly he is not the Satan of Scripture any more than the terrific hideous beings, Sin and Death, created by Milton are the sin and death of the Bible. Satan, in Milton, is a vastly magnified Nimrod—a colossal Napoleon—a being possessed by an extraordinary,

an immeasurable lust of self—boundless pride—inexpressible but in Miltonic words :
> 'To reign is worth ambition, though in hell—
> Better to reign in hell than serve in heaven.'

With this transcendent pride there is united a daring almost its equal, and withal there is a ruined splendour, a grandeur of sufferance, which touches the true sublime, and makes the 'Fiend' an exhaustless source of interest. He has all the high qualities of a great military leader and statesman; the largest designs, the broadest views, in connexion with wiliest cunning, deftest sleight of hand, most wonderful perseverance, most perfect dissimulation, and promptest wisdom of action. But when Milton lets us look into Satan to see his animating motive, the central power which moves all this splendid machinery, we know not which to admire most—the poet's penetration or his fidelity to truth. The world is apt to credit its great political man-hunters with some mysterious motive unspeakably grand and noble, entitling them to 'hero-worship' and what not. Satan's motive, as we are allowed to see it in his soliloquies, is small and mean. The revelation is disgusting, as in that scene in which the 'Veiled Prophet,' whose countenance was supposed to be too bright for earthly eye to behold, in the moment of defeat drops the veil and discloses features of hideous and amazing ugliness. And such to worshippers of fancied nobleness the true motive of most of the world's great ones, if exhibited, would be. At the centre of Satan's being, therefore, as the inmost and original spring of action, Milton allows us to see simply intense selfishness, an 'alcohol of egotism,' as some one has called it; and beside this principle, with all its evil and destructive consequences, he faithfully sets (in the other leading Figure of the poem) its opposite, denial of self, and all the blessed redeeming results that spring from that.

To conceive the great supernatural beings of the poem was not Milton's most astonishing feat; it was still harder to make them speak and act in character. In this one cannot say that

Milton has perfectly succeeded. To do so would have required more than man. Our sense of consistency and of propriety is sometimes offended. Owing to our ideas of what spiritual beings should feel, and say, and do, we meet with incongruities in Milton. Yet we should remember what wonders he has done to prevent this. The triumph of his genius consists in his having surmounted the difficulty so well. He has not, like Dante, told us the height of Satan in feet or yards, or how many men standing on each others' heads would reach his middle ; far better, and more poetically, he speaks of him in the first scene as

> 'Talking to his nearest mate
> With head uplift above the wave, and eyes
> That sparkling blazed ; his other parts besides
> Prone on the flood, *extended long and large*,
> Lay floating many a rood :'

or afterwards raised to his full height,

> 'Like Teneriffe or Atlas unremoved
> His stature reached the sky, and on his crest
> Sat horror plumed.'

This *indefiniteness*, this grand looseness of treatment, enables Milton to cope successfully with the difficulties of his subject ; and yet he avoids the vagueness which would deprive his creations of human interest. The picture of the ruined Archangel addressing his army reassembled after their defeat, is certainly one of the most powerful and pathetic in any literature :

> 'His form had not yet lost
> All her original brightness, nor appear'd
> Less than Archangel ruin'd, and the excess
> Of glory obscured . . . his face
> Deep scars of thunder had intrenched, and care
> Sat on his faded cheek, but under brows
> Of dauntless courage and considerate pride,
> Waiting revenge. Cruel his eye, but cast
> Signs of remorse and passion to behold
> The fellows of his crime, the followers rather,
> Far other once beheld in bliss . . .'He now prepared
> To speak . . .

> Thrice he assayed, and thrice, in spite of scorn,
> Tears, such as angels weep, burst forth.'

Who has ever drawn a Satan like this? Goëthe's 'Mephistopheles' has interest of another kind, but none of this grandeur. Goëthe's Devil is a mean, pettifogging, sarcastic villain, who amuses by his shrewd remarks and his trick of doing mischief of some kind at every opportunity, great or small. How different Milton's Satan, who has but begun an evil course, and appears to us pursuing it not without moments of deep relenting! His first sight of our sun brings bitter remembrance of the state from which he fell; hence, he 'hates its beams,' and is led into some regretful meditation:

> 'O had His powerful destiny ordain'd
> Me some inferior angel, I had stood,
> Then happy; no unbounded hope had raised
> Ambition. . . .
> Me miserable! which way shall I fly
> Infinite wrath and infinite despair?
> Which way I fly is hell; myself am hell;
> And in the lowest deep a lower deep . . .
> O then, at last, relent: is there no place
> Left for repentance, none for pardon left?
> None left but by submission: and that word
> Disdain forbids me, and my dread of shame
> Among the spirits beneath, whom I seduced
> With other promises and other vaunts
> Than to submit. . . . Ay, me! they little know
> How dearly I abide that boast so vain,
> Under what torments inwardly I groan
> While they adore me on the throne of hell,
> With diadem and sceptre high advanced,
> The lower still I fall, only supreme
> In misery; such joy ambition finds.'

Leaving the 'hero' to take a brief parting glance at the general character of the poem, we find that throughout there reigns 'an order, noble, clear, and natural.' The poet has so distinct a vision, so firm a grasp of his subject, that there are no inconsistencies in the vast range of incidents in Hell, in Heaven, and on Earth, which he invents. The characters which he at first stamps on his creations he preserves throughout the lengthened and varied epic narrative; he never forgets at any stage how he had before conceived Satan, Adam, Eve, or any of the other characters. 'Where,' asks Professor Craik, 'in the poetry of the ancient world shall we find anything which approaches the richness and beauty, still less the sublimity, of the most triumphant passages in " Paradise Lost?" The First Book of that poem is probably the most splendid and perfect of human compositions—the one, that is to say, which unites these two qualities in the highest degree; and the Fourth is as unsurpassed for grace and luxuriance as that is for magnificence of imagination. And though these are, perhaps, the two greatest books in the poem, taken each as a whole, there are passages in every one of the other books equal, or almost equal, to the finest in these. And worthy of the thoughts that breathe are the words that burn. A tide of gorgeous eloquence rolls on from beginning to end, like a river of molten gold; out-blazing, we may surely say, everything of the kind in any other poetry.' Finally, Milton's blank verse, both for its rich and varied music and its exquisite adaptation, would in itself almost deserve to be styled poetry, without the words—alone of all our poets, before or since, he has brought out the full capabilities of the language in that form of composition. Most other blank verse (except Shakespeare's) reads like a sort of muffled rhyme—rhyme spoilt by the ends being blunted or broken off. Who remembers, or who can repeat, any narrative blank verse but his? In whose ear does any other linger? What other has the true organ tone which makes the music of this form of verse—either the grandeur or the sweetness?'

SWIFT.

In the year of the Revolution—the glorious 1688—a young student in Trinity College, Dublin, not very distinguished in his classes, was sketching the outline of a strange satirical production, afterwards known to the universe as 'A Tale of a Tub.' In that same famous year was born Swift's great friend and fellow-worker, Alexander Pope. Swift himself came into the world the year after the Great Fire, which succeeded the Great Plague of London—a year (1667) memorable for its own disaster —when the Dutch fleet sailed up the Thames, and insulted England in sight of her capital. Dalziel's dragoons were at that time shooting the Covenanters among the Pentland Hills. But the birth of Swift was a still greater calamity to the Presbyterians, whom he satirized in the 'Tale of a Tub.'

That famous 'Tale' was lying ready for publication when Dryden died. 'Glorious John Dryden' knew nothing of the lampoon which his kinsman Swift had inserted for him in the 'Tale,' as a retribution for his unfavourable verdict: 'Cousin Swift, you will never be a poet.' For Swift, after leaving Trinity College, Dublin, came to stay with his great relative, Sir William Temple, near London, and thus had an opportunity of meeting the old literary dictator, then reigning at Will's Coffee House, and of submitting to his judgment certain 'Pindaric Odes,' whose merit in Dryden's eyes turned out to be disappointingly small. This was all the more annoying to Swift that Dryden's verdict at that time was so powerful that it was thought it could either make or mar the fortune of a young literary aspirant like Swift.

It is a curious fact that Dryden had got from his predecessor Milton a verdict similar to that which he himself gave to Swift. Milton said of Dryden (having only seen his earlier verses): 'He is a rhymer, but no poet.' Had Milton lived to read 'Absalom and Achithophel,' he would doubtless have given a different sentence. And Swift, if not in verse, at least in prose, has triumphed over Dryden in the department of satire where he is greatest.

Swift, indeed, judged by his prose, must be pronounced the greatest of British satirists, and the most original author of his age. His style has not the Roman grandeur of his predecessors: it is free, simple, natural, like that of a man who cares for nothing but the matter: it is, indeed, singularly unornamented, its power apparently depending entirely on the sense which it conveys:—'the sense'—say rather the *demoniacal energy* which moves in it, dishonouring and demolishing any given object of attack. Satire like Swift's would derive no aid from verse. Carlyle has made us acquainted with prose more beautiful, and some more severely satirical, than almost any verse in our language; and Carlyle learned from Swift to discard the trammels of verse, and trust to something more important for the success of his writing.

I was first struck with this idea of Carlyle's connection with Swift while reading long ago the 'Sorrows of Herr Teufelsdröch,' and his famous 'Clothes Philosophy.' To bring out what I mean, let me read to you first a passage from 'Sàrtor,' and then one from 'A Tale of a Tub.' 'Nay, if you consider it,' says Carlyle, 'what is man himself and his whole terrestrial life but an emblem; a Clothing or visible garment for that divine Me of his, cast hither like a light particle down from heaven? . . . . Why multiply instances? It is written the heavens and earth shall fade away like a Vesture; which indeed they are; the Time-vesture of the Eternal. Whatsoever sensibly exists, whatsoever represents spirit to spirit, is properly a Clothing, a suit of Raiment—put on for a season, and to be laid off. Thus in this our pregnant subject of Clothes rightly understood, is included all that men have thought, dreamed, done, and been.'

Compare this with what Swift has written in his 'Tale of a Tub': 'About this time a sect arose [this sect will be seen to resemble Carlyle's " Dandiacal Body"], whose tenets obtained and spread far and wide, especially in the *grande monde* and among everybody of good fashion. They worshipped a sort of idol [a tailor], who, as their doctrine delivered, did daily create men by a kind of manufactory operation. This idol they placed in the highest part of the house on an altar erected about three feet: he was shown in the posture of a Persian Emperor, sitting on a superficies, with his legs interwoven under him. This god had a goose for his ensign: whence it is that some learned men pretend to deduce his original from Jupiter Capitolinus. . . . The worshippers of this deity had also a system of their belief, which seemed to turn upon the following fundamentals. They held the universe to be a large suit of clothes which invests everything: that the earth is invested by the air; the air is invested by the stars; and the stars are invested by the *primum mobile*. Look on this globe of earth: you will find it to be a very complete and fashionable dress. What is that which some call land but a fine coat faced with green? or the sea but a waistcoat of water-tabby? . . . Examine even the acquirements of the mind, you will find them all contribute in their order toward furnishing out an exact dress: to instance no more; is not religion a cloak; honesty a pair of shoes worn out in the dirt; self-love a surtout; vanity a shirt,' etc.—Carlyle is severe upon the superficial fashionable world, but he does not hit harder than Swift.

Though born in Dublin city, Swift, like some other eminent Irishmen, was of English descent. The Roundheads of the preceding generation had plundered his grandfather's house in Yorkshire. Afterwards that grandfather's four sons came over to Ireland to push their fortune. One of these was Jonathan's father, who died before Swift was born, leaving him in charge of Godwin Swift, the most prosperous of the four; a great lawyer, who consigned him to the care of Sir William Temple, a distant relative, and a minister of William III., for whom Swift acted as a kind of private secretary. With his poetic temperament, Swift felt keenly from the first his dependent position, and in considering the formation of his character, this should be taken into account. All his life, indeed, Swift occupied the position of a man conscious of great abilities, yet constantly disappointed as to the results which might naturally be expected from them. There is nothing in his life more striking than this fact, of his always missing the promotion that seemed so easily within his reach. Expecting it first from Sir William, then from Somers, Harley, Queen Anne—waiting for it, longing for it to the last—at sixty years of age he left London disappointed; though he had obtained promotion for hundreds, while wielding or seeming to wield the influence of a Government, yet he never became an English Bishop as he wanted, but died an Irish Dean, which he abhorred. I believe it was thought dangerous to make a Bishop of a man so vastly clever. Nature, we may observe, seems to distribute her gifts so as to maintain a certain balance of power in society. A genius is generally hindered from obtaining high office. That is reserved for some more common-place person; otherwise, were the power of office added to that of genius, individual power would be a dangerous enormity. This might be expressed in a commoner form by saying that men in high office felt the Dean's vastly superior ability, and 'kept him down' simply on the principle of self-defence.

But there were other causes hindering his promotion. It is, in fact, the old story of genius irritating contemporaries to please a future age. Swift has written an amusing address to 'Prince Posterity.' It was not that 'Prince,' however, but Jonathan Swift, who paid for the pleasure so abundantly bestowed on us. That *jeu d'esprit* which makes you rub your hands and laugh, that fine caustic satire which you read with infinite delight, that humorous lampoon which compels you to shout and hold your sides—each of these cost Jonathan something—you would wonder to hear how much. The 'Windsor Prophecy,' for instance, consisting of only twenty rhymes or so: 'I like it mightily,' he wrote to Stella; 'it is a marvellous good one, and the people are mad for it'—what was it about? In the quaint language of Chaucer (Swift's favourite poet), the 'Windsor Prophecy,' we find, shows up the red hair and nefarious practices of a certain Duchess. The town was mightily tickled with it for a time: but what then? A Bishopric became vacant some time after, and Queen Anne was advised by her Ministers to bestow it on Swift. The Queen would have done so, but—mark the effect of a few sarcastic couplets—the red-haired Duchess watches her time, with tears, and kneeling, pours out supplication before the throne of Majesty, holding forth in her hand the offending squib. Sobs emphasize entreaties—*will* her Majesty give the Bishopric to one who shot *this* hateful arrow into the heart of her faithful handmaid—one who also wrote that dreadful 'Tale of a Tub,' which Majesty may remember made her shudder by its irreverent treatment of sacred mysteries? The Queen's answer to her Duchess is not hard to guess. Jonathan again may go without the Bishopric, may go once more and ruminate on the present advantage of pleasing 'Prince Posterity,' and while with some surprise he estimates the effect of the gentle sting which angel woman uses, he may conclude, like Franklin in an after age, that he has 'paid too dear for his whistle.'

Swift's life was in fact a good deal composed of such indiscretions (as wise men who have no genius would call them). Glorious indiscretions they may seem to *us*, whose only concern with them is to read them in a book and enjoy the fun. But it is an historical fact that Swift, with all his friends in court, with all the admiration of his wit with which the nation was ringing, with all the familiarities lavished on him by statesmen and great lords, long enough remained the poor Vicar of Laracor, county Meath; and only at the age of forty-six, by a hard push made by some friends, obtained the despised

Deanery of St. Patrick's, Dublin, his first and last preferment. He has given in well-known vigorous verse, his own account of the advantages and disadvantages of the poetic temperament:

> 'Not empire to the rising sun
> By valour, conduct, fortune won,
> Not highest wisdom in debates
> For framing laws to govern states,
> Not skill in sciences profound,
> So large to grasp the circle round,
> Such heavenly influence require
> As how to strike the muse's lyre. . . .
> . . . Not beggar's brat on bulk begot,
> Not bastard of a pedlar Scot,
> Not boy brought up to cleaning shoes,
> The spawn of Bridewell or the stews,
> Are so disqualified by fate
> To rise in Church, or Law, or State,
> As he whom Phœbus *in his ire*
> *Has blasted* with poetic fire!'

This doubtless explains how it was he had his bachelor's degree from Trinity *by special grace*, having had while a student about seventy penalties in two years. It may also have some bearing on the fact that when he preached at Laracor his audience was so small, sometimes, it is said, consisting simply of the clerk, so that on one occasion he commenced the service, 'Dearly beloved Roger, the Scripture moveth you and me.' His poetic temperament may have had something to do with the fact that when he came as Dean to Dublin he was even less popular, at first, being groaned, hooted, and hustled on the very streets. One with such a temperament, if he meddles with politics, is liable to become a keen and extreme partisan. Swift went far in both Tory and High Church ways; and such a man as he gives more offence to opponents than others whose hostility may be quite as decided.

Perhaps, however, it was in his relations to the fair sex he was most unfortunate of all; and here again, in estimating his conduct, we shall do him injustice if we do not take into account the peculiar temperament of genius. As all the world knows, two of the finest and fairest English women of that age were his devoted slaves, despising reputation and honour, kindred and country, for his sake; and though we may think he might have been happy with either, he was happy with neither, making neither happy: for neither became his acknowledged wife; but he lived in a strange unsatisfactory relationship with one of them till her death. It has often been asked, why did he not marry Miss Esther Johnston, his admired and deeply-loved Stella, since she was young and perfectly beautiful, and since he affirmed she never failed in any company to say the best thing that was said? Or, if there was a private marriage, why was it never acknowledged? Why did he never meet her except a third person was present?

Swift was doubtless to blame; but it is now known that he had some constitutional infirmity, causing a certain 'coldness' of temperament. Besides, he was ambitious; an enormous pride of talent dwelt in the man. He long looked forward with considerable certainty to be called 'my Lord Bishop;' and, with such pretensions, he deemed the first lady in England not too good for him. He probably foresaw that 'Stella' would not be received in society of the first class; and though he loved her, it was not in that high, entire, unselfish way which makes nothing of all other earthly considerations. Whatever the pain—and it was no unreal or trifling pain which visited his heart—he strove to endure it, rather than give love the mastery over ambition.

A not uncommon case. And while pursuing his ambitious schemes in London, he, of course, wrote to his Stella in Ireland with the utmost frequency and tenderness, as the celebrated 'Journal to Stella' fully demonstrates. So far satisfactory; but was there not another lady in the question? How came *she* in to complicate matters? The fact is, one could hardly expect a wit like Swift to live entirely without female society in London, even though dear Stella did pine in the solitude of Trim, or by the willows of Laracor. Though somewhat ungainly and gruff, Swift was very popular with the fine ladies of London, who found his conversation striking and fresh. On being presented to the Princess of Wales, he said, in allusion to the savage lately caught in Hanover, 'he understood her royal highness loved oddities, and that, having lately seen a wild boy from Germany, she was now desirous to see a *wild Dean* from Ireland.' He had a way of dealing with women which they felt to be uncommon. He did not give them prattle and small talk as other men did. He never seemed to be condescending to their understandings, but treated them as if they were mentally his equals, and as if there was no danger, in giving them strong meat as well as milk. This he did quite simply and naturally; but if he had adopted it as a policy to produce success, he could not have been so successful as he was. He liked talking with thoughtful literary ladies, was fond of directing their studies, and indicating the character of their books. His Irish warmth may sometimes have led him farther than was wise in this direction. It requires a *very* wise man to keep perfectly exact when literary unite with other charms to shake his self-possession and make him slip; and Swift, though on paper the very wisest man living, was not quite infallible in conduct. The fact is, having been absent from Stella some years, and having constituted himself a sort of amateur tutor of a certain literary Miss Vanhomrigh, he did not behave just as wisely as he should have done. To this young lady he gave the poetical name 'Vanessa,' as he had given 'Stella' to Miss Johnston. You would hardly expect Swift to state to the latter everything which took place during his absence in London. But he could not hinder Stella from becoming aware that the current which flowed towards her through the medium of letters was no longer so copious or strong as it had been, and being of a reflective turn, she rightly deemed that part of it was going in another direction. But like a gentle, patient, loving soul, as she was, she made no complaint; nor, indeed, had Jonathan any definite intention of deserting her. According to his own way of telling the story, if rhyme is to be believed, he was perfectly astounded when the talented, strong-minded young lady, 'Vanessa,' made to him a declaration of her love, while he, innocent man, was merely aiming at acting the part of a tutor. Hear Swift's rhymed report of what she said:

> 'She well remembered to her cost
> That all his lessons were not lost;
> Two maxims she could still produce,
> And sad experience taught their use:
> That virtue pleased by being shown
> Knows nothing that it dares not own—
> That common forms were not designed
> Directors to a noble mind. . . .
> "Now," said the nymph, "to let you see
> My actions with your rules agree—
> I knew by what you said and writ
> How dangerous things are men of wit,
> Your lessons found the weakest part—
> Aim'd at the head, but reach'd the heart."'

Cadenus (as Swift calls himself in this piece) was, as we have said, astounded by this declaration:

> 'Cadenus felt within him rise
> Shame, disappointment, guilt, surprise;
> His thought had wholly been confin'd
> To form and cultivate her mind.'

And this is how it was turning out! It would be said he was no better than other people—he had been scheming for Vanessa's money all along:

> 'So tender of the young and fair,
> It show'd a true paternal care—
> Five thousand guineas in her purse!
> The Doctor might have fancied worse!'

Whatever the difficulties, however, 'Vanessa' bore herself like one who was in good sad earnest, and meant to win. Having broken the ice, she made a determined plunge—having got the matter begun, she would bear it through valiantly!

> 'But not to dwell on things minute,
> Vanessa finished the dispute;
> Brought weighty arguments to prove
> That reason was her guide in love;'

as an ingenious young lady would! And Cadenus does not deny, but confesses, that in these arguments he took considerable pleasure.

> 'Howe'er it came, he could not tell,
> But sure she never talked so well!
> His pride began to interpose—
> Preferr'd before a crowd of beaux!
> So bright a nymph to come unsought—
> Such wonder by his merit wrought!'

He was pleased, but considering his age, which was forty-four, his Deanship could not promise her love—

> 'But friendship in its greatest height,
> A constant rational delight,
> His want of passion will redeem
> With gratitude, respect, esteem.'

We are not told that 'Vanessa' was satisfied with this—a thing most women would deem unlikely—for the poet suddenly draws up, and stops confession by placing upon it a prudent reserve:

> 'But what success Vanessa met
> Is to the world a secret yet;
> Whether the nymph to please her swain
> Talks in a high romantic strain;
> Or whether he at last descends
> To act with less seraphic ends;
> Or, to compound the business, whether
> They temper love and books together;
> Must never to mankind be told:
> Nor shall the conscious muse unfold.'

Like some men of poetic temperament, Swift, it is to be feared, had an inconsiderate habit of insignificant gallantry which brought bitter pain to himself and others. And 'what success Vanessa met is to the world a secret' no longer! She followed him to Ireland, where both Swift and she were kept in agony for a time by the necessity of concealing her presence from Stella. Vanessa, of course, heard of the latter, being with an old lady, Swift's chief company in Dublin; and after long vexations caused by the gradual lessening of the Dean's visits, Miss Van took the bold and decisive step of writing to Stella to ask the nature of Swift's attachment to her! Stella, in dreadful pangs of jealousy, gave Vanessa's letter to Swift, who, as Scott says, made it serve for Vanessa's death-warrant. He rode at once to her house, entered her apartment, and, in the awfully stern manner which was peculiar to him, laid her letter on the table before her, walked out, and rode off without uttering a word. In a few days after the beautiful and brilliant Vanessa was dead.

Swift had been forced at length to decide between the two ladies; he chose the older friend; the stern expression of his decision had such tragic result;* and, when too late, he lamented his dangling and dilatoriness. He should have decided long before. It is true he discouraged Vanessa from coming to Ireland—true he gave her discouragement when she came; but it had the effect, though not intentional, of fanning the flame instead of blowing it out. Reading the letters he wrote to her, we cannot say their discouraging tone is sufficiently distinct.

His treatment of Stella was still worse. Why did he not now, after Vanessa's death, do her the justice of marrying her? or, if there was a private marriage, why did he not now acknowledge it? At the time of his settlement in Dublin he was forty-six, and he might then have married Stella, but the Vanessa affair compelled him to wait at an epoch of his life when there was no time to spare. There was naturally a pause after the sad explosion that terminated that affair, and Swift began to realize that he was on the borders of old age! 'Yet justice to Stella required that he should marry her even then, if not before.' True; and we must admit, after every explanation which has been suggested, there was some mystery in Swift's unwillingness to marry. It may have been that constitutional defect or ailment which at length, in his old age, ended in lunacy.

There can be no doubt that during the latter part of his life Swift has the bearing of a man who carries some dreadful secret about with him; some think it was the expectation of madness, after he knew that awful visitation was certainly in

* 'There is something in your look so awful that it strikes me dumb.'— *Vanessa to Swift.*

the future. It is indeed hardly too much to say there was a kind of madness in him all along. His 'cousin' Dryden has a famous couplet :

> 'Great wits are sure to madness near allied,
> And thin partitions do their bounds divide.'

Most of us have remarked the sharpness, the excessive logic, which madmen exhibit in drawing their conclusions from wrong premises. And not unfrequently in Swift's pages (*e.g.* his account of the Yahoos), we meet with a fierce enormity of satire which strikes the common mind as a sort of madness. Thackeray, who is far too severe on Swift, expresses an amount of truth when he says, 'he goes through life tearing, like a man possessed of a devil.' There was certainly in Swift's nature a peculiar something, distinct from genius, but allied with it ; and before he could write the humorous-bitter things that came from his pen, his thoughts and feelings must rage like fiends within his soul, which happy expression would then tranquilise. Critics have used the word 'demoniacal' in a good sense to indicate (in accordance with the Greek derivation of the word from $\delta\alpha\iota\mu\tilde{\omega}\nu$) the highest effort of genius, and we are often reminded of this in reading the pages of Swift. We feel that an exorbitant pride of talent—a soaring ambition arising from consciousness of power, 'gnaws at the heart of this furious gifted man.' But there was more—that highest elevation of mind leading to converse with the infinite, the illimitable, the transcendental, the supernatural, which is always the lot of men like Swift. This tendency of the mind to anchor beyond what is seen and temporal, the privilege of all the truly great, has in different individuals different effects. To one after a night of eclipse it brings 'the morn' with which

> 'Those angel faces smile
> Which he had loved long since, and lost awhile.'

To another it brings ' fiends and shapes of horror,' which seem 'tugging at his thoughts from beneath.' Like Hamlet, Swift could say with truth he was 'dreadfully attended.' But, as it is when the tempest gathers blackest, the lightning flashes are most splendid in terrific beauty, so some of the most brilliant pages that do honour to the English tongue proceeded from the sombre intellect of a man who had a tendency to madness.

It is easy to blame Swift—easy to point out his errors—yet ah! what a mystery our fellow man may be! 'The heart knoweth its own bitterness'—few or none know its secret—many misapprehend and misjudge. Who knows what mighty exertions Swift had put forth against the evil spirit that rent him at last? Yet doubtless in order to maintain an average outward evenness and moderation, he struggled long and well. If this be genius, then Sir Walter Scott was right when he thanked God he saw no signs of it in his son. It is a rare and perilous endowment which the world neglects or treats unskilfully while it is incarnate among them—without which, however, a large portion of the world's pleasures would be wanting —for without this dangerous energy, Swift's writings would be insipid, and Shakespeare's would be worth no more than old almanacks.

In estimating Swift, however, we should avoid the common notion in which he appears as a mere incarnation of caustic wit or sarcasm. He was a great deal more. He was a profound politician, a deep moralist, an eminent patriot. To those who knew him intimately he was most admirable—there was none like him. Addison, presenting him with one of his own beautiful writings, inscribed on the blank leaf of the book: 'To Doctor Jonathan Swift, the most agreeable companion, the truest friend, and the greatest genius of the age.' This in Addison's circle was not regarded as flattery, but a just expression of truth. And when we know that the numerous circle of wits in which Addison presided included the brilliant Congreve, the pathetic Otway, the admirable Arbuthnot, the profound and benevolent Berkeley, Prior, Gay, Parnell, and, above all, Swift's great friend and *confrère*, Alexander Pope, we can estimate the meaning of the praise bestowed by a man so judicious and clear-sighted as Addison, who was as eminent for high moral and amiable qualities, as for the excellence of his easy, graceful, charming prose.

Many of the striking contrasts of Swift's character arose from his strong independence of spirit, which is kindred to the something which we call originality. He took care that the genuine promptings of conscience should not be vitiated by the feeling that others were applauding his acts. He regularly conducted prayers with the servants, though his guest might live for months in the house without discovering the fact. While continuing to publish a variety of satires, which appeared to many a strange mixture of cleverness, profanity, and coarseness, he never forgot his daily visit to the small closet in which he performed his private devotions. Swift saw more in religion than mere propriety of speech, precision of ritual, or outward decency, and therefore many weak intellects, whose piety depends on the tone of their nervous system, have been deeply scandalized at Swift's writings. To such people an original thought in religion is as shocking as infidelity. Hence Swift was hated by that kind of ecclesiastics who bitterly contend for the minutiæ of a system which they have learned by rote, and which they love because it secures their worldly revenue. He offended such people, because he avoided the bathos of sanctimonious expression, and hated to admit the cant of a trade into his conception of religion. Hence he was, in his own words,

> 'A clergyman of special note
> For shunning others of his coat;
> Which made his brethren of the gown
> Take care betimes to run him down.'

They, of course, suggested the suspicion that he was an infidel; yet they must have been conscious *they* had never written anything against infidelity so able as his ironical 'Argument against abolishing Christianity,' in which with marvellous power he turns the tables on the scoffers. Take a short specimen: 'I am very sensible,' says he, 'how much gentlemen of wit and pleasure are apt to murmur and be shocked at the sight of so many daggle-tail parsons who happen to fall in their way and offend their eyes; but at the same time those wise reformers do not consider what an advantage and felicity it is for great wits to be always provided with objects of scorn and contempt, in order to exercise and improve their talents, and divert their spleen from falling on each other, or on themselves. And to urge an argument of a parallel nature: if Christianity were abolished, how could the free-thinkers, the strong-reasoners, and the men of profound learning, be able to find another subject so calculated in all points whereon to display their abilities? . . . We daily complain of the great decline of wit among us, and would we take away the greatest, perhaps the only topic we have left? Who would ever have suspected Asgill for a wit, or Toland for a philosopher, if the inexhaustible stock of Christianity had not been at hand to provide them with materials? What other subject through all art or nature could have produced Tindal for a profound author, or furnished *him* with readers? It is the wise choice of the subject that alone adorneth and distinguisheth the writer. For had a hundred such pens as these been employed on the side of religion they would immediately have sunk in silence and oblivion.'

Another of those strange contrasts, apparent or real, which we see in Swift, appears in his political character. While always detesting Ireland, and speaking of it as 'this scoundrel country,' he was one of its truest and most energetic patriots. His achievements on behalf of liberty alone were those which he desired to be inscribed on his tomb.

By his personal influence with the English Government, after long negotiations, he obtained the remission of the first-fruits for the clergy of the Irish Church—a benefit long before enjoyed by English ecclesiastics — though his envious Irish brethren gave him little thanks for his exertions. But he did other and more important services for Ireland.

England in those days took advantage of Irish dissensions to reduce Ireland to the most abject condition. A law was passed in the reign of William III. prohibiting the exportation of Irish woollen goods to any place besides England and Wales, thus destroying the Irish woollen trade to increase that of England. On the same principle any selfish huckster might knock down a neighbouring stall that his own might have a greater run. Certainly the public spirit of the English parliament of that age did not rise above the meanest aims of peddling shop-keepers. The Dean's ire was roused, and he wrote and published, 'A Proposal for the Universal Use of Irish Manufactures, etc., utterly rejecting and renouncing everything wearable that comes from England.' The printer of the pamphlet being prosecuted, immense popular commotion arose, and Government ultimately let the matter drop. But a popular storm still more terrible succeeded, being roused by letters which appeared in a Dublin journal over the apparently harmless signature, 'J. B. Drapier.' This was Swift writing as a business man in a plain business way to advise brethren of his trade, and all whom it might concern, not to accept certain new halfpence which Government had authorised one William Wood, 'tinker and esquire,' to coin. Wood was really an ironmonger of some wealth, who had obtained by treaty with the King's mistress a patent to coin the sum of £108,000 in halfpence. Swift justly regarded this contract as dishonourable in itself, and an insult to the Irish nation; as the patent was obtained by bribing the King's mistress, and without the consent of the Irish Parliament. To effect his object and get the nation to reject the halfpence, Swift insisted on their inferior value, and that those who accepted them would be ruined; though doubtless he knew that the decreased intrinsic value of halfpence did not unfit them for a medium of commerce. But he may also have known that the difference between their intrinsic and their stamped value should have gone, not into the private purse of George I. or his mistress, but into the Irish Exchequer, to lighten the taxation of a country already burdened with some infamous items of the King's pension list. That Irish trade should be ruined by English selfishness was bad enough; but this patent to coin, obtained through so base a channel, and without consulting the Irish Parliament, seemed an expression of contempt such as imperial pagan Rome dared not have put on her meanest conquered province. Wood, however, felt so sure that the English foot was on the Irish neck, that he boasted his coin should be imposed by force if necessary. But Wood had not calculated the effect of one satiric pen. As letter after letter with the signature 'J. B. Drapier' appeared, the nation grew more and more excited, and at length such was the ferment and indignant repugnance roused by Swift's plain but powerful writing, that the Government was convinced it could not carry the scheme without a civil war! At first the letters seemed only to attack Wood and his base halfpence; but as they went on, higher topics were introduced, and Swift expounded in his own forcible way the principles of liberty and free government. He touched on dangerous subjects—on the dependency of the kingdom of Ireland—on 'the power assumed contrary to truth, reason, and justice of binding her by the laws of a Parliament in which she has no representation.' The Fourth Letter contained a remarkable statement touching at once the core of the controversy and the heart of Ireland: 'The remedy is wholly in your own hands, and therefore I have digressed a little in order to refresh and continue that spirit so seasonably raised among you, and to let you see that by the laws of GOD, of NATURE, of NATIONS, and of your COUNTRY, you ARE and OUGHT to be as FREE a people as your brethren in England.' This the Government called sedition, and offered £300 reward for the discovery of the author of the letter. Harding, the printer, was imprisoned; but though offered his liberty and a large bribe, he would not discover the writer. Something wonderful was the excitement of the nation when the trial came on, and the following memorable passage of Scripture was circulated by a Quaker in broad sheet:

'And the people said unto Saul, shall JONATHAN die, who has wrought this great salvation in Israel? God forbid: as the Lord liveth there shall not one hair of his head fall to the ground; for he hath wrought with God this day. So the people rescued Jonathan that he died not.'

Though the grand jury were browbeaten by Chief Justice Whitshed, Harding was released amid the enthusiastic triumphant joy of the nation. Wood afterwards surrendered his patent, receiving £36,000 in compensation.

So ended one of Swift's great battles in the cause of liberty —a cause which he served zealously and effectively by word and deed to the last. If he had never written 'Gulliver's Travels,' 'A Tale of a Tub,' nor any other of those immortal works which place him on high among the sons of men, his noble exertions on behalf of a country so downtrodden, so utterly wronged and wretched as Ireland then was, would have placed his name among the brightest on the records of time. It is sad and strange to read in our times in his 'Short View of the State of Ireland,' or in his 'Present Miserable State of Ireland,' such complaints as still sound in our ears from contemporaries —as if the evils of Ireland were chronic and irremediable. Take a short extract or two. 'Another great calamity is the exorbitant raising of the rents of lands. Upon the determination of all leases made before the year 1690, a gentleman thinks he has but indifferently improved his estate if he has only doubled his rent-roll. Farms are screwed up to a rack-rent—leases granted for a small term of years—tenants tied down to hard conditions, and discouraged from cultivating the land they occupy to the best advantage, by the certainty they have of the rent being raised on the expiration of their lease proportionably to the improvements they shall make.'

Again: 'We are apt to charge the Irish with laziness because we seldom find them employed; but then we do not consider they have nothing to do. Sir William Temple . . . inquires why Holland, which has the fewest and worst ports and commodities of any nation in Europe, should abound in trade, and Ireland, which has the most and best of both, should have none? This great man attributes this surprising accident to the natural aversion man has for labour. . . . But, with due submission to Sir William's profound judgment, the want of trade with us is rather owing to *the cruel restraints* we lie under, than to any disqualification whatever in our inhabitants.'

Once more: 'Another cause of the decay of trade . . . is the unnatural affectation of our gentry to reside in and about London. Their rents are remitted to them, and spent there. The countryman wants employment from them; the country shopkeeper wants their custom. For this reason he can't pay his Dublin correspondent readily, nor take off a great quantity of his wares. Therefore the Dublin merchant cannot employ the artisan, nor keep up his credit in foreign markets.' . . .

The horrible wit of his 'Modest Proposal for preventing the children of poor people in Ireland from being a burden to their parents,' etc., was intended to shock and shame England out of her unjust and barbarous policy. After gravely discussing the good effects of fattening yearly 100,000 poor children for the shambles as a mode of relieving their parents and the country, and gratifying the landlords with a good dish by which the ragged parent would have at least 8s. net profit, Swift pursues his grim jest thus: 'We are told by a grave author, an eminent French physician, that fish being a prolific diet, there are more children born in Roman Catholic countries about nine months after Lent than at any other season; therefore, reckoning a year after Lent, the markets will be more glutted than usual, because the number of Popish infants is at least three to one in this kingdom: and therefore it will have one other collateral advantage by lessening the number of Papists among us.' And concludes with the following melancholy challenge: 'I desire those politicians who dislike my overture . . . that they will first ask the parents of these mortals whether they would not at this day think it a great happiness to have been sold for food at a year old in the manner I prescribe, and thereby have avoided such a perpetual scene of misfortunes as they have since gone through by the oppression of landlords, the impossibility of paying rent without money or trade, the want of common sustenance, with neither house nor clothes to cover them from the inclemency of the weather, and the most inevitable prospect of entailing the like or greater miseries upon their breed for ever.'

In this way Swift strove on behalf of the poor and downtrodden—by his wit getting a hearing where otherwise this would have been impossible. It is astonishing to consider the number of subjects relating to the welfare of his fellow-men he has treated, and all in such a manner as to command attention, and manifesting invariably the goodness of his heart as well as the clearness of his head. A whole cyclopædia of political and moral and even religious wisdom might be gathered from his pamphlets, or even from 'Gulliver' alone. A writer of a 'Sketch of the State of Ireland' (1810), pays to Swift the following just tribute of praise :

'On this gloom one luminary rose, and Ireland has worshipped it with Persian idolatry; her true patriot, her first, almost her last. Sagacious and intrepid—he saw, he dared ; above suspicion, he was trusted ; above envy, he was beloved ; above rivalry, he was obeyed. His wisdom was practical and prophetic—remedial for the present, warning for the future ; he first taught Ireland that she might cease to be the slave of a despot. . . . His mission was but of ten years; and for ten years only did his personal power mitigate the government ; but though no longer feared by the great, he was not forgotten by the wise; his influence, like his writings, has survived a century ; and the foundations of whatever prosperity we have since erected, are laid in the disinterested and magnanimous patriotism of Swift.'

It would be impossible in one chapter to attempt any analysis of his larger works, the ' Tale of a Tub,' or 'Gulliver's Travels.' This is the less to be regretted as these works are so well known —' Gulliver ' especially being still highly popular with young and old, and having the rare quality of being a favourite child's book, while capable of giving instruction to the wisest in old age. Before parting with Swift, let us for a moment compare him with his most distinguished contemporary and friend. After his patriotic exertions for Ireland had successfully ended in the withdrawal of Wood's patent, Swift paid a long visit to his friend Pope, then living in his celebrated villa of Twickenham, London. Swift and he were great friends, and friends to the last. Pope was irritable, and had quarrels with many of the wits of the time—notably with Addison—but he never quarrelled with Swift. One great cause why Swift and Pope agreed so well was Swift's wonderful indifference to literary distinction or fame. Though certainly the ablest literary man of his day, he would have disdained to designate himself a man of letters. Not literary reputation, but POWER, ecclesiastical and political, was the mark he aimed at. His most celebrated works were never owned by him; though his style was so full of character that the public knew his anonymous work almost as easily as his friends knew his handwriting. Swift hardly ever wrote as an artist who delights in his work for its own sake; he wrote for an object distinct from art; and that object being accomplished, the writing became in his eyes almost as valueless as a spent cartridge. Pope was just the opposite in this respect. To him literary reputation was everything. To him fine writing was a final end and aim. For literary effect—for literary reputation—he laboured incessantly day and night, as constantly and as long as his frail, sickly constitution would allow. The two friends did not love the same thing, so they did not quarrel about it. Swift could see Pope enjoying the reputation of the greatest poet of his day without the least jealousy; nor, since Swift gave freely his powerful help to Pope's literary projects, could the latter feel jealous of a man so generous and so indifferent to poetic glory. Swift would say he envied Pope his style, by way of praising him—that was all.

> 'In Pope I cannot read a line,
> But with a sigh I wish it mine;
> When he can in one couplet fix
> More sense than I can do in six,
> It gives me such a jealous fit
> I cry, " Pox take him and his wit !"'

Swift would say this to make the town prize Pope. It was simply his manner of praising. Yet he was not accustomed to praise any man beyond his merits; and in these lines he indicates exactly Pope's peculiar excellence—his power of condensing. And while Swift loved Pope so generously, it is honourable to the heart of the latter—though he commonly gets little credit for heart—that in the sardonic verses, written by Swift on his own death, he predicts that Pope, of all his friends, will mourn longest:

> 'Poor Pope would grieve a month, and Gay
> A week, and Arbuthnot a day.'

STERNE.

As the astronomer loves to contemplate that beautiful belt in the heavens in which constellation succeeds constellation at regular intervals, so the student of English literature delights in distant acquaintance with those brilliant assemblages of wits which have succeeded one another in the literary heaven of London from the Restoration to the present day. Dryden and his brilliant circle at Will's was succeeded by Addison and his brilliant circle at Button's, including Swift, Pope, Steele, Arbuthnot, Gay, Congreve, Bolingbroke, a genial and splendid constellation—we cannot easily fellow it; yet it is succeeded by another, the central luminary of which is the Great Bear himself, Dr. Samuel Johnson, who, owing to his manifold mental powers, deserves to be likened to the 'Seven Stars' rather than a single one. He has before now been called the Great Bear in a less flattering sense.

Open almost at any page that famous biography, 'Boswell's Life of Johnson,' and you must be struck with the literary richness of the time. Such familiar names as Burke, Reynolds, Gibbon, Garrick, Fielding, Hume, gleam up here and there, often associated with *one* that wears a peculiar attraction—Goldsmith, or 'Goldy,' as he is called by the huge Doctor—as strange a combination of weakness and strength, of envy and generosity, of humility and vanity, as will be found in the case of any other genius. Who is not interested when Goldsmith's name turns up—whether we are to see him strutting about with lunatic grimaces in his showy scarlet frock, or behold him held in durance vile by his landlady, who has converted his lodging into a debtor's prison ; or find him gulled into giving his last guinea, or his watch, to some vulgar rogue? Who is not interested in Goldsmith—endeared to our hearts by a thousand fascinating pages, wherein he at one time searches as with a lighted candle all the secret depths of human nature and at another depicts it so humorously that we make merry over all its faults—Goldsmith, who 'writes like an angel,' but in actual life

> 'He seems to me, begging your grace's pardon,
> Like one of those long-legged things in a garden,
> That fly about and hop and spring,
> And in the grass the same old chirrup sing.'

In these interesting pages of Boswell we meet, sometimes in connexion with that of Goldsmith, the name of another humourist, whose humour is of a finer quality than even Goldsmith's, and who must live with 'my Uncle Toby,' even as Shakespeare does with 'Jack Falstaff.' I refer to Laurence Sterne, whose life extended from 1713 till 1768. Opening Boswell somewhere near the middle, we find him saying: 'I censured some ludicrous fantastic dialogues between two coach-horses and other such stuff, which Baretti had lately published. Dr. Johnson joined with me and said, ' Nothing odd will do long. "Tristram Shandy" did not last.' This growl of the Great Bear, who seems to have had some dislike to Sterne, was given about eight years after his decease. It would appear, therefore, that at that date Sterne's greatest work was regarded by Johnson as something that had had its day—had grown old, and was ready to vanish. 'Tristram Shandy did not last,' said Johnson. Well! it is now over one hundred years since the date of that oracular verdict, yet Sterne is living, and we venture to predict that even at the end of another hundred years no Englishman, who has any voice in such matters, will announce that 'Tristram Shandy did not last.'

The style of Sterne is so different from the stiff dignity of Johnson that we hardly expect an appreciative or fair verdict from that clear-sighted, but severe, and often prejudiced old autocrat. From Goldsmith, a far more kindred spirit, we might expect some appreciation for Sterne; but poor human nature was not perfect in Goldsmith, who, with all his good and genial qualities, was a little addicted to envy. Take another scrap from Boswell: 'It having been observed that there was little hospitality in London—JOHNSON: Nay, sir, any man who has a name, or who has the power of pleasing, will be very generally visited in London. The man Sterne, I have been told, has had engagements for three months. GOLDSMITH: And a very dull fellow. JOHNSON: Why, no, sir.' Johnson had met Sterne in company, and did not think his tone was what the tone of a clergyman of the Church of England ought to be. Goldsmith had also met Sterne, and one would have expected from Goldsmith the more favourable verdict, yet Johnson has to contradict him on Sterne's behalf. Johnson disliked Sterne, no doubt, but the charge of dulness seemed too absurd. Though Vicar of Sutton and Prebendary of York, he was in Johnson's mind only 'the man Sterne,' since the mercurial Laurence too lightly regarded the dignity of his office. But Johnson knew better than to receive Goldsmith's epithet 'dull' as descriptive of a man whose fascinating powers of conversation he had heard of and felt; a man whose society was sought for by the finest ladies and the ablest men in London—whose dinners were sometimes three months deep. We are not always to believe what one wit says of another. While Goldsmith's 'Chinese Letters' (or 'Citizen of the World') was enjoying a languid popularity, 'Tristram Shandy' was the rage of the town. Was *this* why Goldsmith called his fellow humourist dull? Was *this* why in one of those 'Chinese Letters' Goldsmith censured so severely the 'license' of 'Tristram,' though in that very 'Citizen of the World,' engaging as it is, we occasionally come to passages exhibiting very considerable license? In the passage referred to Goldsmith thus chastises Sterne: 'It is very difficult for a dunce to obtain the reputation of a wit, yet by the assistance of some freedom this may be easily effected, and a licentious blockhead often passes for a fellow of smart parts and pretensions; every object in nature helps the joke forward, without scarce any effort of the imagination.' So that, according to Goldsmith, instead of genuine humour, pervaded by the most beautiful, and touching, and tender elements, you have only some improper allusions and coarse jokes in Sterne. *That* is the justice of a rival wit. And why did Goldsmith express such special disgust at the author of 'Tristram Shandy'? Were there not Fielding and Smollet, and twenty others in that age, far more indecent than he? Was Goldsmith himself always free from coarseness?

That age was one not eminent for its high spiritual aspirations, or its high ideal of duty. We are all familiar with the state of the Church, against which Whitfield and Wesley rose to protest. Sterne was not the only clergyman of those days who seemed to those great evangelists in a state of spiritual death. You could find the Gospel in the moral writings of a heathen philosopher quite as readily as in most of the sermons of that age. Gibbon, 'sapping a solemn creed with solemn sneer' was fashionable; and Hume, the 'Prince of Sceptics,' was then publishing his subtle and seductive essays, followed by his yet more attractive but misleading history. Scotch clergymen were generally 'Moderates' and Unitarians; while those of England were sometimes even avowed infidels. Even in Puritan Scotland, the Reverend Mr. Home had dared to write the 'Tragedy of Douglas,' in which suicide is applauded; and Dean Swift, a dignitary of the Irish Church, had published things unspeakably shocking to those who reverenced his holy calling. Sterne himself has said: ' As Swift always kept a good distance off Rabelais, so I always keep a good distance off Swift.' In justice to Sterne, we must, I think, admit the truth of this statement, which means, in plain language, that Rabelais is as much coarser than Swift as Swift is coarser than Sterne. Be it remembered, all three were ecclesiastics—one French, the other two Irish born. Against all three charges of infidelity and immorality have been preferred, and of all three we may now say that, though the license of their writings gives countenance to these charges, no foundation for them has been found in their lives.

Though Sterne lived during the last thirty years of the life of Swift, there is an interval of half a century between the appearance of 'A Tale of a Tub' and that of 'Tristram Shandy.' We may note the fact that these two (our greatest) prose humourists, were born and bred in Ireland; and, adding Goldsmith and Steele, we may say our four greatest prose humourists were Irishmen. There may be something in the Irish climate—in our variable, genial, cloudy, sunshiny, salubrious, uncertain, impracticable climate—that favours the growth of wit and humour. The English, when transplanted to Ireland, we find from history, become more Irish than the Irish themselves. And though Sterne studied in Cambridge, and was afterwards for twenty years an unnoticed pastor in Yorkshire, he seems never to have lost a peculiar raciness which he derived from the soil on which he first drew breath. That was at Clonmel, where his father's regiment was stationed at the time. But, though his father was a soldier, Sterne was the scion of an old ecclesiastical stock, his great grandfather having been Archbishop of York, and his uncle, Jaques Sterne, a famous fighting dignitary of the Church. The intimate knowledge of military affairs apparent in 'Tristram Shandy' is accounted for by the fact that Sterne's boyhood was spent in barracks with soldiers at Mullingar, Wicklow, Carrickfergus, Londonderry, and other places besides Clonmel, where he was born. What was Irish in Sterne's nature was doubtless after all chiefly derived from his mother, who was an Irishwoman, a daughter of a noted sutler of Clonmel, named Nuttle. The lady was a captain's widow at the time Sterne's father married her; and there is reason to think he had not the felicity of making a love-match, the fact that he was in debt to the sutler being against that supposition. Laurence was the second child of a large family, of which few besides himself survived childhood, mostly all being 'of a fine delicate frame not made to last long,' as Sterne himself tells us.

At the age of seventeen Sterne lost his father, who had quarrelled with another officer about a goose, got run through the body and literally pinned to the wall of a room in Gibraltar, where the duel was fought. From the effects of this wound he afterwards died at Jamaica. As he is known to be the original of the famous 'Uncle Toby,' it is important to note what his son has written of him. 'My father,' says Sterne, 'was a little smart man, active to the last degree in all exercises, most patient of fatigue and disappointments, of which it pleased God to give him full measure. He was in his temper somewhat rapid and hasty, but of a kindly sweet disposition, void of all design, and so innocent in his own intentions that he suspected no one; so that you might have cheated him ten times in a day, if nine had not been sufficient for your purpose.'

After his father's death Sterne went to Cambridge, being enabled to do so by the kindness of a cousin, and having the celebrated Dr. Dodd and the poet Gray among his fellow-students. At college Sterne had the reputation of an odd man —one who had no harm in him, but had parts, if he would use them. He learnt a great deal, but in his own desultory whimsical way—and he never learned to spell. When writing the works that have made him famous, he would spell 'aches' with a *k*, 'buyer' without the *u*, 'sought' with an *a*, and 'magazine' with two *ee*'s. We are not of opinion, however, that his genius was anything greater on that account. His uncle, an ecclesiastic of many titles, and a famous fighting dignitary of the day, got him the living of Sutton, a quiet country cure, not far from the city of York. He got two additional livings after his marriage; but here, at Sutton, he lived for twenty years almost unnoticed and unknown to fame, until he at length emerged by going up to London with the first two MS. volumes of 'Tristram Shandy' in his pocket, being then nearly fifty years of age. He had lived in the quietest way down there in Yorkshire, never being a man of robust health, but hollow-chested, asthmatic, and hectic-looking, with a terrible tendency to bursting blood-vessels. Possibly owing to delicate nerves, he courted retirement and avoided the rougher scenes of life. He was an artist in more than a literary sense, being musical, fond of his bass violin, and addicted to painting also, to his knowledge of which art his books doubtless owed some of their peculiar expressiveness.

Sterne married a lady of York, and to judge from an incident of the courtship which he relates, seems to have made quite a love-match. The lady, he says, had resisted his addresses for two years, concealing her affection, and then fell into consumption. 'One evening that I was sitting by her,' says Sterne, 'with an almost broken heart to see her so ill, she said, "My dear Laurie, I can never be yours, for I verily believe I have not long to live! but I have left you every shilling of my fortune." Upon that she showed me her will. It pleased God she recovered, and I married her in the year 1741.' Sterne was then only twenty-seven, yet this consumptive wife, with one daughter, long survived her husband.

On Sterne's expression just quoted, 'with an almost broken heart to see her so ill,' Thackeray makes the comment that 'the Reverend Mr. Sterne's heart was a good deal broken in the course of his life.' Surely this is uncalled-for. Whatever Sterne became twenty years afterwards, when he went to live in London, or further on when he travelled in France, he certainly manifested during his long residence at Sutton a deep and genuine affection for both his daughter and his wife. Thackeray, to countenance his sneer, has produced a letter of Sterne's in dog-Latin, penned in some London tavern, to the effect that he was 'sick and tired' of his wife, and has artfully set this beside the courtship scene as exhibiting the result of 'not many years.' But this is a misstatement; for Mr. Fitzgerald has shown that the dog-Latin letter dates nearly twenty years after the courtship scene. No doubt a man *should* not be 'sick and tired' of his wife even at the end of such a period, but it may not be just so bad then as at the end of 'not many years.' In twenty years a good many things may happen. When fine ladies of the great London world began to *fête* our obscure country parson and listen to his sparkling talk with rapturous eyes, it was not so wonderful that a man so sensitively organized sometimes lost his self-possession. We should not be quickly moved to charge this hollow-chested, hectic-hued, spare parson from the country with the gross sins with which he stands charged in Thackeray's ferocious satire. Irregular flashes of wit, or even unseemly license of speech, does not always mean this.

Sterne's wife was a great contrast to those literary ladies who swarmed round the author of 'Tristram Shandy.' He could hardly feel in her presence an impetus to brilliancy. She would accept quietly, in perfect unconsciousness of wit, the most extravagant statements which his humour could prompt him to make. She never could see the meaning of metaphors and other sorts of unliteral speech. She was, in fact, the prototype of Mrs. Shandy, whose husband once exclaimed, after an ineffectual *tête-à-tête* with his better half : 'What a pity to be master of one of the finest trains of reasoning in the universe, and unable to hang up a single inference within my wife's head !'

Sterne, when his genius blazed out before the world, became suddenly acquainted with spiritual beings of a different type; and if then he did sometimes feel his wife's company a tiresome contrast—of course, he was wrong; but if his fault was really not greater than this—a fault simply of feeling, and confined to mere sentiment—surely he was not the monster depicted in Thackeray's terrible irony. Thackeray, of course, puts the worst construction on Sterne's friendship with a certain Mrs. Draper, an invalid lady whose husband was in India, and who met Sterne while he was performing his 'Sentimental Journey' in France. She is the 'Eliza' connected with Sterne's somewhat as 'Stella' is with Swift's fame. This lady possessed an enlightened and cultivated mind, refined and tender feeling; she could fully appreciate Sterne's literary work, and could herself write beautiful letters. I do not wish to defend, but to condemn Sterne's warm attachment to her; but there is absolutely no evidence that there was anything more than sentiment in the case. She certainly was a great contrast to his wife, though Sterne should not have felt the contrast as he did. The fulness of literary appreciation from a lovely tender woman was something new in his life, and beyond his dreams. He was wrong to allow this to influence him as it did; but a mercurial sentimentalist like Sterne must not be judged altogether by the common rule. There are expressions in his last latter to 'Eliza,' when she was taking ship to India, which cannot be defended; but it closes with words of advice which are surely not those of a villain: 'Adieu—adieu! and with my adieu let me give thee one straight rule of conduct, that thou hast heard from my lips in a thousand forms—but I concentre it in one word—REVERENCE THYSELF.'

But the special pleading of Thackeray is relentless. He puts forward in evidence of Sterne's baseness another passage from these letters to Eliza, and his comments seem triumphantly damaging. The passage is this:—

'And indeed I begin to think you have as many virtues as my Uncle Toby's widow. Talking of widows, pray, Eliza, if you are ever such, do not think of giving yourself to some wealthy Nabob, because I design to marry you myself. My wife cannot live long, and I know not the woman I should like so well for her substitute as yourself. 'Tis true, I am *ninety-five* in constitution and you but twenty-five: but what I want in youth I will make up in wit and good humour. Not Swift so loved his Stella, Scarron his Maintenon, or Waller his Saccharissa. Tell me in answer to this that you approve and honour the proposal.'

'Approve and honour the proposal!' echoes Thackeray in his most savage tones; 'the *coward* was writing gay letters to his friends all this while, with sneering allusions to this poor foolish Bramine (Eliza). Her ship was not out of the Downs, and the charming Sterne was at Mount Coffeehouse with a sheet of gilt-edged paper before him, offering that precious treasure his heart to Lady P——.'

'Shocking!' cries every reader of Thackeray's lecture. You are now utterly disgusted with Sterne. You would not, after this, touch his book with the tongs. And you are right—on one condition—a simple one and easily forgotten—namely, that Mr. Thackeray has presented us with *facts*. His lecture on Sterne is powerfully and dramatically written. Himself a brilliant wit, Thackeray experienced the usual temptation to sacrifice tasteless truth to theatrical conditions. If somebody's reputation is rendered very black, what matter? The genius of Thackeray has gained a splendid triumph.

Now, we may ask, how did Thackeray know that before Eliza was 'out of the Downs' Sterne was addressing another lady on gilt-edged paper? He would know by comparing the dates of the letters. The believer in Mr. Thackeray will therefore learn with surprise that the 'gilt-edged' note is *undated*, while internal evidence shows it was written long before the commencement of Sterne's acquaintance with Eliza! Here is a pretty play. Mr. Thackeray writes with the printed collection of Sterne's letters before him, and of course is quite able, by affixing arbitrary dates, to fill into Sterne's life some exciting or disgusting inconsistencies. The world will read the pungent production, while the writer has saved himself the trouble of accurate research. Mr. Percy Fitzgerald, who has written a full biography of Sterne in two volumes, is not by any means so trenchant or dramatic a writer as Thackeray; but Mr. Fitzgerald is content to possess less attractiveness and more truth. As we have seen in the case of Goldsmith, one wit cannot always be trusted with the reputation of another wit. By Mr. Fitzgerald's calm judgment and quiet industry poor Sterne has been saved from the effects of Thackeray's passionate eloquence, when he erroneously places near that courtship scene in which the will appears a letter which was written about twenty years afterwards; and, still worse, when he makes Sterne write the 'gilt-edged' note while Eliza is in the Downs.

But admitting Fitzgerald's corrections of Thackeray, it will be said the ugly facts remain—that Sterne wrote so warmly to Eliza—that he wrote (though at a different date) so warmly to Lady P——, that he talked of marrying Eliza when he and she were free, etc. This was all wrong, but not so wrong as if Sterne had been a more literal and a less sentimental individual. His love for Eliza was like that of Swift for Stella, Waller for Saccharissa, etc., that is, like the love of men of genius, which seems to flourish best in the absence of the lady and in sonnets devoted to her praise. Perhaps we have all heard an honest virtuous man say to an honest virtuous woman he would have her for his second wife, without fancying he meant any harm. It is not an uncommon joke. And when we take into account the sentimental state out of which Sterne spoke, we must see that many of his warmest proposals could amount to little more than jokes. This letter, for instance, in which he proposes to Eliza, is the letter of a delicate man of fifty who feels he is 'ninety-five in constitution,' and as the letter itself mentions, was written just after being 'at the verge of death,' while yet weak from fearful loss of blood caused by the bursting of a blood-vessel in his breast. What should we think if we heard a kindly old slippered pantaloon of fourscore address a nice young woman of twenty-five, and say he would marry her if ever she became a widow? Should we make fools of ourselves by stopping our ears and crying out 'horror!'

It should be remembered, also, that at the time he was writing these letters to Eliza—which fairly examined will be seen to have in them more of the affectionate father and kind protector than of anything worse—he was writing letters to his daughter Lydia, which even Thackeray admits do honour to his heart and his fatherhood. It is hard to see how the pure and tender paternal affection of these letters to Lydia is compatible with the existence, at the same time, of a guilty passion such as Thackeray suggests: especially as we find Sterne does not conceal, but openly avows, his liking for Eliza in these letters to the daughter, whom he loved so fondly and to the last.

We have a letter written almost with his dying hand in that lonely lodging-house in Bond Street, London, where he breathed his last—a letter that might go far with feeling souls to vindicate him from deep or radical badness of any kind. It is addressed to his tried and faithful friend Mrs. James, and its subject is—Lydia:

'Your poor friend is scarce able to write—he has been at death's door this week with a pleurisy—I was bled three times on Thursday and blistered on Friday—the physician says I am better—God knows, for I feel myself sadly wrong, and shall, if I recover, be a long while of regaining strength. Before I have gone through half this letter I must stop to rest my weak hand above a dozen times. . . . Do, dear Mrs. James, entreat Mr. J. to come to-morrow or next day, for perhaps I have not many days, or hours, to live—I want to ask a favour of him, if I find myself worse—that I shall beg of you, if in this wrestling I come off conqueror—my spirits are fled—'tis a bad omen: do not weep, my dear lady—your tears are too precious to shed for me—bottle them up, and may the cork never be drawn. Dearest, kindest, gentlest, best of women, may health and happiness prove your handmaids! If I die, cherish the remembrance of me, and forget the follies which you so often condemned—which my heart, not my head, betrayed me into. . . . . Should my child, my Lydia, want a mother, may I hope you will (if she is left parentless) take her to your bosom—you are the only woman on earth I can depend upon for such a benevolent action. I wrote to her a fortnight ago and told her what I trust she will find in you.'

Surely this is not the letter of a 'coward,' a 'wretched, worn-out old scamp,' a 'vain, wicked, witty, feeble wretch!'—terms applied to him by Thackeray. 'Alas for the rarity of Christian charity under the sun!' Sterne, as he himself confesses, had follies on account of which he was admonished by good and wise friends, but they were follies into which his heart, not his head, betrayed him. If he was more universally sympathetic, more kindly, more alive to beauties of character and form than others, these were with regard to the world's wisdom and the world's morality disadvantages connected with his peculiar nature. He could not so easily control and regulate his feelings as those who had a weaker emotional nature. His original nature did not accord with the conventional morality: he chose to act by his own light; and the flippant superficial judge whom we call Society condemned him after giving him great encouragement. That matters little, since there is a court of appeal which he has now entered, and since we may still listen to eloquent pleadings by himself in his own defence like these:

'Ye whose clay-cold heads and lukewarm hearts can argue down or mask your passions, tell me, what trespass is it that a man should *have* them? or how his spirit stands answerable to the Father of spirits but for his conduct under them? If nature has so wove her web of kindness that some threads of love and desire are mingled with the piece—must the whole web be rent in drawing them out? Whip me such stoics, great Governor of nature! said I to myself: wherever Thy Providence shall place me for the trials of my virtue; whatever is my danger—whatever is my situation—let me feel the movements which rise out of it, and which belong to me as a man—and if I govern them as a good one, I will trust the issues to Thy justice; for Thou hast made us, and not we ourselves.'

True, if one has not first planned the circumstances out of which the passions grew, their existence may be comparatively innocent: the less he is responsible for those circumstances, the less guilty he must be held to be: the tares are not guilty for striking root and making growth, since some one has gone and deliberately planted them in the field. But it is sometimes in human power to avoid the circumstances which would create passion; or, the passion being inadvertently created, it is in human power to diminish it by avoidance of such circumstances—perhaps even to destroy it altogether: this being the case, we should beware of taking comfort from a doctrine that makes our Creator responsible for our sins; though, no doubt, a man may fairly plead some excuse in the original defects of his constitution, caused by his parents or ancestors. We perceive how deeply—too deeply—poor BURNS has drunk of Sterne when he wrote that wild verse:

> 'Thou know'st that Thou hast formèd me
> With passions wild and strong,
> And listening to their witching voice
> Has often led me wrong.'

But the world pays little regard to such pleadings on behalf of men of feeling: it deals with them by a sterner logic. How many, after Horace Walpole, have sneered at Sterne for 'snivelling over a dead ass' while neglectful of the wants of his own mother? The numerous enemies which his satires in 'Tristram' made him gave currency to accusations of this sort. Mr. Fitzgerald has shown that Sterne actually gave his mother all the help he could. But at what time is Sterne said to have shown unfeeling conduct towards his mother? It could not have been at the time or near the time when he wrote the celebrated piece on the 'Dead Ass': it must have been, if at all, some twenty years before, when his mother was still alive, and when he was a young man, dependent on his relatives for support at college.

Truly, the vitality of lies is wonderful, and if put into epigrammatic shape (like this of Walpole's) they will fly to the ends of the earth and fill millions of gaping mouths. The effect of the last-mentioned lie has been to make people turn away from the 'Dead Ass' picture almost with the feeling that it was disgraceful for Sterne to have made it. Yet, notwithstanding some depreciatory remarks from high quarters, I venture to give this scene as a specimen of Sterne:

'——"And this," said he, putting the remains of a crust into his wallet—"and this should have been thy portion," said he, "hadst thou been alive to have shared it with me." I thought by the accent it had been an apostrophe to his child; but 'twas to his ass, and to the very ass we had seen dead on the road, which had occasioned La Fleur's misadventure. The man seemed to lament it much, and instantly brought into my mind Sancho's lamentation for his: but he did it with more true touches of nature.

'The mourner was sitting upon a stone bench at the door, with an ass's panel, and its bridle on one side, which he took up from time to time—then laid them down—looked at them, and shook his head. He then took his crust of bread out of his wallet again, as if to eat it, held it some time in his hand— then laid it upon the bit of the ass's bridle—looked wistfully at the little arrangement he had made—and then gave a sigh. The simplicity of his grief drew numbers about him, and La Fleur among the rest, whilst the horses were getting ready: as I continued sitting in the postchaise, I could see and hear over their heads.

'He said he had come last from Spain, where he had been from the farthest borders of Franconia; and had got so far on his return home when his ass died. Everyone seemed desirous to know what business could have taken so old and poor a man so far a journey from his own home.

'It had pleased Heaven, he said, to bless him with three sons, the finest lads in all Germany; but having in one week lost two of the eldest of them by small-pox, and the youngest falling ill of the same distemper, he was afraid of being bereft of them all, and made a vow if Heaven would not take *him* from him also, he would go in gratitude to St. Iago in Spain.

'When the mourner had got thus far on his story, he stopped to pay Nature his tribute—and wept bitterly.

'He said, Heaven had accepted the conditions, and that he had set out from his cottage with this poor creature, who had been an excellent partner of his journey—that it had ate the same bread with him all the day, and was unto him as a friend. Everybody who stood around heard the poor fellow with concern. La Fleur offered him money. The mourner said he did not want it—it was not the value of the ass, but the loss of him. The ass, he said, he was assured, loved him; and upon this he told them a long story of a mischance upon their passage over the Pyrenean Mountains, which had separated them from each other for days, during which time the ass had sought him as much as he had sought the ass; and that they had scarce either ate or drank till they met.

' " Thou hast one comfort, friend," said I, " at least, in the loss of thy poor beast; I'm sure thou hast been a merciful master to him."

' " Alas !" said the mourner, " I thought so when he was alive —but now that he is dead I think otherwise. I fear the weight of myself and my afflictions, together, have been too much for him—they have shortened the poor creature's days, and I fear I have them to answer for."

' " Shame on the world !" said I to myself—" did we but love each other as this poor soul loved his ass, 'twould be something !" '

As a note taken by the way during his 'Sentimental Journey,' surely this is admirable. In his unjust lecture on Sterne, Thackeray says : 'There is not a page in Sterne's writing but has something that were better away, a latent corruption, a hint as of an impure presence.' ' One can't give the whole description.' Now, in the above extract, which occupies much more than a page, I have not left out even a syllable, and I ask you where is the 'latent corruption ?' where is the 'something that were better away ?' I defy the most critical powers of vision to detect in this exquisite little tale anything 'that were better away.' And we can say of Sterne what cannot be said of every novelist, that there is never in any of his pictures a redundant feature—a stroke that could be spared. It is true, indeed, that in the interests of morality we could spare some entire pictures; but even in these, speaking artistically, there is no such thing as a careless or unnecessary stroke—all exhibit the most perfect, sometimes even exquisite, finish. As to the indelicacies, the world's taste has greatly altered since Sterne's day, for we read that his writings had the approval of all the bishops ; yet almost the only thing in Thackeray's lecture with which I can heartily agree is his closing reference to the purity of Dickens : ' I think of those past writers and of one who lives amongst us now, and am grateful for the innocent laughter and the sweet and unsullied page which the author of "David Copperfield" gives to my children.'

This is just, so far as Dickens is concerned, though Dickens would have been the last to desire such a compliment at Sterne's expense. Nor have I any hesitation in affirming that there are in Sterne many pages as 'sweet and unsullied,' while manifesting greater power and more exquisite literary skill than anything we have from Dickens.

A certain feeling of incongruity has been experienced on finding a volume of Sermons bound up with 'Tristram Shandy' and the 'Sentimental Journey.' Yet that extract on the Dead Ass is itself a little sermon on a subject that needs frequent handling to this hour. There are little towns known to us where the most rigid orthodoxy seems to flourish in conjunction with a cruelty to animals unheard-of on the wildest African shore. We whose ears are accustomed to the heavy thud of the cudgel on the poor donkey's ribs may feel inclined to sneer at Sterne's 'Dead Ass' as a piece of mere sentimentalism. Yet it may be even possible that the infamous treatment often received by inferior creatures from those who claim to be their superiors has been in some indirect manner mitigated by that little chapter which I have quoted from Sterne. Who knows? At any rate, the world would be none the worse, were minute differences of dogmatic theology sometimes supplanted by preaching of this sort. And surely amid the hatred of cliques and sects and lodges in which we live and breathe, it might be no harm at times to look into the meaning of Sterne's closing remark : ' " Shame on the world !" said I to myself—" did we but love each other as this poor soul loved his ass, 'twould be something!" '

Indeed, I know of no writer who makes mutual love and forbearance so delightfully attractive as Sterne. Reading those delightful scenes between Mr. Shandy and 'my Uncle Toby,' you may conclude you have a very bad heart if you do not feel it growing palpably better as you read. It is in 'Tristram Shandy' also that the incomparable 'Story of Le Fevre' occurs, with the immortal passage about Uncle Toby's oath and the tear of the recording angel. There are, we lament it, in Sterne many things offensive to the purity of the present age; but he must not be condemned wholesale. It is to be remembered, the hard, virtuous moral temperament may have its vices as well as the soft, easy and sensuous one: and while the vices of the former are less frequently denounced, they are perhaps even more ugly and injurious than the others. There is often a beggarly meanness and callous cruelty in the so-called 'respectable' classes, that may fairly be said to be unmatched by any other kind of wickedness or immorality. But whatever be the indelicacy laid to Sterne's charge, we were not prepared for the accusation of *false* sentiment. Here is the way in which Thackeray refers to the passage we have quoted: 'Tears and fine feelings, and a white pocket-handkerchief, and a funeral sermon, and horses and feathers and a procession of mutes, and a hearse ... with a dead donkey inside! Psha! Mountebank! I'll not give thee one penny more for that trick, donkey and all!'

Is that fair criticism? Is that a *just* representation of Sterne's manner? The passage reads like the simplest account of an incident in an ordinary letter written home to a friend by an eye-witness: yet Sterne is accused of using all manner of theatricals. I believe Thackeray never wrote words more unfortunate for himself: and were his fame not so firmly established by other (meritorious) writings, this one on Sterne would seriously damage it.

The genius of Sterne is sufficiently vindicated by the fact that so many of the characters he has drawn are well-known living realities to this hour. Men know Corporal Trim almost as familiarly as their next-door neighbour. We begin to have some taste of geniality at the bare mention of Uncle Toby's name. How kindly familiar we feel towards the queer old crotchety philosopher, Mr. Shandy, with his hobby horse;

Dr. Slop we may ridicule, but like to see him come out and in among our friends. And though more dangerous, we are quite as willing to tolerate Widow Wadman. Even the inferior creatures—Sterne's Starling, his Dead and his Living Ass— have acquired a kind of prescriptive right in the domain of memory. Mrs. Quickly, or Pistol, or even Falstaff himself, is not more of a living reality and perpetual denizen of the world than some of Sterne's creations.

Look at this one little picture, and say whether you do not think the world is the better for possessing it:

'I need not tell the reader, if he keeps a hobby horse, that a man's hobby horse is as tender a part as he has about him; and that these [my father's] unprovoked strokes at my Uncle Toby's [viz., the miniature siege conducted by him and Trim in the garden] could not be unfelt by him. No—as I said before, my Uncle Toby *did* feel them, and very sensibly too. Pray, sir, what said he? How did he behave? Oh, sir! it was great: for as soon as my father had done insulting his hobby horse—he turned his head without the least emotion from Dr. Slop, to whom he was addressing his discourse, and looked up into my father's face, with a countenance spread over with so much good nature—so placid—so fraternal—so inexpressibly tender towards him; it penetrated my father to his heart. He rose up hastily from his chair, and seizing hold of both my Uncle Toby's hands as he spoke: " Brother Toby," said he, " I beg thy pardon; forgive, I pray thee, this rash humour which my mother gave me " . . . . " My dear, dear brother,". answered my Uncle Toby, rising up by my father's help, " say no more about it; you are heartily welcome, had it been ten times as much, brother" . . . . " But it is ungenerous," replied my father, " to hurt any man—a brother worse; but to hurt a brother of such gentle manners—so unprovoking—and so unresenting—'tis base, by heaven! 'tis cowardly " . . . . " You ' are heartily welcome, brother," quoth my Uncle Toby, " had it been fifty times as much " . . . . " Besides, what have I to do, my dear Toby," cried my father, " either with your amusements or your pleasures, unless it were in my power to increase their measure?"'

In Sterne we see that exquisite mixture or combination of the ludicrous and the pathetic which is to be found only in humourists of the first class—in Shakespeare and Cervantes and others—if there be other such. His beauties are not, as some suppose, rare spots amid extensive pages of rubbish; he seems to have aimed in every line at the most exquisite finish; the manuscripts he left were full of corrections, manifesting the utmost painstaking even in the lightest and easiest sketches. Goldsmith, indeed, in the spirit of a rival wit, ridiculed him for his dashes and strokes, which, Goldsmith slily says, passed for wit; as if there were in Sterne's page no strokes of wit but those grotesque dashes. But Goldsmith knew better: the printer might in many cases omit Sterne's strange punctuation and still preserve his English as amusing and excellent as before. Sterne's work, however, was not one which was dependent for its value on nice attention to grammatical proprieties. His genius enabled him to seize with unfailing accuracy the point on which every man is a humourist. His pictures of life, *e.g.*, the begging monk at Calais, are not detailed descriptions, but skilfully given by allusive hints. His satire is not that fierce, truculent, stormy sort which we see in Swift, but is perhaps even harder to bear, because it is so constantly pervaded with gaiety and good-humour. His character of Dr. Slop procured Sterne a score of remonstrating medical visitors, who each fancied *he* was aimed at. The frivolous objects on which large learned folios are sometimes expended are finely ridiculed in the account of a huge folio by Dr. Slawkenbergius on the Philosophy of Noses; and we have a most comical instance of the terror produced among the learned by this imaginary Dr. Slawkenbergius in the fact that the celebrated Dr. Warburton, the commentator of Pope and others, actually sent Sterne a purse of gold and some fine complimentary letters, through pure fear that he would be drawn under some such whimsical name in some of the concluding volumes of 'Tristram Shandy.'

We cannot give you a better idea of Sterne's character as a man, or of his power as a writer, than by transcribing his picture of Yorick, the curate in 'Tristram Shandy,' whose name Sterne often appropriated to himself. We must admit that Sterne was, like Yorick, 'a fellow of infinite whim,' of nimble penetrating wit, delighting doubtless too much in the humorous-satiric vein, but capable of deep affection, and a genuine man after all. Instead of possessing 'that cold phlegm and exact regularity of sense and humours' which was looked for, Yorick was, says Sterne, 'as mercurial and sublimated a composition—as heteroclite a creature in all his declensions, with as much whim and *gaité de cœur* about him, as the kindliest climate could have engendered and put together. With all this sail poor Yorick carried not one ounce of ballast; he was utterly unpractised in the world; and at the age of twenty-six knew just about as well how to steer his course in it as a romping unsuspicious girl of thirteen; so that upon his first setting out, the brisk gale of his spirits, as you will imagine, ran him foul ten times a day of somebody's tackling: and as the grave and slow-paced were oftenest in the way—you may likewise imagine it was with such he had generally the ill-luck to get entangled. For aught I know there might be some mixture of unlucky wit at the bottom of such *fracas;* for to speak the truth, Yorick had an invincible dislike and opposition in his nature to GRAVITY—not to gravity as such; for where gravity was wanted, he would be the most grave or serious of mortal men for days and weeks together; but he was an enemy to the affectation of it, and declared open war against it, only as it appeared a cloak for ignorance or for folly: and then, whenever it fell in his way, however sheltered and protected, he seldom gave it much quarter. Sometimes in his wild way of talking he would say that gravity was an arrant scoundrel, and, he would add—of the most dangerous kind too—because a sly one—and that, he verily believed, more honest well-meaning people were bubbled out of their goods and money by it in one twelvemonth, than by pocket-picking and shop-lifting in seven.

In the naked temper which a merry heart discovered, he would say, there was no danger—but to itself: whereas, the very essence of gravity was design, and consequently, deceit—it was a taught trick to gain credit of the world for more sense and knowledge than a man was worth; and that, with all its pretensions, it was no better, but often worse, than what a French wit had long ago defined it: viz., *a mysterious carriage of the body to cover the defects of the mind*—which definition of GRAVITY Yorick, with 'great imprudence, would say, deserved to be written in letters of gold. But, in plain truth, he was a man unhackneyed and unpractised in the ways of the world, and was altogether as indiscreet and foolish on every other subject of discourse where policy is wont to impress restraint. Yorick had no impression but one, and that was what arose from the nature of the deed spoken of; which impression he would usually translate into plain English, without any periphrasis, and too oft without much distinction of either person, time, or place—so that when mention was made of a pitiful or an ungenerous proceeding—he never gave himself a moment's time to reflect *who* was the hero of the piece—what his station—or how far he had power to hurt *him* hereafter, but if it was a dirty action—without more ado—the man was a dirty fellow—and so on. And as his comments had usually the fate to be terminated in a *bon mot*, or to be enlivened throughout with some drollery or humour of expression, it gave wings to Yorick's indiscretion. In a word . . . . he had but too many temptations in life of scattering his wit and his humour, his gibes and his jests about him. They were not lost for want of gathering. . . . . The mortgager and the mortgagee differ the one from the other not more in length of purse than the jester and the jestee do in that of, memory. . . ." For every ten jokes thou hast got a hundred enemies," said his friend Eugenius to Yorick. But Yorick somehow always neglected advice. A few hours before he breathed his last, Eugenius stept in with an intent to take his last sight and last farewell of him. Upon his drawing Yorick's curtain, and asking how he felt himself, Yorick, looking up in his face, took hold of his hand—and after thanking him for the many tokens of his friendship to him, for which, he said, if it was their fate to meet hereafter, he would thank him again and again—he told him he was within a few hours of giving his enemies the slip for ever. . . . "For my part," continued Eugenius, bitterly crying as he uttered the words, "I declare I know not, Yorick, how to part with thee, and would gladly flatter my hopes," added Eugenius, clearing his voice, "that there is still enough left of thee to make a bishop, and that I may live to see it." "I beseech thee, Eugenius," quoth Yorick, taking off his nightcap as well as he could with his left-hand—his right being still grasped close in that of Eugenius— "I beseech thee to take a view of my head." "I see nothing that ails it," replied Eugenius. "Then, alas! my friend," said Yorick, "let me tell you that it is so bruised and misshapen with the blows which * * * * and * * * and some others have so unhandsomely given in the dark, that I might say with Sancho Panza, that should I recover, and mitres thereupon be suffered to rain down from heaven as thick as hail, not one of them would fit it." Yorick's last breath was hanging upon his trembling lips ready to depart as he uttered this—yet still it was uttered with something of Cervantic tone, and as he spoke it Eugenius could perceive a stream of lambent fire lighted up for a moment in his eyes—faint picture of those flashes of spirit which (as Shakespeare said of his ancestor) were wont to set the table on a roar! He lies buried in a corner of his churchyard in the parish of ———, under a plain marble slab, with no more than these three words of inscription, serving both for his epitaph and elegy—

'"Alas, poor Yorick!"'

BURNS.

At Sterne's death, Robert Burns was ten years old; and, from a note in his 'Commonplace Book,' we discover the fact that 'Tristram Shandy' was with the poet a bosom favourite. By comparing a certain passage in it with a celebrated stanza in Burns, I have been led to the conclusion that some of the praise that has been given to Burns by Coleridge and others should be divided with Sterne. ' " I declare," quoth my uncle Toby [after hearing the curse of Ernulphus repeated], "my heart would not let me curse the devil himself with so much bitterness." . . . " He is the father of curses," replied Dr. Slop [who, as a good Catholic, defends the 'Curse']. . . . "So am not I," replied my uncle. . . . "But he is cursed and damned already to all eternity," replied Dr. Slop. . . . "*I am sorry for it*," quoth my uncle Toby.' The celebrated stanza in which Burns's unspeakable charity is indicated by a hope for the devil's amendment was doubtless suggested by these last words of 'my uncle Toby,' which are equivalent to Burns's

'I'm wae to think upo' yon den;'

but Burns deserves full credit for the still more original idea expressed in the other line:

'O wad ye tak' a thocht *and men*' !'

There are those whose idea of Burns is that of a coarse uneducated peasant; and if by uneducated they mean he was little indebted to 'schools and schoolmasters,' other than those described by his countryman, Hugh Miller, they are right. It should be remembered that, stone-mason though he was, Hugh Miller took a high position among the highest literary men of his day, and was probably better educated than most professors in our colleges; and Burns, besides the English masters, had read a good many French authors in the original, and had gone through Euclid and many a volume of history and metaphysics at his fireside in the winter nights. There have been, and there are, families in humble life in which a superior kind of education is obtained by the members without the 'pomp and circumstance,' and also without the apathy, of colleges. Burns's intelligent father, his brother Gilbert, his sisters, and himself, made at the dinner-hour in their cottage quite an interesting group of students, reading or arguing while they ate, and exhibiting an uncommon eagerness for information.

Carlyle, in his fine essay on Burns, affirms that the poet was 'born in an age the most prosaic Britain had yet seen,' which is surely stating the matter too strongly. Certainly the nation then possessed some of its ablest literary men. Burns was fifteen years of age at the death of Goldsmith, twenty-five at the death of Dr. Johnson, seventeen at the death of David Hume; Gibbon died two years, and Dr. Robertson three years, before Burns's death. Edmund Burke, Adam Smith, and Dr. Paley, were Burns's contemporaries. So were the sentimental poet Beattie, the elegant Gray, and the satiric Wolcot ('Peter Pindar'), none of whom are forgotten. But, above all, Chatterton, the 'mad genius' of Bristol, was a contemporary of Burns —born seven years before the birth, and dying by arsenic twenty-six years before the death of the Ayrshire bard—having proved himself a wonderful poet at eighteen—and having had for his portion genius and hardship during a term precisely one-half of that occupied by Burns's own short life. The celebrated Dr. Hugh Blair was the patron both of 'Ossian' (Macpherson) and Burns. Crabbe, whom Byron has styled 'Nature's sternest painter, yet her best,' was born five years after Burns's birth. The 'School for Scandal,' and other plays of Sheridan, and 'Percy's Reliques,' a collection of ballads, which caused the revival of romantic poetry, were published in Burns's lifetime. The French Revolution was then, like a series of earthquakes, shaking the nations of Europe, and its tumultuous life leaped in the veins of Burns before it was felt by Wordsworth, Coleridge, or Shelley. Walter Scott was twenty-five years of age at Burns's death, Wordsworth twenty-six, Coleridge twenty-four, Moore seventeen, Byron eight, and Shelley four. In view of the remarkable flood of poetic light which came afterwards, the poems of Burns might be called 'songs before sunrise.' But fairly examined, Burns's own age cannot be called 'prosaic.' If his own name will not redeem it from that reproach, we should not forget that a great poet was singing in South Britain, while Burns was making North Briton vocal with his lays. 'The Cotter's Saturday Night,' and 'The Task,' appeared about the same time. An age is not prosaic which produces a William Cowper and a Robert Burns.

Should two such names ever be mentioned together? Has the serious, timid, Calvinistic, preaching Cowper anything in common with the broadly humorous, bold, sceptical, revolutionary, sometimes profane Burns? No doubt the two characters form a strong contrast; but, after they are closely examined, we discover the artist nature essentially the same in both.*
Both wrought at the same national task, which had for its object the revival of true poetry in Britain, by recalling it from affectation to nature, from complex, artificial formalities to simple, lively, and genuine expressions of emotion. And it were hard to say, whether to Burns or Cowper Britain is most indebted for the glorious sunburst they preluded—the poetry of this nineteenth century!

Though many stumble at this Scottish poet found on the British roll of fame, to Ulstermen he is not more, but less, of a foreigner than the others. A large portion of the natives of Down and Antrim take him in the fullest sense for a

---

* Burns carried the 'Task' about with him on Excise expeditions. He calls it a 'glorious poem;' and, with the exception of some points of Calvinism, approves of the religion set forth in it.

'prophet of their own.' I know certain parts of county Antrim where Burns is as keenly relished as he can be in Ayrshire itself. The Scotch of Ulster generally feel they are of Burns's race—a transplanted portion of those old western Whig martyrs whom Claverhouse tried to subdue. We still feel one with the yeomen who fought in the ranks of Wallace on that soil sacred to liberty,

'Where Bruce ance ruled the martial ranks,
And shook his Carrick spear.'

And we think that soil doubly sacred, because it was tilled by an inspired ploughman, whose strains are among those that touch the universal sympathies of the human race. I can yet recall the impression which, when a mere child, I received from relatives, Ulster Scotsmen, regarding Burns. Affection as for an excellent, a wonderful, though erring, brother of whom they had been recently bereft by death—deep affection, combined with reverence, and including a tinge of blame—such, as I recollect it, was the feeling which these Ulster Scots manifested at the mention of Burns's name. I thought I knew him long before I could read his book. He was to me first a great and deeply interesting man, and *then* an author.

Very few besides the Scotch and Scotch-Irish can fully appreciate Burns. There has grown up of late, however, among Scotsmen and Ulster Scotsmen, a class pretending to refinement, who are ashamed of the language of the great Scottish bard. Such persons may be met in our social gatherings, who take offence if perchance the accents of this dead or dying tongue should 'come between the wind and their nobility'— who resent a quotation from Burns as an offence against the rules of good society. The refinement of these people—bless the mark!—being external and easily acquired, teaches them to reject Doric songs as vulgar, because they have discovered that the Attic style prevails in certain high quarters.

Utterly unconscious of the fact that Lowland Scotch was once the language of a brilliant court and an independent nation— utterly unconscious of the literary treasures which that language contains, and on account of which intelligent foreigners have gone to great trouble in acquiring it—these recreant Scotch, these would-be refined, are willing to cast away the advantage of being able to relish Burns with the keenness of a native. Shall this snobbery prevail? Will the time ever come when the SONGS of Burns shall be excluded from our feasts as vulgar? —such strains as these:

> 'Now in her green mantle blithe Nature arrays,
> And listens the lambkins that bleat o'er the braes,
> While birds warble welcome in ilka green shaw,
> But to me it's delightless—my Nannie's awa'!

> 'The snowdrop and primrose our woodlands adorn,
> And violets bathe in the weet o' the morn,
> They pain my sad bosom, sae sweetly they blaw,
> They mind me o' Nannie—and Nannie's awa'.'

The importance of songs which speak to the heart of a nation, and by which a nation speaks out its heart, has not been perceived by some thoughtless persons as it was perceived by the statesman Fletcher, when he said, 'Let me make the songs of a nation, who will may make its laws.' A truth may be hidden by its very commonness; but those who agree with Fletcher must acknowledge the importance of Burns, who is perhaps the greatest of all song-makers. We do not value lightly his other writings, but we think it is mainly by his songs that he continues to be a living power among us still. He is one half of the answer to his own prayer at the close of the 'Cotter's Saturday Night:'

> 'O Thou that pour'd the patriotic tide
> That stream'd thro' Wallace's undaunted heart,
> Oh never, never, Scotia's realm desert,
> But still the *patriot* and the *patriot bard*
> In bright succession raise, her ornament and guard!'

We think 'the patriot and the patriot bard' have both appeared in Scotland with a superiority of splendour which other nations might envy. To her heart her hero-warrior and her hero-poet are both transcendant in glory, and powerful to produce its loyal and enthusiastic applause. Her hero in deeds is her Bruce of the fourteenth century; and not till the eighteenth century did another equally heroic soul appear fully able to enter into the spirit and meaning of the hero's deeds, and express them to the satisfaction and delight of the nation in befitting words. Thus the glory of Bruce by the force of genius has been joined to the glory of Burns; and, 'like two bright particular stars which have no fellows in the firmament,' they shine for ever in conjunction on the heaving heart of Scotland. If Burns had sung but *one* song he would have been immortal as Homer—*that* song which Carlyle says 'should be sung with the throat of the whirlwind'—'SCOTS, WHA HAE.' The idea of this magnificent war-ode rushed like an inspiration into Burns's heart as he was once riding through a storm with his friend Syme, with whom he had been visiting the field of Bannockburn. The great lyric was afterwards finished under an impulse given by a report of the startling success of the French Revolution. In his letter enclosing the song to Mr. Thomson, Burns says he was one evening 'roused by the accidental recollection of that glorious [Scottish] struggle for freedom, associated with glowing ideas of some other struggles of the same nature not quite so ancient.' Greater definiteness was not prudent in a Government official at such a time of intense, almost wild, conservatism; but Burns's mind had evidently been dwelling with some delight on the recent victories of the young French Republic over its Royalist foes. Roused and inspired by contemplating an actual war of independence so near, Burns was soon in imagination on the field of Bannockburn, addressing the soldiers of Bruce:

> 'Scots, wha hae wi' Wallace bled,
> Scots, wham Bruce has aften led,
> Welcome to your gory bed,
>   Or to victory!

> 'Now's the day, and now's the hour:
> See the front of battle lour,
> See approach proud Edward's power,
>   Chains and slavery!

> ' Wha will be a traitor knave?
> Wha can fill a coward's grave?
> Wha sae base as be a slave?
>   Let him turn and flee!
>
> ' Wha for Scotland's king and law
> Freedom's sword will strongly draw,
> Freeman stand, or freeman fa'?
>   Let him follow me!
>
> ' By oppression's woes and pains!
> By your sons in servile chains!
> We will drain our dearest veins
>   But they shall be free!
>
> ' Lay the proud usurper low!
> Tyrants fall in every foe!
> Liberty's in every blow!
>   Let us do or die!'

'The art of art,' says Emerson, 'the glory of expression, and the sunshine of the light of letters is simplicity. Nothing is better than simplicity—nothing can make up for excess, or for lack of definiteness.'* And if ever a powerful simplicity has been manifested in writing, it is manifested in this prince of war-songs; for these six brief stanzas are themselves sufficient to preserve the flame of freedom brilliant in the bosoms of Scotsmen till the world's end. It is delightful to freeborn men to observe how often true genius is allied to love of liberty. About the same time at which Burns produced this ode, the famous 'Marseillaise Hymn' had leaped like sudden flame from the living heart of France.

Indeed, Burns's sympathy for the cause of the people in France was but too well manifested. Too well for his own personal happiness. It lost him promotion from Government, and helped to make the miserable circumstances in which he died. While an humble officer of his Britannic Majesty, he had the imprudence to send a present of two small carronades, accompanied by a letter of encouragement, to the French

---

* 'There is a quality more necessary than either pathos, sentiment, or point in a song, and which is the very essence of a ballad: I mean simplicity.'—*Burns to Thomson*, April, 1793.

Assembly; and by democratic epigrams and witty sayings, which ran like wildfire to official ears, he provoked wrath in high quarters.

Burns was, indeed, a very imprudent man as the world goes. Hardly any piece of song or verse which he wrote but showed this. Very often they were personal satires on near neighbours; and when they were not, they involved loss of time to a poor man. The good narrow people of his neighbourhood did not appreciate this verse-making. They thought he should have worked closely at his farming or flax-dressing. They thought his circumstances required hard work, and that he had no time to spare for rhyming. When not actually working with his hands, he should have been planning and calculating beforehand; and thus he doubtless would have been as prosperous as other small farmers round Mossgiel. But by his sociality, his verse-making, and so forth, his farming and his flax-dressing failed, and he got into debt.

Prudence, according to the standard of his well-doing neighbours, Burns had none. They saw his errors—they were patent to all: too much falling in love, too much social drinking, too much verse-making, too much personal satire. He was by no means unconscious of them himself. Referring to a matrimonial project, he says:

> 'I lo'e her mysel', but daurna' weel tell,
> My poverty keeps me in awe, man:
> For making o' rhymes, and working a times
> Does little or naething at a' man.'

His rhyme-making was detrimental to his worldly prospects in more ways than one. Satirical verses that cause only pleasant laughter *now*, were felt to be somewhat galling by his neighbours at the time when they were written. How would the elders of one of *our* congregations like to see their minister appear in print as Burns sets forth the Rev. Mr. Peebles?

> 'See, up he's got the Word o' God,
> An' meek an' mim has view'd it,
> While Common Sense has ta'en the road,
> An' aff, and up the Cowgate,
> Fast, fast that day!'

. Suppose, madam, your clergyman was named Mr. Moodie—what would be your feelings on perusing in print the following lines?

> ' Should Hornie, as in ancient days,
>   'Mang sons o' God present him,
> The vera sight o' Moodie's face
>   To 's ain het hame had sent him
>   Wi' fright that day.
>
> ' Hear how he clears the points o' faith
>   Wi' rattlin' and wi' thumpin' !
> Now meekly calm, now wild wi' wrath,
>   He's stampin' and he's jumpin' !
> His lengthen'd chin, his turn'd-up snout,
>   His eldritch squeel and gestures,
> O, how they fire the heart devout,
>   Like cantharidian plasters,
>   On sic a day !'

It may be true that such pictures have helped to banish bad taste, or something worse, from Scotch and Irish pulpits: but, meantime, Burns cannot hope to be a favourite with neighbours of influence like the Rev. Mr. Moodie and his kirk session. Something very different from favour he may expect from them, should his interests happen to fall in *their* way—or in that of a yet more terrible champion of orthodoxy at hand, Rev. Mr. Russell, whom the poet profanely designates as ' Black Jock '—a somewhat gigantic personage with a powerful voice, who was accustomed to invade the streets of Kilmarnock on Sabbath evenings, with an immense cudgel which he called his 'ruling elder,' and with which he made Sabbath strollers disappear like chaff before the wind. Neither the Rev. Mr. Russell nor his worshippers would speedily forgive the author of the following lines :

> ' But now the Lord's ain trumpet touts
>   Till a' the hills are rairin',
> And echoes back return the shouts,
>   Black Russell is na sparin' !
> His piercing words, like Highlan swords,
>   Divide the joints and marrow,
> His talk o' hell, where devils dwell,
>   Our vera sauls does harrow ! . . .

> The half-asleep start up wi' fear
>   And think they hear it roarin','
> When presently it does appear,
>   'Twas but some neighbour snorin',
>   Asleep that day.'

The last verse is certainly very comical; but his wise agricultural neighbours doubtless thought he would have been better employed at the plough, or in calculating the price of his flax, than in writing these remarks on the Rev. Mr. Russell's preaching. To those inclined to join in this verdict, there must be considerable comfort in the reflection that very few of our small farmers have ever been, or shall ever be, tempted to commit the imprudence that Burns was guilty of. It must be comforting to think how many small farmers have managed their farms better than Burns, with all his wisdom, managed his; but it is only fair to bid them, in his own words,

> ' Discount what scant occasion gave
>   The purity ye pride in.'

Persons entirely devoid of the poetic temperament can easily enough refrain from committing imprudences in rhyme.

The point lies here. To the ordinary machinery of the human frame suitable for its purpose as an instrument of worldly work, there is *something added* in the case of the poet; call it, if you will, an extra quantity of sensibility, or soul. And just as your engine with too much fire is in some danger of flying off the rails, while one with a moderate amount of fire, or without any, is safe: so Burns had more to do to keep within the bounds of what is called prudence, than many other people have. Let me put the question to men of the world of the average intelligence. Was it, therefore, only a *disadvantage* to Burns that he possessed this extraordinary portion of sensibility, or soul? We hear that he was a good farmer when he liked, and discerning people like Professor Dugald Stewart, who knew him personally, said Burns had such general ability as would make him distinguished in *any* profession or business. But in the narrow business point of view his poetic temperament was a loss to him : for example, he ploughed badly for a few minutes after the coulter ran through a certain 'moosie's nest,' while the fit was on him, and while there was taking place within him a strange sort of fermentation which resulted in some well-known stanzas. Perhaps the furrow went slightly 'a-gley' just then, and some time was lost. Would the strictest and sternest man of business have grudged it to his ploughman? If a man of discernment, if a man with a soul, you would have said, on reading the verses, 'This is not lost time: this is evidence that besides the talents divinely bestowed on ordinary men, an additional one has been given to this ploughman by his Creator, and this gift also may have its legitimate exercise in God's world. This man is gifted to teach whole nations humanity, sincerity, love of freedom, generosity, highest and noblest truth on all subjects; and he may be allowed to do this, though his ploughing shall be somewhat less valuable in consequence.' True: Mr. Worldly Wiseman *allows* the poet to do this work, though thereby he shall lose, say, one-sixth of his salary, which is just £7 sterling per annum—an inspired man will be allowed to give illumination to the nations, to endow them with gems of sentiment and thought, on these munificent terms!

Yes! on these munificent terms—not on others: for who knows that Burns is a distinguished peasant *until* he distinguishes himself? So rare a miracle does not obtain instant credence: you excuse yourself in exercising at least a preliminary scepticism respecting one of your frieze-coated neighbours: even when at length you believe in him, you can hardly be expected to act on your own opinion until it is strengthened and backed up by unquestionable authority: and by the time *that* appears the poet is dead of hunger. It is the old story—of Spenser—of Butler—of Chatterton—of Scotland's king of song! We know what grand mausoleums and monuments have been erected in Scotland to the memory of Burns: we know also that an attorney's letter for £7 of debt so agitated the poet, that the rheumatic fever from which he was recovering became fatal. Notwithstanding the monuments, his own fate necessarily recalls the lines he wrote on his predecessor Ferguson's sad end :

> 'My curse upon your whunstane hearts,
>   Ye Edinbro' gentry !—
> A tithe o' what ye spend at cartes
>   Wad stowed his pantry !'

It has been observed, that in reference to the productions of genius, the ordinary law of supply and demand does not work: for those who have most need of such products always refuse to believe they have any need of them. 'The writer of a fine poem,' says Carlyle, 'is not even now rewarded as well as the inventor of a spinning-jenny.' The poet may happen not to be rewarded at all; but if he be rewarded in some measure, it is by those who are more or less cultivated by means of older writings which were themselves unrewarded in their day.

We do not wish to represent Burns as faultless, throwing undue blame on his countrymen. We admit he had grave faults, for which no excuse can be made. As he often said, he was himself his own worst foe. His vast attractive power, which, far from being diminished, goes on increasing, is owing to the strong human interest that naturally pertains to a life in which base and glorious elements are so strikingly commingled. Looking at him from this distance of time, our eyes free from the rancorous fire that biased the glance of his more bigoted contemporaries, we must say: *There* was a man, not faultless indeed, but a noble fellow in ways; generous in deeds as well as in his fine honest words; enthusiastic, eloquent, sincere; loving flow of soul in unrestrained social intercourse; and much more admirable, it was said, in his talk than in his best pieces of 'song genius;' a hater of policy and cunning, and all hypocrisy; an open genuine MAN, full of clear natural light, and anon equally full of the finest, most scathing fire; a great subject of the tender passion, and withal not by any means easily duped by a specious argument or cowed by imposing authority; a fearless inquirer for facts, and a bold scorner of doctrines unsupported by reason; full of the shrewdest wit and the most delicious convulsive humour; capable of high flights of speculation, and of truest practical wisdom in common things; as fierce and terrible a satirist as ever wove a verse, and yet the author of the most delicate, sweet-flavoured, and impassioned love songs that the 'daughters of music' have yet chanted. The faults of such a man we may lament, but they increase our interest in him; we know our own failings, and are touched to see them exemplified on a theatre so noble as Burns. Hence the strong fascination which the Epitaph that he wrote for himself exercises over us; remembering there was a time in his life when he appeared to those who saw him, to be 'the gayest, brightest, most fantastic fascinating being to be found in the world,' it touches the human heart in us to stand at his headstone and read:

> 'Is there a whim-inspired fool,
>   Owre fast for thought, owre hot for rule,
>   Owre blate to seek, owre proud to snool?
>   Let him draw near,
>   And owre this grassy heap sing dool,
>   And drap a tear.
>
> 'Is there a man whose judgment clear
>   Can others teach the course to steer,
>   Yet runs himself life's mad career,
>   Wild as the wave?
>   Here pause, and thro' the starting tear
>   Survey this grave.
>
> 'The poor inhabitant below
>   Was quick to learn and wise to know,
>   And keenly felt the frindly glow,
>   And softer flame,
>   But thoughtless follies laid him low,
>   And stain'd his name!'

We do not think any good purpose would be served now by dwelling on the indiscretions which he here so deeply deplores. We would rather set forth what we may call his 'noble imprudence'—his forgetfulness to calculate the chances of worldly gain in connexion with his vast literary power. Had he devoted himself to making money by writing, he might have thus found an easy end of his difficulties. But had he been capable of this calculation, he probably would have been incapable of filling his high office of national bard. It was impossible in the nature of things that the generous and noble inspiration which moved the depths of his being should become a marketable article. We read of some newspaper offering him £50 a year for occasional contributions. Was it boundless sentimental pride, or reverence of the heavenly gift lodged within him, that made so poor a man promptly refuse the offer? Mr. Thomson, the publisher of his songs, once enclosed him £5, and in the most delicate manner begged him not to return the cheque. This is Burns' reply : 'I assure you, my dear sir, that you truly *hurt* me with your pecuniary parcel. It degrades me in my own eyes. However, to return it would savour of affectation : but as to any more traffic of that debtor and creditor kind, I swear by that HONOUR which crowns the upright statue of ROBERT BURNS'S INTEGRITY, on the least hint of it, I will indignantly spurn the by past transaction, and from that moment commence entire stranger to you! BURNS's character for generosity of sentiment and independence of mind will, I trust, long outlive any wants of his which the cold unfeeling ore can supply; at least I will take care that such a character he shall deserve.'

Burns wrote this near the end of his brief life of hardship and struggling, when he knew there were some small debts against him which he could not pay. But it hurt him beyond endurance to take money for those songs which he meant as no mercenary service, but as sacred patriotic offerings made in purest disinterestedness at his country's shrine. As this collection of Scottish songs was a labour of love on the part of Mr. Thomson, so Burns meant his contributions to be. For another example of such delicacy we shall search the lives of British poets in vain. In view of the practice of literary men in our age, it may seem over-sensitiveness ; but it strikingly presents Burns in the light of a noble-hearted, high-souled man. 'Not as a hired soldier,' says Carlyle, 'but as a patriot would he strive for the glory of his country; so he cast from him the poor sixpence a-day, and served zealously as a volunteer. Let us not grudge him this last luxury of his existence—let him not have appealed to us in vain! The money was not necessary to him; he struggled through without it: long since these guineas would have been gone, and now the high-mindedness of refusing them will plead for him in all hearts for ever.'

What cannot be said of all poets can be said of Burns— the man was more than the poet. However great the impression made by his poetry, the impression he made personally was greater still. Good judges who knew him have told us that even his book of brilliant poems gives little idea of what was in the man. The power of his presence and conversation was at once felt, in whatever circle, high or low, he appeared. Ostlers and servants gathered at the inn-door, if they heard he was there—a duchess said she felt as if his talk were carrying her off her feet! In his poems, as far as they go, we have himself. There is no affectation, no laboured or artificial expression. Vigorous common sense pithily expressed distinguishes his poems quite as much as brilliancy of fancy or strength of imagination. Hence we have often found men who have no taste for other poetry delighting in Burns. By talented practical men of the world he is often the only poet read. Many of his lines read like proverbs, and in some parts of the country actually do duty as such. In his poetry, what do we find but a man speaking out directly, manfully, fearlessly the thought that is kindling his heart, or the thing that he clearly sees? For if he is pre-eminent as a man of feeling, he is equally so as a man of strong understanding. We find in him that CLEARNESS which, as Carlyle notes, is the unfailing characteristic of genius. His keenness of insight equals his keenness of feeling. Therefore we discover in him not only the form of originality, but the power also.

As a set-off against all these unquestionable merits, it will be said by some that Burns is coarse. So far as this charge points to the *dialect* in which the finest effusions of his poetic spirit are clothed, we treat it as we would treat any other piece of ignorant snobbery—with contempt. The Scottish language, one of the original English or Saxon dialects, is in many respects a more refined, because more expressive, language than the modern English. True, Burns speaks the language of the common people of his own rank, but those who can distinguish the thought from its russet clothing, will not rashly make the charge of common vulgarity. We feel well assured that the main current of his thought and sentiment, as traceable in his book, reaches a level very far above what is common or vulgar. It is surely not needful at this time of day to affirm that a man may belong to the so-called lower classes without being deficient in the essentials of true refinement or delicacy of feeling. I believe the essentials of true refinement are as well preserved in many poor homes in Scotland, as in the richest and most splendid mansions. We should remember that Burns's father was no ordinary man, and a better proof of the genuine worth of the members of his family cannot be given than the fact that their poverty did not hinder them from obtaining from their neighbours an altogether exceptional respect. Burns's behaviour in Edinburgh, when, after the publication of his poems, he was lionized at the houses of the great, was such as we should expect from one of nature's noblemen. The refined and intelligent ladies whom he conducted to table, and conversed with on those occasions, did not complain of his coarseness. On the contrary, his self-possession, natural dignity, equally distinct from servility and presumption, and his instinctive delicacy, were noticed and admired by people of the best taste in the Scottish capital. We find one lady writing to him as follows: 'Our last interview has raised you very high in my esteem. I have met with few, indeed, of your sex who understood delicacy in such circumstances.' The idea of coarseness connected with Burns, so far as it is correct, arises from the folly of those who gathered up and printed every thoughtless stray rhyme which escaped from him in moments of excitement or levity when he condescended to suit himself to his company. Almost with his dying breath he deprecated the publication of these things, which he feared would take place.*

Yet, after all, but little expunging is needed to make Burns presentable. Let us dwell on the bright and beautiful, the noble and elevating things which he has left, and forget the others, which he better than any of us knew were unworthy of him. All men and women love his 'Cotter's Saturday Night:' take a single picture in one stanza:

> 'Wi' joy unfeigned brothers and sisters meet,
>   And each for other's welfare kindly spiers,
> The social hours swift-wing'd unnoticed fleet,
>   Each tells the uncos that he sees or hears,
> The parents partial eye their hopeful years,
>   Anticipation forward points the view;
> The mother wi' her needle and her shears
>   Gars auld claes look amaist as weel's the new,
> The father mixes a' wi' admonition due.'

How well he has painted the poor man's joys and pleaded the poor man's cause in this fine poem, in 'The Twa Dogs,' and in 'Hallowe'en'! What a piece of brilliant humour, full of force, instinct with life and genius, is 'Tam O'Shanter'! What a tremendous satire we have in 'Holy Willie'! Who will not forgive some slight improprieties of speech for sake of the genial and harmless humour that runs through the wonderful lampoon on Wilson the quack-doctor—immortal 'Hornbook'? It is impossible to resist the comic familiarity with which we see the poet approaching the awful 'Something' with whom he foregathered what time

> 'The rising moon began to glower
> The distant Cummock hills out owre,'

---

* Writing to a lady, Burns says: 'As I have some little fame at stake—a fame that I trust may live when the hate of those who "watch for my halting," and the contumelious sneer of those whom accident has made my superiors, will with themselves be gone to the regions of oblivion—I am uneasy now for the fate of those manuscripts. Will Mrs. Riddel have the goodness to destroy them or return them to me?' This request, we believe, was not complied with.

when the effects of the 'Clachan yill' are indicated by his deliberate attempt to count her horns.

> 'I there wi' Something did foregather
> That put me in an eerie swither;
> An awfu' scythe out-owre ae shouther
> Clear-dangling hang,
> A three-ta'ed leister on the ither
> Lay large and lang.
>
> Its stature seem'd lang Scotch ells twa,
> The queerest shape that e'er I saw,
> For fient a wame it had ava'
> And then its shanks,
> They were as thin, as sharp and sma'
> As cheeks o' branks.'

After this gruesome description, we have the poet's neighbourly address to the ghastly Shape:

> '"Guid-e'en," quo' I, "Frien', hae ye been mawin',
> While ither folk are busy sawin'?"'

After an explanation of peaceable intentions on the part of the Spectre, we have the poet's almost patronizing rejoinder:

> '"Weel, weel," says I, "a bargain be't;
> Come, gie's your han', and sae we're gree't—
> We'll ease our shanks and tak' a seat!
> Come, gie's your news;
> This while ye hae been mony a gait,
> At mony a house."'

And thus DEATH is induced to enter upon his tale, which is, in brief, a complaint against 'Hornbook,' who deprives him of his lawful prey by the manifold drugs and 'new uncommon weapons' of the 'bauld apothecary'—the only adversary that has effectually resisted Death for 'sax thousand years!'

Still more powerful is Burns's treatment of another awful Being of ghostly character:

> 'Whyles ranging like a roarin' lion,
> For prey a' holes an' corners tryin',
> Whyles on the strong-wing'd tempest flyin',
> Tirlin' the kirks;
> Whyles in the human bosom pryin'
> Unseen thou lurks.

'I've heard my reverend granny say,
In lanely glens ye like to stray,
Or where auld ruin'd castles gray
　　　Nod to the moon,
Ye fright the nightly wanderer's way
　　　Wi' eldritch croon.

'Ae dreary windy winter night,
The stars shot down their sklentin' light,
Wi' you, mysel', I got a fright
　　　Ayont the lough;
Ye, like a rash-bush stood in sight,
　　　Wi' wavin' sugh.'

A large section of Burns's poetry sprang out of the religious battles of his time. Before glancing at this, a remark or two regarding the poet's religion may not be inappropriate. To many serious people, even in our own day, Burns is nothing better than one of the profane, an utterly irreligious man, or even a monster of profanity. Now, if we conceive the Scottish people of that age as divided, like the people of Judæa, into two great classes of Pharisees and Publicans, we must admit that, constitutionally and otherwise, Burns belongs to the latter. On this all parties agree; the only question is whether we cannot find in him the Publican's penitence, as well as the Publican's excesses. There is, indeed, ample evidence that the sins to which he was addicted were not the cold, hard, severe vices of pride, covetousness, and hypocrisy, but those errors of unlimited indulgence and headlong passion which are the bane of generous natures and warm hearts. We may admit that Burns at times shows too much leniency towards his own besetting sins, while showing no toleration for the opposite vices. We find him pretty often indulging a strain like this:

'O ye douce folk wha live by rule,
Grave, tideless-blooded, calm, and cool,—
Compar'd wi' you,—O fool! fool! fool!
　　　How much unlike! . . .
Your hearts are just a standing pool,
　　　Your lives a dike!

*　　*　　*　　*　　*

'Awa', ye selfish warldly race,
　Wha think that havin's sense and grace,
　E'en love and friendship, should give place
　　　　　　To catch-the-plack!
　I dinna like to see your face,
　　　　　　Nor hear your crack!

'But ye whom social pleasure charms,
　Whose hearts the tide of kindness warms,
　Who hold your being on the terms,
　　　　　　"Each aid the others,"
　Come to my bowl, come to my arms,
　　　　　　My friends, my brothers.

＊　　＊　　＊　　＊　　＊

'Were this the charter of our state,
　"On pain o' hell be rich and great,"
　Damnation then would be our fate
　　　　　　Beyond remead;
　But, thanks to heaven, that's no the gate
　　　　　　We learn our creed.

'For thus the royal mandate ran,
　When first the human race began,
　"The social, friendly, honest man,
　　　　　　Whate'er he be,
　'Tis he fulfils great Nature's plan,
　　　　　　And none but he!"'

There is no doubt, however, that Burns carried these liberal principles quite too far; and that while scorning, perhaps too vehemently, the coldness and precision of the Pharisees, he found himself too often in the wretched outcast condition of the Publican. But the following scrap from his private papers may be some evidence that 'this man went down to his house justified rather than the other': 'I have been this morning looking at my past life—a rueful prospect! What a scene of thoughtlessness, weakness, and folly! My life reminded me of a ruined temple. What strength, what proportion in some parts! What unsightly gaps and prostrate ruin in others! I kneeled down before the Father of mercies, and said, "Father, I have sinned against heaven and in Thy sight, and am no more worthy to be called Thy son." I rose, eased and strengthened.'

Burns was not an orthodox Presbyterian, though we believe he did the Presbyterians great good by satirizing the extravagances and follies to which they were once addicted. His early training had led him to adopt the Arminian and Arian views professed by the 'New Light' or Broad Church party of the time. His father, a man of genuine piety and uncommon intelligence, had drawn out in writing for the guidance of his children a statement of views in which he differed from the orthodox standards. Beginning thus on the liberal side, Burns early threw himself with characteristic vehemence into the polemical theology which, he tells us, 'was driving the country half mad.' In the discussions which frequently sprang up in the churchyard on Sabbath mornings before the service, Burns would at times astonish an improvised audience with the vigour of his reasoning powers and the boldness of his arguments. It is probable that as he grew older his creed did not acquire any new articles, but rather lost some of the old ones: but, with dogmas or without them, religion, he always maintained, was his favourite subject and strongest sentiment.* Though certainly a warm partisan of the New Light or Rationalistic party, it was not, we should observe, the dogmas of the Orthodox, but their practice, on which the terrible vials of his satiric muse were poured. In the 'Holy Fair' itself there is a certain negative reverence; for though the extravagances of the preachers, the follies and inconsistencies of the superstitious mobs are exposed, there is not even the slightest or most distant reference to the Sacrament itself. The carnival-like concomitants of those extraordinary gatherings were fair game for his wit. He held his vivid picture up before the eyes of the Scottish public—Scotland was once for all made ashamed of

---

* 'Nor would I quarrel with a man for his want of religion any more than I would for his want of musical ear. I would regret that he was shut out from what to me and to others were such superlative sources of enjoyment.'—*Burns to Mrs. Dunlop.*

those scenes, and from that moment they began to disappear. In the same way Burns's scathing satire destroyed and burnt up many of the spiritual evils in the party to which he was opposed. Want of candour, vehemence of bigotry united with weakness of understanding, tyranny combined with superstition and nonsense, self-righteousness working with deceit to screen the scoundrel and with pitiless pride to crush the more candid transgressor who disregards a form—*these*, with the peculiar severity and meanness of an ill-natured sanctimonious revenge, were the evils in the orthodox which, rather than their orthodoxy, Burns attacked so powerfully. The better we apprehend the true spirit of Christianity, the more ready we shall be to sympathize with the spirit of such attacks, which are made on the grandest scale in the sacred writings themselves, in such passages as Isaiah lviii. and Matt. xxiii. Burns, we believe, never did a piece of work of this kind more effectively than in the following strong passage in the 'Dedication to Gavin Hamilton:'

'As master, landlord, husband, father,
He doesna fail his part in either—
But then, nae thanks to him for a' that,
Nae godly symptom can ye ca' that,
It's naething but a milder feature
Of our poor sinfu' corrupt nature . . . .
That he's the poor man's friend in need,
The gentleman in word and deed,
It's no through terror o' damnation—
It's just a carnal inclination ! . . . .
No : stretch a point to catch a plack,
Abuse a brother to his back . . . .
Be to the poor like ony whunstane,
And haud their noses to the grunstane,
Ply every art o' legal thievin'—
Nae matter, stick to sound believin'!
Learn three-mile prayers, and half-mile graces,
Wi' well-spread looves and lang wry faces,
Grunt up a solemn lengthen'd groan,
Condemn a' parties but your own :
I'll warrant then ye're nae deceiver—
A steady, sturdy, stanch believer !'

A shock of this kind from Burns was dangerous, and he gave the Orthodox party more than one or two. We are, we hope, admitting the justice of the rebuke, by endeavouring to make it no longer applicable. I am not sure, however, that there are not *still* certain parties (Arminian as well as Calvinist) to whom a little of this physic would be useful.

Burns was too true a poet to introduce discussions of dogmatic theology into his writings. It is manners rather than dogma with which he deals. Yet by one satire he probably did more for the New Light or Broad Church party than M'Gill, Taylor, and the rest of them did by their books and sermons. This satire, which, though on the wrong side, seems to me as a composition nearly perfect, and not surpassed by Pope's or Dryden's best work, appears as a trifling 'POSTCRIPT' added to one of the rhymed letters which Burns was in the habit of writing to his friends. In this allegorical postscript, Calvinism, or the Old Light, appears as the astronomy before Copernicus, and Arminianism, or the New Light, as the true astronomy, which the ignorant *vulgus* reject.

'In days when mankind were but callans
At grammar, logic, and sic talents,
They took nae pains their speech to balance,
   Or rules to gie,
But spak' their thoughts in plain braid lallans,
   Like you or me.

'In thae auld days they thocht the moon,
Just like a sark or pair o' shoon,
Wore by degrees till her last roun'
   Gaed past the viewin',
And shortly after she was done
   They gat a new one.

'This pass'd for certain, undisputed,
It ne'er cam' in their heads to doubt it,
Till chiels gat up and wad confute it,
   And ca'd it wrang;
And muckle din there was about it,
   Baith loud and lang.

'Some herds weel learn'd upo' the beuk
   Wad threep auld folk the thing misteuk,
   For 'twas the auld moon turn'd a neuk
                     And out o' sight,
   And backlins-comin', to the leuk
                     She grew mair bright.

'This was denied—it was affirm'd—
   The herds and hissels were alarm'd—
   The reverend grey-beards raved and storm'd
                     That beardless laddies
   Should think they better were inform'd
                     Than their auld daddies.

'Frae less to mair, it gaed to sticks,
   Frae words and aiths to clours and nicks,
   And mony a fallow gat his licks
                     Wi' hearty crunt;
   And some to learn them for their tricks
                     Were hang'd and burnt. . .

'The New Light herds gat sic a cowe,
   Folk thought them ruin'd stick and stowe—
   Till now, amaist on every knowe
                     Ye'll fin' ane placed,
   And some their new light fair avow,
                     Just quite barefaced!

'Nae doubt the Auld Light flocks are bleatin',
   Their zealous herds are vex'd and sweatin',
   Mysel', I've even seen them greetin'
                     Wi' girnin' spite,
   To hear the moon sae sadly lied on
                     By word and write.

'But shortly they will cowe the louns!—
   Some auld-light herds in neibor touns
   Are mind't, in things they ca' balloons,
                     To tak' a flight,
   And stay ae month amang the moons,
                     And see them right.

'Guid observation they will gie them,
   And when the auld moon's gaun to lea' them,
   The hindmost shaird they'll fetch it wi' them
                     Just in their pouch;
   And when the New Light billies see them
                     I think they'll crouch!'

A poet who is distinguished for humour can usually, when he likes, show himself a master of pathos. Burns is not always equally successful when he attempts a purely sentimental strain, but we might easily load our pages with specimens from him of powerful convulsive humour and pathetic verse. At times, brimful of genuine fun, the slightest occasion makes it flow from him. He receives the income-tax query-sheet from his friend Aikin, and at once sits down and writes:

> 'For men, I've three mischevious boys,
> Run-de'ils for rantin' and for noise,
> A gaudsman ane, a thresher t'other,
> Wee Davoc hauds the nowt in fother;
> I rule them, as I ought, discreetly,
> And aften labour them completely,
> And aye on Sundays duly, nightly,
> I on the *Questions** targe them tightly,
> Till, faith, wee Davoc's grown sae gleg,
> Tho' scarcely langer than my leg,
> He'll screed you aff "Effectual Calling"
> As fast as ony in the dwalling.'

Or, after an election, he thinks of writing a petition to the Scottish M.P.'s on a subject then exciting the country, and urges them to address the House with vigour, thus:

> 'In gathering votes ye were na slack,
> Noo stand as tightly to your tack,
> Ne'er claw your lug, nor fidge your back,
>   And hum and haw,
> But raise your arm and tell your crack
>   Amang them a'!'

Concluding with expressions of good-will still more comical:

> 'God bless your honours a' your days
> Wi' sowps o' kail and brats o' claes,
> In spite o' a' the thievish kaes
>   That haunt St. Jamie's,
> Your humble poet sings and prays
>   While Rab his name is.'

Though his pathetic touches are not so frequent, they are

---

* The 'Shorter Catechism' of the Westminster Divines.

quite as powerful in their way as the strokes of humour. That 'Bonny Doon' can still touch the heart, though it has been the common possession of the world for nearly a century, proves it to contain an original inherent source of power, such as even Goldsmith's famous verses on a similar subject—'When simple woman stoops to folly'—do not contain. From what other author than Burns can you produce such a 'concentrated essence of a thousand romances' as this?—

> 'Had we never lo'ed sae kindly,
> Had we never lo'ed sae blindly,
> Never met, or never parted,
> We had not been broken-hearted.'

We might challenge the world to produce from all the poets since Homer a finer stanza than the following:

> 'I see her in the dewy flowers,
>   I see her sweet and fair,
> I see her in the tunefu' birds,
>   I hear her charm the air;
> There's not a bonnie flower that springs
>   By fountain shaw or green,
> There's not a bonnie bird that sings,
>   But minds me o' my Jean.'

Not only the charms of youthful lovers, but those of gentle wifehood, and of pure domestic bliss, are wonderfully depicted by him who uttered the noble words:

> 'To make a happy fireside clime
>   To weans and wife,
> That's the true pathos and sublime
>   Of human life;'

and wrote the manly song:

> 'She is a winsome wee thing,
> She is a handsome wee thing,
> She is a bonnie wee thing,
>   This sweet wee wife o' mine!
> The warld's wrack we share o't,
> The warstle and the care o't,
> Wi' her I'll blithely bear it,
>   And think my lot divine.'

Let us remember, in estimating Burns, that the author of these exquisite things was no professed *littérateur*, but one who lived a laborious life to win daily bread; and that most of what has been preserved of him were spontaneous outbursts of the moment, or effusions without effort, or, like his own 'Mountain Daisy,' cropping out in its beauty amid every discouragement:

> 'Cauld blew the bitter biting north
> Upon thy early humble birth,
> Yet cheerfully thou glinted forth
>   Amid the storm.'

Yet this poet of humble life does not shrink from comparison with the best of those who may be called poets of the higher classes. This poor man's poet has somewhat effectively stood up for the native nobility of man. He sang that grand lyric of human-kind—'A man's a man for a' that.'

> 'For a' that, and a' that,'
>   Our toils obscure and a' that,
>   The rank is but the guinea-stamp,
>   The man's the gowd for a' that.

He may have erred in that at times he 'grudged a-wee the great folks' gift wha live sae bien and snug.' Carlyle regrets that he did not more constantly find in poetry its own great reward. This is easily said by men whose means of living are secure. But we know well that Burns, while partaking of all the uncertainties and hardships of the poor man's lot, knew his dignity as the national poet, and took in his lyre a boundless delight. His most beautiful poem, 'The Vision,' is proof enough of this. As he sits in a desponding mood by the ingle-cheek in the 'auld clay biggin',' and is just about making a rash vow to be 'rhyme-proof' to his last breath, the national goddess, Coila, suddenly appears, and presents to him the laureate wreath, with words of exquisite poetic beauty:

> 'I saw thee seek the sounding shore,
> Delighted with the dashing roar,
> Or when the north his fleecy store,
>   Drove thro' the sky,
> I saw grim nature's visage hoar
>   Struck thy young eye.

'Or when the deep green-mantled earth
  Warm-cherished every floweret's birth,
  And joy and music pouring forth
        In every grove,
  I saw thee eye the general mirth
        With boundless love.

'When ripen'd fields and azure skies
  Call'd forth the reaper's rustling noise,
  I saw thee leave their evening joys
        And lonely stalk
  To vent thy bosom's swelling sighs
        In pensive walk.

'When youthful love, warm-blushing, strong,
  Keen shivering shot thy nerves along,
  Those accents grateful to thy tongue,
        The adorèd name,
  I taught thee how to pour in song,
        To soothe thy flame.

'I saw thy pulse's maddening play
  Wild send thee Pleasure's devious way,
  Misled by Fancy's meteor-ray,
        By Passion driven;
  But yet the light that led astray
        Was light from Heaven.*

'I taught thy manners-painting strains,
  The loves and ways of simple swains,
  Till now, o'er all my wide domains
        Thy fame extends,
  And some, the pride of Coila's plains,
        Become thy friends. . . .

'Then never murmur nor repine,
  Strive in thy humble sphere to shine;
  And, trust me, not Potosi's mine,
        Nor kings' regard,
  Can give a bliss o'ermatching thine,
        A rustic Bard.'

To conclude with one or two general remarks. Burns's style is remarkably natural, his great virtue being, as Carlyle

* This has been censured; but the poet only refers to his imaginative susceptible temperament, as at once the source of his poetry and the cause of his falls.

says, sincerity, or freedom from affectation. His writing is compact, pregnant, pithy—not even Pope's verse is so full of matter as Burns's. He is thus the father of many proverbial phrases. His descriptive power is vivid, seizing with brevity and judgment the points of interest, and avoiding wearisome complexity. A single word will sometimes with terrible distinctness set the scene before us—as when he speaks of the Scots under Wallace pressing onward '*red-wat-shod.*' His words invest with the strongest interest any natural phenomenon that he touches—the 'burn' in 'Hallowe'en' becomes in his page little less than a portion of animated nature. By his deep and marvellous love of nature, like that of the mother to her child, he is able to teach with power his high lesson of humanity, as in ' Winter Night ':

> 'Ilk happing bird, wee helpless thing,
> That in the merry months o' spring
> Delighted me to hear thee sing,
>   What comes o' thee?
> Where wilt thou cower thy chittering wing,
>   And close thy ee?'

Some who loudly blame Burns's indelicacy may find that, though he too often sins in this respect, he has a delicacy superior to their own. He has, at any rate, a warm all-comprehending fellow-feeling, of which the hot-house plants of modern prudery know nothing. However this may be, the historian must recognise the fact, that a certain Ayrshire farmer, struggling with poverty and misfortune, has vindicated for himself a foremost place among the most considerable men of the eighteenth century. When we consider the millions whom his thoughts and sentiments have affected, it seems not too much to say that this ploughman has fairly beat all the great scholars and wits of his age. 'He begs no indulgence on account of the circumstances in which his poems were produced—they are intrinsically so remarkable that the circumstances cannot add to our astonishment.'* Rheumatic-fever cut him off at thirty-

---

* Craik.

seven—what might he not have accomplished had he lived till three-score? Calumnies, according to their own base nature, seem peculiarly ready to cluster round genius—they have even polluted his grave, as if it were that of a drunkard slain by his dissipation. This was what some saw in the sad event, in which deeper eyes beheld a gift too soon recalled from a nation that learned too late to prize it. I will not admit that his faults were such as to excuse the neglect of his countrymen; for his faults he has himself pleaded such excuse as the candid and generous will not reject:

> 'Who knows the heart, 'tis He alone
>   Decidedly can try us,
> He knows each chord, its various tone,
>   Each spring—its various bias ;
> Then at the balance let's be mute,
>   We never can adjust it ;
> What's done we partly may compute,
>   But know not what's resisted.'

SAMUEL JOHNSON.

THE Johnson clan is an extensive one, and has contained potentates of no mean order, from 'Rare Ben,'[*] who jested with Shakespeare at the Mermaid and wrote plays for Elizabeth, to this 'Great Sam,' who brow-beat Bozzy at the Turk's Head when George III. was King. Out of all the Johnsons which have existed, or exist, we choose for our companion for an hour that very remarkable one born at Lichfield in the year of grace 1709—for this one reason, among others, that the good people among us who fear and scorn and hate literature may hear of an undoubtedly pious man whose life was devoted to it. Though that life is set forth in the most popular and most perfect of biographies by Boswell, there may be something for a short paper to accomplish which a large book cannot do. A few points presented vividly is all that will take effect in this busy age; and if any have time for more, this sketch may quicken their interest in books and give additional life to their reading.

Saith picturesque Macaulay: 'The old philosopher is still among us in the brown coat with the metal buttons, and the shirt which ought to be at the wash, blinking, puffing, rolling his head, drumming with his fingers, tearing his meat like a tiger, and swallowing his tea in oceans.' With some such picture before her eyes, a lady once said in my hearing she 'just hated' big Sam Johnson, he was so overbearing and dogmatic! Had this lady seen him—had she invited him to her table—she would probably have liked him rather less. She would have found his soul was attached to an unwieldy mass

[*] Jonson.

called his body, which certainly was not as perfectly in working order, nor as well-balanced, as a newly patented, newly polished, newly oiled coffee-grinding steam-engine. It was much less securely uniform than either that machine or any ordinary specimen of our modern genteel society. Johnson's body was, in fact, a large territory, and all the provinces were not equally under control: for a similar reason his mind also may have been harder to keep in order than that of others who have less. According to the theology of the Dandiacal Sect, the unpardonable sin is to be queer; for it is a fundamental dogma of their creed that every distinct individual of the human race should be turned out as articles of commerce are turned out—*so* that on laying two together you can perceive no difference amounting to more than a scratch on the surface between the one and the other. Johnson was, therefore, as is well known, condemned to the limbo of the Dandiacal Sect by its then reigning great Lama, Lord Chesterfield, who wrote certain 'Letters to His Son,' against which our Great Bear growled as containing 'the manners of a dancing-master and the morals of a ——.'

Dismissing for the present Johnson's body, which at the current date cannot be supposed to affect us much, let us turn our attention to the more important question—What is his value otherwise? How does his *mind* affect us? What are his literary merits? The fact that Carlyle treats of Johnson under the heading 'The Hero as a Man of Letters,' is a sufficient proof that Johnson's special gift was literary. WHAT, then, has he written? and HOW has he done it? What work of Johnson's do we find still successfully battling against oblivion and claiming to be an element of the present intellectual life?

We do not commend his style. In it he appears

> 'Pedantic, stiff—some statue, you would swear,
> Stept from its pedestal to take the air!'

Some blame the fashion of the age—but no! For Addison's light graceful slip-shod English was before him; and it was even Johnson's self who uttered the maxim: 'If you would learn to write English, spend your days and nights in reading Addison.' Why did he so little 'reck his own rede'? You cannot blame the fashion of the time for Johnson's suit of cumbrous buckram; for there is Goldsmith, his intimate friend, whose style is so easy and natural, who in one of his happiest hits has handed Johnson down to us as one who in writing an allegory of little fishes would make them all speak like whales! Carlyle calls Johnson's style 'a measured grandiloquence, stepping or rather stalking along in a very solemn way, grown obsolete now; sometimes a tumid *size* of phraseology not in proportion to the contents of it: all this you will put up with.' I fear not: I rather think this age of ours does *not* put up with it. Who of us has read six papers of the once famous, always ponderous, now dimly remembered 'Rambler'? We would almost as soon engage six of the lengthy discourses of Isaac Barrow or tough Thomas Cartwright. Even 'Rasselas,' though still mentioned among us with respect, is not greatly read. One takes it up on account of the fame it has, but soon finds that a few pages of those undulating masses called sentences has the effect that rocking the cradle has on young brains. So much for the style of Johnson's prose.

As to his poetry—for being truly a literary man, Johnson was necessarily something of a poet—there are a few couplets from Johnson's 'Vanity of Human Wishes' with which we have somehow got acquainted, *e.g.*, that one on Charles XII.—

> 'He left a name at which the world grows pale
> To point a moral, or adorn a tale.'

And of the couplet which with deep personal feeling and intense bitterness of spirit he wrote in his 'London,' we know at least the line he printed in small capitals:

> 'SLOW RISES WORTH BY POVERTY DEPRESS'D.'

But Johnson's poetry is now generally regarded as considerably beneath the 'highest heaven of invention,' and is little read. If you belong to the school that discusses the question: 'Was

Pope a poet?' I fear for Johnson's reputation in your hands. In his day poetry had not acquired the natural flow and perfect sincerity which we see in it now as it leaves the working brain of a Tennyson or a Browning. In neither poetry nor prose has Johnson left us the example of a really good style, nor has he done much work in which genius, or the genial element, is very conspicuous. We think we can now afford to do very well without his works—dictionary included—all, perhaps, but one. That once world-renowned dictionary is now obsolete as well as the 'Rambler,' yet it would be possible for any of us to spend an hour occasionally over the original edition of the dictionary with both pleasure and profit, for it is a wonderful collection of good extracts from English authors. But the book which we reserve from the oblivion to which his other works are delivered is undoubtedly his 'Lives of the Poets,' a book which I have sometimes fancied has been injured by the author's name on the title-page; for if it were supposed to be written by any other than the ponderous moralist of the 'Rambler,' there are several lively persons among us who would make its acquaintance. I venture to affirm that no person who has even dipped into that book has ever after been able to despise Dr. Johnson. It contains the condensed result of a world of thinking on men and things, the cream of knowledge preserved so that all generations after may know what is worth knowing of the leading spirits of an age. The essence of Johnson's good sense, the excellence of his understanding, the force of his masculine intellect, are there. One will not have much leisure to find fault with the style if he gives attention to the matter of this book.

It was in his old age, when all his Grub Street troubles were long over; after he had fought, as it were, with beasts for food; after he had drudged for the booksellers, and once in his rage with a great book knocked down one of them, the greedy Osborne; long after this, when he was enjoying his royal pension and reigning as the 'great Cham of literature,' no fewer than forty-four booksellers waited on him to request that he would undertake certain 'introductions' to a series of poetical works then about to be published. It was thus that near the age of seventy he was started to work at his *chef d'œuvre!* He could do something respectable at verse-making, he could write moral disquisitions and criticisms in an impressive and dignified style, he could build up the immense pile of a huge Dictionary — doing for English what forty Frenchmen could not do so well for French—he was also a wonderful talker and debater; but, after all, his main work has proved to be his account of the lives and appreciation of the merits of literary men. Quite recently a man so distinguished for literary culture ('sweetness and light') as Matthew Arnold has presented a volume of these 'Lives' in a new dressing to the cultivated circles of his countrymen, saying, 'Take this book and read it: for as yet we have got no better pabulum of this sort.' No! even Mr. Arnold himself could not write a Life of Dryden or a Life of Pope as good as Johnson's.

Johnson's criticisms on his authors are generally penetrating and judicious, his judgments are often final. We cannot enter into these matters here; but by way of discriminating Johnson's own special literary character we shall refer to one of his pronouncements. There is one of his criticisms too notable to be omitted even in a short paper: his emphatic and severe condemnation of the poetry of 'Lycidas.' 'In this poem,' says Johnson, 'there is no nature, for there is no truth; there is no art, for there is nothing new. Its form is that of a pastoral, easy and vulgar and therefore disgusting; whatever images it can supply are long ago exhausted; and its inherent improbability always forces dissatisfaction on the mind. . . . We hear how one god asks another, what is become of Lycidas, and how neither god can tell. He who thus grieves will excite no sympathy; he who thus praises will confer no honour.' . . . and so on; finishing up with this final blow: 'Surely no man could have fancied that he read "Lycidas" with pleasure had he not known the author.' Those of us who remember Ruskin's description of a true book, and the example he gives, will smile at Johnson's criticism. Ruskin says: 'Whatever bit of a wise man's work is honestly and benevolently done, that bit is his book, or his piece of art. It is the piece of true knowledge or sight which his share of sunshine and earth has permitted him to seize. He would fain set it down for ever, engrave it on a rock, if he could; saying, "This is the best of me; for the rest, I ate, and drank, and slept, loved and hated like another; my life was as the vapour, and is not; but *this* I saw and knew: *this*, if anything of mine, is worth your memory."'

Ruskin says this, and then proceeds with his masterly exposition of 'LYCIDAS' *as an example of the 'true book' he had just described!* How vast the interval this reveals between cultured minds who are scarcely one century apart! How different Ruskin's light from Johnson's! When we remember that the reading of 'Lycidas' has been in our days used as a test by which a man may discover whether he possess a true taste for poetry, we can understand the effect of Johnson's critique on his own reputation. His judgment on Milton's Sonnets is at least equally damaging to the critic: 'They deserve not any particular criticism; for of the best it can only be said that they are not *bad;* and perhaps only the eighth and twenty-first are truly entitled to this slender commendation.'

However ridiculous these decisions may appear to critics in our days, they ought to admire their manful honesty—especially those critics whose chief business is to re-echo the common cry. Nor is it necessary to decide against Johnson's claims as a literary man; for as there are different schools of painting, so there are different schools of poetry; and in both cases we can find disciples of one school depreciating the products of a different school. Certainly the school of poetry founded by Coleridge and Wordsworth contrasts strangely with that of Pope and Johnson; but I fancy we are now coming round to think that the soaring transcendental school of these last times has sometimes taken up, in reference to its predecessor, a somewhat intolerant attitude. At any rate, there is no danger in affirming that Johnson's 'Lives' contains much sound instruction and valuable criticism, notwithstanding these unfortunate criticisms on 'Lycidas' and the Sonnets.

The style of the book is better, more easy, and less pedantic, than that of his other prose-writings, for this reason, that the writer had now been for many years a chief talker in the first literary circles of London, where he had gathered some of the most valuable things in his biographies. Johnson as a talker, even as he still talks to us in Boswell's 'Life,' surpasses Johnson as a writer. We are sure we cannot now estimate the greatness of this man from his writings, as we might have done had we known him in his glory, surrounded by the foremost men of England in the Turk's Head.

Here, after all, was his real triumph. This 'strange' individual that genteel folks had shrunk from—this once poor child of a Lichfield bookseller; this diseased son of a diseased father, his face marred and his sight greatly injured by scrofula; this odd companion, prone to strange rollings and extraordinary gestures; this quondam awkward, uncouth, rusty denizen of a garret, who had been told he was fitter to wear a porter's knot than to do elevating literary work—was, indeed, the central light, the elected king, in those brilliant societies where Reynolds and Burke, Goldsmith and Garrick, Gibbon and Hume, Adam Smith and Sir Wm. Jones were members. Yes; poor old Sam, with all his odd convulsions and queer, superstitious ways, was a king *there* by native right which none disputed. His clever retorts, his deep sayings, his acute remarks, made in those societies impromptu, and taken down by the assiduous Boswell, are now considered more important than all he has written. The fact that Reynolds deferred to him proves something, but more is proved by the deference of Burke, the greatest of modern political philosophers. Genteel persons who may still feel inclined to sneer at him because, as Macaulay says, 'he dressed like a scarecrow and ate like a cormorant,' would probably have been very proud to make his acquaintance in one of those brilliant assemblages at the Turk's Head, where his word was law.

Had one of your acquaintances who claims to be 'sensible' and not literary met Johnson, he would have cheerfully admitted his title to at least two characteristics—great good sense and largeness of heart. But his great good sense was, in other words, his genius, with which fearful and wonderful gift that of melancholy is for ever allied. Whether genius itself be the result of disease I leave an unsettled question; but it was surely a strange sight to see, in that huge diseased frame of Johnson, genius and melancholy, like an angel and a fiend, locked in the death-grapple. I sometimes think such minds are emblematized in the weird fancy of Coleridge of 'the lovely Lady Geraldine,' who charms all eyes, but wears about her night and day a concealed, a nameless, an unspeakable horror. How often a saying of Johnson's makes us exclaim, 'This is a clear-sighted man! Here is strong good sense piercing the centre of the subject!' while we may forget at the moment how long the dull, painful fire of melancholy had worked beneath the smoke before that light was at last emitted. On this subject hear one of the gifted themselves speak:

> 'The wise
> Have a far deeper madness, and the glance
> Of melancholy is a fearful gift;
> What is it but the telescope of truth,
> Which strips the distance of its fantasies,
> And brings life near in utter nakedness,
> Making the cold reality too real!'

I forgive Byron fifty foolish things for saying that so well—with such strength and accuracy. Before those good things could be emitted from Johnson's mind in the club, what oppressive seasons of gloom, what inward wasting, what feelings of helplessness and despair, what terrors of night and day, had kept him company! Knowing what we do of men like Johnson, their 'good things' remind us too forcibly of moments of exuberant joy which some patients experience after the racking pangs of an intermittent malady.

Johnson's great good sense appeared in the strong, honest attempts which he made to see things as they are—to get rid of the self-delusion that occurs where the 'wish is father to the thought.' No matter how comfortless the bare fact appeared, he persisted in looking at it naked, without any of those softening, modifying influences which fond hope usually lends to it. If, for example, one talked to him about the pleasures of literature, the happiness of the poet in conceiving and executing some fine work of imagination, 'Sir,' Johnson would growl, 'no man but a blockhead ever wrote except for money.' In this way he liked to cut down high-flown expressions, and cut away the flowery margin of impractical ideas.

In this respect he much resembled that other great old talker Socrates. The two are nearer akin than we might at first suppose. There is much of the Socratic spirit in Johnson's famous imperative: 'Clear your mind of cant.' The long-continued process of talking with his fellow-citizens, and discovering to them the respective delusions under which they laboured, and by means of which they were more or less happy —this long-continued process, which made the Athenian philosopher so unpopular, and at length brought about his death, was not unlike the work which Johnson performed in the societies and clubs of London. It has struck me as a remarkable coincidence to find two sages in some respects so similar in ages so distant, who lived simply for the purpose of talking to their neighbours, and convincing them of the unreality of their knowledge and worth. Both Socrates and Johnson had a faculty for laying hold of an inflated idea and squeezing it very small. They were both preachers who were contented to preach to mankind simply, without the aid of vestments or solemnities. The market-place or the club-room, the porch or the tavern, made good enough preaching-houses for them— the only pulpit Johnson wanted or would accept was his tavern chair. He was once offered a living in the Church, but he preferred preaching what Gospel he had in his own way. Ultimately he preferred the way of talking to that of writing. After many years spent in the use of the latter method, he at length gave up written sermons, and betook himself to the extemporary method. He prepared beforehand, and deliberately aimed at talking well. Writing had made him an 'exact' man, and then conference made him a 'ready' man. In retort or repartee he became as unfailing as powerful. Thus the foundation of Johnson's fame seems largely to lie in the impression created by his presence and conversation; and it so happens that while the books of other men preserve their memory, Johnson's memory has preserved his books.

It was, therefore, a good deed of George III. to pension this preacher in his old age—to grant him the royal bounty, and set him up just to talk in London for the remainder of his days, though it is true that in his Dictionary he had somewhat unfortunately defined a *pension* as 'payment given to a hireling for betraying his country.' Poor Johnson wrote that in 'Grub Street,' when he had no pension and saw less deserving men who had. In that great undertaking for the public advantage (his Dictionary), he received no help or sympathy from the great. My Lord Chesterfield was then politely allowing him to shift for himself—to struggle through 'seven lean years' with his heavy undertaking; if he succeeded, it would be time enough to notice him *then*. He *did* succeed, and then Chesterfield, like a true son of flunkeydom, bustled about and puffed Johnson's work in the *World*, in order that he (Chesterfield) might flourish as a Patron on the first page of the Dictionary. For once, it would not do. The poor man for once *did* afford to give the rich man a rebuff. He wrote a letter to Lord Chesterfield. People read it with relish even to this day, as one of the permanent things in literature. The literary man generally does his best when his personal feelings are thoroughly stirred. Though we may have read this celebrated letter, it will bear reading again. Here it is:

'February 7, 1775.

'My Lord,—

'I have been lately informed by the proprietor of the *World* that two papers in which my Dictionary is recommended to the public were written by your lordship. To be so distinguished is an honour, which, being very little accustomed to favours from the great, I know not well how to receive, or in what terms to acknowledge.

'When, upon some slight encouragement, I first visited your lordship, I was overpowered, like the rest of mankind, by the enchantment of your address, and could not forbear to wish that I might boast myself *le vainqueur du vainqueur de la terre*—that I might obtain that regard for which I saw the world contending; but I found my attendance so little encouraged, that neither pride nor modesty would suffer me to continue it. When I had once addressed your lordship in public, I had exhausted all the art of pleasing which a retired and uncourtly scholar can possess. I had done all that I could; and no man is well pleased to have his all neglected, be it ever so little.

'Seven years, my lord, have now passed since I waited in your outward rooms, or was repulsed from your door; during which time I have been pushing on my work through difficulties of which it is useless to complain, and have brought it at last to the verge of publication without one act of assistance, one word of encouragement, or one smile of favour. Such treatment I did not expect, for I never had a patron before.

'The shepherd in Virgil grew at last acquainted with love, and found him a native of the rocks.

'Is not a patron, my lord, one who looks with unconcern on a man struggling for life in the water, and when he has reached ground encumbers him with help? The notice which you have been pleased to take of my labours, had it been early, had been kind; but it has been delayed till I am indifferent and cannot enjoy it; till I am solitary and cannot impart it; till I am known and do not want it. I hope it is no very cynical asperity not to confess obligations where no benefit has been received, or to be unwilling that the public should consider me as owing that to a patron which Providence has enabled me to do for myself.

'Having carried on my work thus far with so little obligation to any favourer of learning, I shall not be disappointed though

I should conclude it, if less be possible, with less; for I have been long waked from that dream of hope, in which I once boasted myself with so much exultation,

'My lord,

'Your lordship's most humble, most obedient servant,

'SAM. JOHNSON.'

In this letter we have Johnson as a prose writer nearly at his best; uniting dignity with severity, reasonableness with indignation, independence with politeness, lofty satire with strong rebuke, self-possession with self-assertion, and modest self-estimate with touching complaint. Here are no unnecessary words, and none of them seem unnecessarily long. If in these respects he was faulty in other writings, he is not so here, where he is moved by strong personal feeling, and where the useless and insolent patronage of the grandee stings him to the quick. Johnson's letter to Chesterfield may be regarded as sounding the death-knell of patronage, and authors have since had something better than the pocket of one rich man to look to—better ways of getting paid for literary work than by what Burns called their 'fleechin', flatterin' Dedications.' They have now considerable access to the more extensive pocket of that august personage, the reading public—thanks to the labour and courage of Johnson and other pioneers, who, to bring in a glorious future, scorned the present and were content to 'rough it.'

No! we may rest assured that the pension which Johnson received was *not* a 'payment to a hireling to betray his country.' It was at worst only a sort of stipend or Regium Donum, on the strength of which Johnson was able to give up his pen and preach independently. It was, indeed, a very plain and practical Gospel that he preached, insisting mainly on two things—(1) 'That in a world where so little can be known and so much is to be done, the main thing is to do well whatever one can see to be his duty;' and (2) 'In any case, and at all risks, clear your mind of cant.' It would, indeed, be interesting to form a brief table of Johnson's opinions on all subjects, as one finds them reported by Boswell from his conversations. Though one might not always be able to agree with Johnson, we should certainly find instruction in each judgment—the thought being always at once honest and energetic. We could not, for example, help being struck with the peculiar type of High-Toryism he preaches, and his strong attitude *against* America in its struggle with the mother country. He seems almost to have believed in the Divine nature of the Stuarts as a sort of British Brahmins, who could not by any crimes be denuded of their godship. With what we call popular government he did not agree any more than with another kind of liberalism called free-thinking. 'Scoundrels,' who wished freedom in their wicked acts, turned upon the King because they hated his righteous restraints; and 'scoundrels,' carrying their authority farther, wrote books of infidelity. Or else these men were restless, tired of the old because it was old; and because so much had been said on the orthodox side, something was said on the other to rouse attention and—doubtless—to get one's book sold! This we admit to be a somewhat narrow way of looking at the rise and progress of modern scepticism and the struggle with doubt in inquiring minds. Still valuing it at its proper worth, and not undervaluing or despising it, Johnson's account of the matter will be seen to contain some common-place truth—not the less true because it is common-place. There are many common-place truths that show great signs of permanence, and are likely to be influential when some of our highly prized originality is quite dead and forgotten. Johnson could open his eyes and look steadily at plain prominent facts, and fairly apprehend their meaning. Not every man—not every genius—can do that. Some are able with great ingenuity to apprehend far-off, obscure, and difficult things; but do not discern the significance of those obvious patent facts by which men live. Not so Johnson. He firmly believed in the 'powers that be.' He recognised the meaning and potency of constituted authority. He admitted even its right to persecute. In what other way can truth be better discovered than by burning those who hold it ? If a man is willing to die for his opinions, there is likely to be something in them both valuable and true.

Johnson was not one of your 'rose-water' reformers who have framed a philosophy far too 'nice' for this rough and naughty world. He would defend flogging in schools, for example, by such reasoning as follows : If a boy has not learnt his lesson, being idle, he is flogged, and there is an end of it : but to excite the evil passions of envy, jealousy, emulation by 'prizes' would result in permanent evil to the boy's character which would be felt in maturer years. He had a satirical (sometimes slightly offensive) way of dealing with certain theories that could not be conveniently discussed. On the question of woman's rights he would vehemently affirm that 'a wife was *not* the worse for being learned,' but would add, 'a woman preaching is like a dog walking on his hind legs. It is not done well, but you are surprised to find it done at all.' Possibly I should have given this as an illustration of the 'prejudices' for which Johnson was so famous; but a clearer and no less amusing illustration will be found in his opinion of the Scotch.

His anti-Scotch prejudice was so notorious, that poor Boswell, when first introduced to him, blurted out in a kind of terror : 'Sir, I come from Scotland, but I cannot help it.' Johnson's quick reply was pointed and pitiless : ' Sir, that is what a great many Scotchmen cannot help.' When at another time a Scotchman attempted to recommend his country to Johnson, and spoke of its scenery—the many noble 'prospects' (fine views) which one could have in it—Johnson replied, 'Sir, the noblest *prospect* which a Scotchman ever sees is the high road to England.' The national prejudice was sometimes expressed with an extravagance in which there was a good deal of concealed humour, not quite pleasant to an opponent. On one occasion, when the faults of the North Britons formed his theme, and Johnson descanted with great force on their greed and meanness and pride, and knavery, their peculiar mixture of bigotry and cant, shrewdness and superstition, Boswell, by way of protest, as strong as he dared, put in, 'Well, sir, God made the Scotch.' 'Yes, sir,' said Johnson, 'and He made worse beings in a worse place.'

To the amazement and amusement of all beholders, Johnson gave effect to a strong combination of the High-Tory and anti-Scotch prejudices, when he made his memorable invasion of Scotland, and met in mighty conflict the old Laird of Auchinleck, the father of Boswell. It must have been a lively scene. In high anger and extreme disgust, Johnson heard this old laird express his admiration of Cromwell—the admiration of a Whiggish Scotch Presbyterian for the very leader of regicides. 'Sir,' said Johnson, in his loudest, sternest manner, 'sir! what did Cromwell do for the country?' 'What did he dae for the country?' repeated Auchinleck, with equal pungency in a different style—'he gart the Kings ken they had a lith in their neck.'

A word or two on Johnson's relations with women, and a few on his religion and benevolence, will bring this brief sketch to a close.

A man so awkward, so ungainly, and in some respects so forbidding and rude, will naturally be supposed to have been no favourite with women. On examination, however, we find the fact to be different. We are told, indeed, by Leslie Stephen, that the old moralist had always in hand a flirtation or two—ever, of course, within proper limits. Mrs. Porter, the widow lady who became his wife, remarked, after the first interview, 'That is the most sensible man I have ever met;' and there is no doubt that other ladies saw in him what justified this comment. Johnson, in fact, while expressing a philosopher's scorn for a 'set of wretched unidea'd girls,' enjoyed above most men the company of intelligent women: and there is every reason to believe the enjoyment was mutual. For women are ever more ready than men to overlook faults in appearance and manner where they once recognise a real living centre from which warmth and good sense radiate: and one may even find in such cases that the worship of women is rather intensified than otherwise by the ugliness of their idol. The secret of this seems to be their discovery in said idol of a *kind* of sympathy which they rarely get from men. This, it seems, Johnson could bestow abundantly, and it was found that Mrs. Porter had not wrongly estimated him. Garrick could in any company raise an uproar of laughter by mimicking the endearments of two strange lovers (Johnson and his wife, with whom he had once been a boarder); but it is certain that Mrs. Johnson understood and appreciated her husband when few of his fellow-men did so : naturally, therefore, and rightly, he valued her opinion of his writing more than that of any other. When she died he was *alone*, in a sense which only hearts like his can understand: he sought relief from agony in hard work : and there is pathos in the fact that to this cause much of the astonishing labour which he spent on his Dictionary may be attributed.

There is some further proof that Johnson's nature was not entirely filled with dry logic and definitions of moral philosophy. Mrs. Thrale was certainly a woman of intelligence, wit, and fashion ; and notwithstanding her marriage with Piozzi in the end, she must be set down as one who was attached to Johnson with no ordinary affection. Their friendship, we find, was one of sixteen years' standing. He had a separate room in Streatham for his own use; and when at last she went off to Italy with the musician, Johnson's ebullition of feeling was, we must think, rather more than a fatherly one.

As to Johnson's religion, a good many curious points might be noted, his life being in some respects so like that of a thorough man of the world, and in other respects so 'serious,' so full of awe and reverence. John Wesley and he were fellow-students at Oxford ; and though the lives of the two men seem so different, I have no doubt that Johnson was at times as deeply ' serious ' as even Wesley himself. We find that he had in early life read the well-known religious book, Law's ' Serious Call,' and at that time experienced something like the Wesleyan conversion; and though he made little profession, and lived so much like his companions, he seems to have held to this first impression with more or less tenacity through life. Wesley took to 'evangelizing the masses,' and Johnson to literary work—both with the same purpose of serving God; and certainly it were hard to say which did the world most good, or which most evil; for, alas! every man's influence is twofold! In each of these two the religious element had a different nature to work in. The literary nature was not Wesley's—it was Johnson's. Why, then, should religion be expected to manifest itself in exactly the same way in both? Certainly Johnson has done that for religion by his connection with literature which Wesley could never have done by his preaching. He has given religion a position in minds that Wesley could never have reached. Yet, are there not in this curious religious age unapproachably good people who will sigh over the sad fact that Johnson was writing 'Rasselas' or the 'Lives of the Poets' when he should have been preaching the Gospel to the denizens of Whitechapel?

To the ordinary religious convictions of a Christian country Johnson seems to have adhered with remarkable steadiness through life. He was never ashamed of them in the presence of brilliant wits. Rather, he made the wits ashamed when they attacked these *loci communes* of the Christian religion. His last request on his death-bed to Sir Joshua Reynolds was to read the Bible, and not to paint on Sundays. To a man of fashion who visited him then he said: 'I fear I shall be one of those who will be damned;' and when this polite person returned a shocked inquiring look, Johnson replied he meant he feared he would 'go to everlasting punishment.' A manful, straightforward soul with the courage of his convictions, it must be admitted that his religion was of the gloomy sort. It gave him little joy. He saw the light from heaven, but it did not cheer—it only guided him. The world will not soon forget the spectacle at Lichfield of Johnson, when old, standing at what was once his father's bookstall for an hour in the rain with his hat off, doing penance for an act of youthful disobedience!

That honest speech on his death-bed about 'everlasting punishment' is not less touching. Yet he must not be mistaken for one of those who deal with the Bible in that literal, unimaginative, realistic way that makes religion so repulsive to the truly thoughtful mind. To a young lady who had changed her religion and become a Quaker, and who fancied she understood her Bible as easily as she comprehended the items of her grocer's account-book, Johnson put the question *under what guidance* she had been led to take a step so serious. 'Oh, I had the New Testament,' she 'said. 'Madam, the most difficult book in the world,' said Johnson. A sentence of Goldsmith's, in the dedication of 'She Stoops to Conquer' to Johnson, neatly sums up the matter: 'It may serve the interests of society to inform them that the greatest wit may be found in a character without impairing the most unaffected piety.'

It would, however, be a grave error to conclude the shortest paper on Johnson without a special reference to the kindness of his heart. It is said that out of his pension of £300 he spent £230 in alms, leaving only £70 for his own support. The most touching thing in his history, or perhaps in any man's history, is the account we have of that strange collection of helpless beings whom he kept in his house in Fleet Street, nursing and bullying, scolding and feeding them by turns. This stern old dogmatist, who at times spoke with some harshness, was the kindest heart in England. He alone of all the great men I have read of dared literally to fulfil Christ's precept: 'When thou makest a feast, bid the poor, the maimed, the lame, the blind: and thou shalt be blessed; because they have not wherewith to recompense thee: for thou shalt be recompensed in the resurrection of the just.' Yes, Johnson has been known to take up on his huge shoulders the helpless one whom he found at the corner of the street at night, and bring him home thus. These wretched ones who came to live on his bounty were not always grateful; but then this great-souled Johnson did not work for gratitude. Their murmurs and contentions sometimes forced him to flee from his own home, or even to beat them; but when they died he felt as a man—felt his life sadder and more lonely. One never forgets his treatment of the old dependent Chambers in her last moments—how he prayed at her bedside—spoke that kindly farewell in which all human distinctions were utterly ignored—even gave a parting kiss in token of all that, as friend to dying friend! In his position as a great English man of letters he was the equal of a duke—and indeed he fully held the maxim, that 'the scholar's life, like the Christian's, levels all distinctions.' But that he acknowledged practically as he did his kinship and brotherhood in these poor suffering, even disgusting, fellow creatures was better than nobility, and more than his title to the [chair of literature, though that was the proudest seat in England.

GOLDSMITH.

GOLDSMITH'S popularity, which is perhaps as great to-day as ever it was, depends on the charming English of his genial prose, on some pictures in verse that live in the memory by a kind of native right, and doubtless not a little on some rich blunders with which his name is associated. We think of him getting quartered in a gentleman's house and mistaking it for an inn—or giving away his watch to a sharper who wanted it just for an hour or two to pawn for present need—or thoughtlessly bestowing his bedclothes on some needy person and having to take shelter among the feathers. We have heard a certain country spoken of as 'a very good country to live out of,' and we suspect that Goldsmith in his day was very often regarded as a very pleasant man 'not to know.' We read of Miss Reynolds (daughter of Sir Joshua) proposing in company this toast, 'The ugliest man in the world!' warmly responded to by other 'nice' ladies there—it is to be hoped in Goldsmith's absence. We are told that this genius had a pock-marked face, that his presence wanted dignity, that he lacked the air of good society, that in conversation he made very silly remarks, and that in company he was often quite ignored. Yet Goldsmith was a popular character in his day, even as he is a popular author now. It is Boswell, I believe, who tells the story of some one wondering in the presence of Dr. Johnson that people generally liked Goldsmith, since he conversed so badly and made so poor a figure in society. 'Why, sir,' said Johnson, 'every man is flattered at being able to beat in conversation the finest writer of the age.' Such is human pride, that often we cannot love except where we in some respects despise. Perhaps some absurdity and folly is necessary to go along with genius in order that the world may like it. When rolled in the sweet ingredients made from these depreciating stories it can be swallowed pleasantly; though, otherwise, it would be a bitter pill indeed.

We may be farther advanced in the present age, yet I do not think we would now treat a Goldsmith any better did he appear among us. We have learned an important science—the using of what is usable and keeping clear of what is not—even more perfectly than our ancestors. We would therefore admire our Goldsmith—and snub him; we would flatter him, and then go away and talk of his weaknesses; we would lionize him at our *soirées* and fail to recognise him on the street. While his graceful verses lent an additional charm to the pretty mouth that uttered them, the owner of that mouth would persist in refusing to know in what back lane or in what garret the poet lay concealed, and would think herself fully entitled to enjoy the grace and flavour of the beautiful things he had composed by purchasing a copy of the book. One thinks one should have the name of possessing literary appreciation, and the advantage of being classed with the cultured, as cheap as possible. There are even some of the wealthy who might be asked, What does their ostentatious appreciation of literature amount to? At what price have they valued it? Not at so much as the discomfort of one awkward presence among their fashionables: not at so much as the suspicion of what they esteem a low acquaintance: not at so much as the hazard of one sanctimonious recognition: not at so much as the extinction of a single rivulet that feeds the mighty muddy mercenary stream of their river of life! Well has Ruskin arraigned this generation, and with a prophet's eloquence brought home the charge: 'Ye have despised literature!'

I know of none of the poets whose personal history can be separated from his writings without lessening their significance and value. This remark applies to Goldsmith. All that now lives of what he wrote sprang in some sense out of his own personal experience; and much of it, as if reflected in the clearest stream in Longford, was the simple and perfect expression of what had been seen and felt by the gifted soul within him in its moods of joy and sorrow. The strange irregular, sometimes romantic, sometimes wretched life he led rouses our interest; and after examining his writings we have to admit that such a life must be lived in order that such products may be produced. One who succeeds in getting free from the tainted air of civilization so far as to climb the mountain or scour along the moor, may stop to admire the freshness of the wild-flower that crops up in his path; he may then shout:

> 'Away ye gay landscapes, ye gardens of roses,
> In you let the minions of luxury rove!'

and holding up the heathbell in triumph may cry, 'This is far better!' But the philosophic mind that grasps the whole truth in all its length, and breadth, and depth, and height will possibly find some element of sadness to mingle with such joy, in reflecting that it requires the *uncultivated* moor to produce the heathbell: it is the wild, unregulated, verdant, heathy, miry moor, not your patch of hoed and harrowed, trimmed and tended garden, which produces the floweret whose freshness and fragrance strike you as unique. There are also flowers produced by original genius which have a certain peculiar freshness that is very charming, but it may be necessary that the life from which they spring be barren in some other respects. There is nothing more likely to make a life barren than the want of an aim; and yet there may be circumstances in which the aimless mortal has his advantages. If you set before you the reading of the most beautiful piece of writing as a work to be accomplished, a duty to be done, you may find your interest growing dull, and even your mental powers seeming to grow feeble under the sobering pressure, the heavy weight of your *aim*. But sit down to read the same book without any such moral millstone round your neck, sit down to it simply as an amusement, or, to give still greater zest, sit down to it as a *forbidden* thing—it is wonderful how thoroughly awake your faculties are; how easy, how enjoyable, yea, effective is the entire spiritual man.

Goldsmith's life appears to me to have been so thoroughly aimless, that I am surprised it was not more barren of all kinds of products, commonplace and original. Should any one have asked him : 'Goldsmith, what are you living for?' I cannot imagine what the answer would have been. Had he religion as an all-absorbing object or purpose in life? I can find no trace of anything like this. Did he live for family duties—devoted to wife and children? No; he spent his five-and-forty years utterly unconscious of all such responsibilities. Were his aims social or political?—was he one 'who to party gave up what was meant for mankind'? He left that for his friend Burke, whom he satirised so severely, but kept himself free from all trammels of sect or party. Life was never a very grave matter to Oliver; like a truant schoolboy, he pursued the journey chiefly on account of the enjoyments of the way—the wild berries in the hedge—the wild music of the songsters of the grove: he enjoyed these things when they came, and fasted over long dreary stretches which were void of such delights. With keen joys and acute sorrows the journey was filled, and the end came, of course, unexpectedly. His life may be summed up thus: he enjoyed such things as fell in his way—he enjoyed *writing* as one of these things.

Should any political economist or worshipper of the hearth goddess Utility search for the uses of Goldsmith's life, he might be disappointed. Should he ask, What has Goldsmith accomplished as an historian, as a scientist, as a scholar? the reply would not be easy. His histories, though famous as schoolbooks, were mere second-hand compilations, sometimes heedless misrepresentations of what was best in human kind, and became dangerous channels along which unjust and furious bigotry has flowed down through the ages. As for his scientific works, Johnson archly said Goldsmith was writing natural history, which he would make 'as interesting as a Persian tale.' This speech of the literary Dictator, though it has been taken literally, had doubtless a mystical meaning. He seems afterwards to have indicated its meaning in plain prose thus: 'If he can tell a horse from a cow, that is the extent of his knowledge of zoology.' Goldsmith was not a man of great scientific attainments. Macaulay, indeed, affirms in his striking way: 'He knew nothing accurately.' And though we know how Macaulay loved little sentences like this, unencumbered with details, sent off with admirable force like an arrow from the string, and may believe he would accept some abatement of the absolute meaning, yet it is certain that Goldsmith at no time of his life could set up for a ripe or accurate scholar. There appears to be still some mystery about his medical degree, said to have been obtained at Padua, and on account of which men styled him 'Doctor' Goldsmith. He afterwards went to an examination for surgeon's mate and was 'plucked.' He went to other examinations with a similar result. He had not in youth or afterwards the faculty of active enduring effort by which college honours are won. In that respect he was rather soft. Patient memorising in making up dry details was not his forte. Also, with what Bacon calls 'dry light' he was poorly furnished. Mathematics was very distasteful to him. He would even treat with contempt that queen-empress of sober, useful subjects. To his genial soul it was stale, flat, and unprofitable—'a subject,' he said, 'suited for the meanest capacity.' And though he appreciated the classics much more highly, and could, he affirmed, 'turn an ode of Horace with any of them,' yet he was far from being in this respect the scholar that Johnson was.

Indeed, for the greater part of his life, Goldsmith appeared to himself and others to be a perfectly unsuccessful and useless human being. He seemed weaker than ordinary men, or as one who has some natural defect. Both at school and college he was registered a dunce. He was, in fact, the ugly duckling who could not be got to square with the dimensions of any ordinary duck. Looking back on his youth and a portion of his manhood, he could see all his efforts made beside those who were succeeding to be failures. Even as the poor usher of a school he could not hold his own. He was not able to hold his position as one of a band of strolling players. He would not do as an apothecary's assistant. He could not live on the halfpence he collected by means of his flute. What on earth was he good for?

As there are monomaniacs—men who are perfectly sane in all other ways, but perfectly mad in one—so there are men who are fools in many respects, but exceedingly wise in one—who are utterly weak in many respects, but very strong in one. After all, though the world was long in recognising it—though Goldsmith himself was long in recognising it—he had a gift; and most of his mistakes arose from his inability sooner to recognise and believe in that gift. His was the artist nature, unsuitable for many ordinary purposes to which ordinary human nature is applied, but perfectly suitable to its own purpose, once that is discovered. And it is the creature who is dowered with this extraordinary artistic gift who so often 'plays such fantastic tricks before high heaven as make the angels weep.' For at first for a long time he is unconscious of the strange endowmnet. He is perplexed and harassed, on trying to force his nature into the ordinary moulds, to find that it will not suit. He is, therefore, apt to exhibit a certain *étourderie*—wandering about to and fro—wasting time—conscious of some half-defined object—seeking rest and finding none—till at length he lights upon the instrument of music, and touches it so as to thrill his own inner deeps, and then to thrill the listening world from east to west.

Even when Goldsmith was making his bread by his pen, he was still far from recognising literature as his end in life. It was only a make-shift. He was dreaming about 'written mountains' in the East—rocks inscribed with Arabic—which he thought the Government might send him out to decipher, if it did not give him some other commission, such as an inquiry into the state of the useful arts in various countries. A more feasible idea was to get out to India to practise as a surgeon on Government pay. All this was treason against his higher nature—unfortunate or culpable forgetfulness of

> '—that one talent which 'twere death to hide,
> Lodged with him useless.'

It was well for the world that he never prospered in any of his manifold worldly schemes—well, if the poet be truly a 'star' of greater or smaller magnitude, 'if he indeed derive his light from heaven,' and if that light be his most precious possession. But Goldsmith himself was long in getting to believe such doctrine. He tells us he could at times, in the interest of literary conversation, be led to forget the meanness of his circumstances; but he was long of seeing, if he ever fully saw, that literature is its own great reward. Now we all can see that his chief work on earth was not that for which he received most wages from publishers, but consists simply of the pure literature he has left us. There is a vast heap of writing from his hand, but a much smaller amount of pure literature, the direct and simple product of his artistic gift—the kind of work which he did when, in his own words, he 'struck for honest fame.' He wrote the 'Traveller,' and almost instantly rose from an obscure bookseller's drudge to the position of a legitimate classic. He drew the Man in Black, Beau Tibbs, the village Schoolmaster, above all, the Vicar, and at once a new magician of the literary kind was acknowledged by an admiring world. The excellence of the work was beheld even by the artists with admiration and despair; and when he died the ablest living judge of literature inscribed this sentence on his tomb: 'There was hardly any species of writing which he did not touch, and he touched nothing that he did not adorn.' With him, as with others, the foundation and formative principle of his artist work was a simple human feeling, strong and genuine. Take an example. All the time he lived in London he never got wholly free from an affectionate longing for the little Irish village in which he was born. From time to time we meet in his letters humorous and other references to this chronic home-sickness, or *maladie du pays*. He confesses it 'is unaccountable *he* should still have an affection for a place, who never when in it received above a common civility, who never brought anything out of it except his brogue and his blunders.' Then, we imagine, with a grotesque smile intended to disguise his pain, he compares his affection to that of the Scotchman, 'who refused to be cured of his rheumatism, because it made him unco thoughtfu' of his wife and bonny Inverary.' Many a man has had *maladie du pays* as strong as Goldsmith, but in the artist nature such human feeling may produce peculiar results—such celebrated music as this :

> 'Where'er I roam, whatever realms to see,
> My heart untravell'd fondly turns to thee,
> Still to my brother turns with ceaseless pain,
> And drags at each remove a lengthening chain.'

Or, on another occasion, a burst even better known :

> 'I still had hopes, for pride attends us still,
> Amidst the swains to show my book-learn'd skill:
> Around my fire an evening group to draw,
> And tell of all I felt, and all I saw ;
> And as a hare whom hounds and horns pursue
> Pants to the place from whence at first she flew,
> I still had hopes, my long vexations past,
> Here to return, and die at home at last.'

The 'Deserted Village,' from which the last extract is taken, Goldsmith's finest work, is the expansion of a sentiment with which we have since become wonderfully familiar. It is the grief of an 'Irish emigrant' or exile, expressed in one long melodious wail. In it we see the bitterness of soul produced by the hopeless severance of old ties—we see despair of the old country yet unmodified by blissful visions of the new. From the distress of his country, vividly realized in his own experience, Goldsmith turns to look with indignation on the cause of such misery. He arraigns capital, and commerce as the producer of capital. It is capital that enables one man to buy up whole scores of farms, and make 'deserted villages' of such pleasant little hamlets as Goldsmith's loved

Lissoy. He and the old Hebrew prophets are cordially agreed on one subject at least, for the poem to which we refer might almost be called a sermon on the text (Is. v. 8): 'Woe unto them that join house to house, that lay field to field, till there be no place, that they may be placed alone in the midst of the earth.' Hence, when cargoes of bullion are brought to our wharfs the land should lament. It is only 'fools' (says Goldsmith) who shout their welcomes to such ships. In brief, Goldsmith preached up peasant proprietorship and denounced large estates as zealously as any of his countrymen since. He believed that more people should live in the country and fewer in towns, and that men, in departing from a rural life, were departing from a Divine institution, and adopting unnatural modes of living, resulting in disease and misery.

These are great questions—not to be settled, I fear, by any amount of fine verses. It may, indeed, be noted as a fact of some significance, that at the very moment when Goldsmith was wooing his unworldly muse in the manner I have indicated, ADAM SMITH was laboriously piling up the huge volume intituled 'The Wealth of Nations,' whose doctrine is just the opposite of Goldsmith's. By the strenuous preaching of SMITH, and later divines of the Church of Mammon, a sufficient antidote has been provided for the heretical opinions of the poet, whose doctrine has thus become depreciated to such an extent that, but for the music of his verses and the truthfulness of his pictures, he would not be read at all. Macaulay, with a true nineteenth-century reverence for utility, instances Lucretius and Goldsmith as two eminent examples of good poetry founded on bad doctrine. But Goldsmith's doctrine was wonderfully different from that of Lucretius! While Lucretius taught materialism in its worst form, Goldsmith's chief objection to wealth was its materializing tendency. To some it may seem but idle speculation to inquire whether our spiritual condition as a nation would be higher if we were poor. It is a curious fact, however, that in some old Jewish writings there are statements which confirm Goldsmith's view. These statements tend towards the opinion that those who are rich materially are often spiritually poor—that they can seldom attain the inward righteousness, peace, and joy in which God's kingdom consists —that having 'received their consolation,' they have nothing to look for in the future but the 'miseries that shall come upon them'—that, in short, 'they that will be rich fall into temptation and a snare, and into many foolish and hurtful lusts, which drown men in destruction and perdition.' But when we read such statements, or hear them read in a drowsy humdrum way, it never occurs to us to fancy that an increase of our yearly income up to two or three thousand pounds, or so, would be any harm. Such language, if we ever trouble to reflect on it, we conclude must have some far deeper 'spiritual' meaning than a bare reference to the state of our pockets. Would it not be *beneath the dignity* of such a Book to make any reference to a man's income? Surely there is some high allegorical —or, at least, some fine Oriental significance in these apparently plain and disagreeable words, could we but find a cautious and cunning divine to expound them!

Meantime, till such expositor can be had, it may be interesting by way of contrast to note how emphatically a later (a living) poet has contradicted Goldsmith's theory about the evil effects of wealth. A 'Farmer' who, it seems, has never heard of 'Sweet Auburn' or the disastrous effects which result

'When wealth accumulates and men decay,'

shows us there is another side of the question discussed in Goldsmith's lays:

'Breäk me a bit o' the esh for his 'ead, lad, out o' the fence!—
Gentleman burn! what's gentleman burn? is it shillin's an' pence?
Proputty, proputty's everything 'ere, an', Sammy, I'm blest
If it isn't the saäm oop yonder, for them as 'as it's the best.
'Tisn't them as 'as munny as breaks into 'ouses an' steäls,
Them as 'as coäts to their backs and taäkes their regular meäls;
Noä! but it's them as niver knaws where a meäls to be 'ad—
Taäke my word for it, Sammy, the poor in a loomp is bad!'

This view of the matter is indeed different not only from

Goldsmith's, but from the more ancient doctrine which says, 'Blessed are ye poor!' The blessing of poverty, like the blessing of affliction, is not, however, greatly sought after in our time.

Whatever we may think of Goldsmith's doctrine, let us keep in mind the fact that the essence of his poetry is not doctrine, but feeling presented in artistic form. We should guard against the mistake of confounding his melodious lines, instinct with life, with a certain poor wooden manufacture named 'didactic poetry.' There is indeed an amount of philosophy in Goldsmith's poetry. Macaulay pays the following high compliment to the 'Traveller': 'No philosophic poem ancient or modern has a plan so noble and at the same time so simple. An English wanderer seated on a crag among the Alps, near the point where three great countries meet, looks down on the boundless prospect, reviews his long pilgrimage, recalls the varieties of scenery, of climate, of government, of religion, of national character which he has observed, and comes to the conclusion, just or unjust, that our happiness depends little on political institutions, and much on the temper and regulation of our own minds.' This is all very well; we do not object to a fine poem having a noble philosophical plan; and we believe that the finest poetry always contains a subtle admixture of philosophy. Nevertheless, those parts of Goldsmith which are most truly poetical are not in the ordinary sense either philosophical or didactic. It is when he forgets his text and gives us pictures, when he comes before us in the power of his pictorial and dramatic faculty, not when he philosophizes or preaches, that he is most truly poetical. Nor is it on account of his doctrines, communistic or otherwise, nor on account of his philosophy, that he now lives in the hearts and on the lips of men; but on account of pictures like *this*:

> 'Beside yon straggling fence that skirts the way,
> With blossom'd furze unprofitably gay,
> There, in his noisy mansion, skill'd to rule,
> The village master taught his little school:
> A man severe he was and stern to view;
> I knew him well, and every truant knew;

> Well had the boding tremblers learn'd to trace
> The day's disasters in his morning face;
> Full well they laughed with counterfeited glee
> At all his jokes, for many a joke had he;
> Full well the busy whisper, circling round,
> Conveyed the dismal tidings when he frown'd!
> Yet he was kind, or if severe in aught,
> The love he bore to learning was in fault.
> The village all declared how much he knew;
> 'Twas certain he could write and cipher too!
> Land could he measure, terms and tides presage,
> And even the story ran that he could gauge!
> In arguing, too, the parson own'd his skill!
> For even though vanquish'd, he could argue still.
> While words of learnèd length and thundering sound
> Amazed the gazing rustics ranged around;
> And still they gazed, and still the wonder grew,
> That one small head could carry all he knew!'

Examining a piece of workmanship like this, one may feel prompted to ask—How came it to be executed by a man of careless habits, a man so unsystematic, so impulsive, so deficient in the faculty of order as Goldsmith?—a man, too, on whom the ordinary incentives to ambition were utterly powerless, and one who in the ordinary affairs of life often seemed to lack discretion. It may seem difficult to understand how extreme accuracy and perfect delicacy can be combined in the same person with rawness, blundering, and improvidence. Yet certainly in human nature such mysteries exist. The careless habits, the unseemly indolence too generally visible in the conduct of life, are not perceptible in the composition. As the almost 'dying wick' which smokes offensively in the common air, in every sense a despicable and even disgusting thing, will, if introduced into a volume of ozone, suddenly break forth into the clearest, most brilliant, most beautiful light—so is this dull and stupid and worthless-looking Goldsmith transformed into something angelic, 'a burning and a shining light,' when he leaves the common atmosphere of every-day life, and breathes the purer ether of the 'Aonian mount.'

> 'He wrote like an angel, and talked like poor Poll.'

We are compelled to admit that Goldsmith did not always shine in conversation. Notwithstanding all that Washington Irving and Forster have done to rebut the charge contained in Garrick's epigram, we must accept it as a truth, though not a whole truth. In the conversations which have been preserved of the famous 'Club,' an unprejudiced reader will admit that Goldsmith sometimes sustains his part well, when he is matched with Reynolds, or Burke, or even Johnson himself. But in company Goldsmith was apt to be seized with an eager restlessness arising from consciousness of his great name as a writer, and desire to make his conversation equal to that. Under excitement of this sort he acted as if talking were to be performed by the mere action of the muscles of the head, while disregarding the fact that one must have something to say. But this accounts for Goldsmith's oft-noted deficiency only in part. That extreme delicacy of nervous organization which is invaluable to the literary artist, pen in hand, becomes a strange encumbrance to him when he attempts sustained discourse before a listening and doubtless critical company. The artist's nervous delicacy will often be such that the pressure of the presence of an audience will reduce him uniformly to silence, as it did to Addison and Cowper; or it will make him appear stupidly silent at one time and foolishly flippant at another, as it did to Goldsmith. The practice of *fine* composition is not always of use for public speaking; for the mode of marshalling the words is so utterly different in the artist's product, that in attempting extempore discourse he will at times feel something like the embarrassment and difficulty of one who uses among foreigners a foreign tongue which he has learned imperfectly. Also that keen and utter accuracy, unknown to ordinary speech-makers, but engrained in the artistic nature, becomes, like a knife too sharp for its work, an impediment in this comparatively coarse extemporary composition, and an additional cause of the nervousness and stammering which the poor 'man of feeling' exhibits in company. May I not mention here, with all reverence, as a further illustration of this, the case of one who had all the finer feelings and nobler gifts of an artist along with higher endowments, 'whose letters were weighty and powerful, but his bodily presence was weak and his speech contemptible.'

Some foolish person (Boswell, I think) has accused Goldsmith of imitating Johnson; but the truth is, Johnson as a writer is no more to be compared to Goldsmith than Goldsmith as a talker is to be compared to Johnson. With all his excellences, Johnson wrote in a style which was hard and stilted compared with Goldsmith's. In the prose of Goldsmith we have the genuine literary thing, in that of Johnson the genial element is greatly in abeyance. In Johnson the sense is good, and presented with the precision of a regiment drilled by the 'immortal Gustavus'; but Goldsmith is wine, and Johnson a soberer beverage; in him there is wanting that deeply interesting glow, that indescribable pleasure, which we recognise in the undiluted ruddy moving creature of genius. A triumphant geometrical demonstration is one thing—the natural outburst of an impassioned song another. We are instructed by Johnson; we admire his good sense; we receive with reverence and conviction his weighty decisions: but Goldsmith we take away with us into a quiet corner to have a pleasant talk over old times; we enjoy him, we luxuriate in him, we love him. Thackeray indeed pronounces Goldsmith the 'most beloved' of all our English authors. The characteristic of his style, says one critic, is 'perfect ease'—unfortunately, poor 'Goldy' was never perfectly at ease in anything else. His style is not, indeed, one of the most powerful, and therefore he ran a risk of being lost amid a crowd of second-class writers. But he was saved by the exquisite warmth of his colouring and his inimitable grace.

One of the noblest things about Johnson is that, though much tempted by the flattery of his adorers to do so, he never depreciated Goldsmith, but always backed him; was never jealous of his merit, but always fully and warmly acknowledged it. We read how, when Goldsmith was about to make a remark to his neighbour in the 'club,' this Scotch worshipper of Johnson interrupted him with, 'Stay! Dr. Johnson is going to say something!' But Johnson was very far from encouraging the opinions of such moon-struck visitants. It is pleasant to recall the relations of these two eminent men. One likes to remember their first meeting. Johnson came to Goldsmith for dinner, dressed with the utmost care, looking unusually neat and genteel. On some one remarking this, Johnson said: 'Why, sir, I hear that Goldsmith is a sloven, and is in the habit of quoting me for an excuse of his carelessness; and I must try to put it out of his power to do so.' It should be remembered to Johnson's lasting honour how he behaved like a big brother to Goldsmith all through—never allowing anyone to brow-beat him except himself. It should be particularly remembered how he sent him that famous guinea when the exasperated landlady had shut him up in his rooms as her prisoner; how Johnson afterwards came rolling into the rooms and found Goldsmith had already made a hole in the guinea by the bottle of wine which stood before him; how the great old literary sage then solemnly put the cork in the bottle and grandly invited the thoughtless one to a serious consultation as to how money might be procured; how the MS. of 'The Vicar' was thereupon produced, and part of it read by the Dictator of Letters; how he went off with it to a bookseller, and came again to hand Goldsmith £60, the result of skilful negotiation, and the cause of Goldsmith's exuberant joy; how Goldsmith thereupon took on airs with his landlady, and proudly paid her bill, with no small exhibition of insulted dignity and injured worth! All this is for ever memorable. And in a world so much accused of selfishness, and specially of dealing hardly with men like Goldsmith, it is pleasant to remember how many stories of this kind can be told to Johnson's credit, notwithstanding the peculiar jealousy that is said to infect the literary tribe, and notwithstanding Johnson's own frequent avowal of selfish theories of life. Not the least generous of Johnson's acts was the speech he made shortly after Goldsmith's death: 'He had raised money, and squandered it by every artifice of acquisition and folly of expense; but let not his frailties be remembered—he was a very great man.'

It is not a little curious, when one reflects on it, that a man who suffered so much from the evils of poverty should write a fine poem on the disadvantages of wealth; but Goldsmith was himself an eminent example of what he has noted in the Irish peasantry—that they are always sprightly in a degree proportioned to their wants. And his own acts were often illustrations of the unselfish, sympathizing spirit which dwells among the poor more abundantly than among the rich. He could feel for another's woe—he could feel for his last guinea then as if he were lord of thousands. Therefore it is we feel his verse come over our spirit, not as ordinary music, but as ministering balm from heaven, bearing the assurance :

> 'Man wants but little here below,
> Nor wants that little long.'

Though he was so far from perfect, I question whether we could love a perfect man as well. His propensity to gambling was one of his greatest faults; but in this, as in other things, the extremes to which he went were partly owing to the temperament of genius. He should have the benefit of his own original verse:

> 'Extremes are only in the master's mind.'

Had he never been excited to play high, had he been incapable of that terrible 'abandon,' he would not have been Goldsmith the famous writer, nor the Goldsmith who sometimes—nay, often—enjoyed life so gloriously! A compound of 'Tony Lumpkins' and 'The Vicar,' of 'Beau Tibbs' and 'Lien Chi Altangi,' this mixture was needed to give to his best work that exquisite flavour which makes it unique in literature. No doubt his egotism often seemed very foolish, but it was of a simple and harmless nature. Nor should we forget that a certain sort of egotism forms the cocoon from which some of the most brilliant webs of poetry are woven. Egotism is offensive in the social circle, but not in music like that of Shelley's

'Skylark' or 'Ode to the West Wind.' It is easy for great people to ridicule his girlish vanity of dress and absurd strutting in showy colours; but you should first have gone with him into the depths of penury, and seen him herd with homeless creatures like 'poor Tom,' in order that you might judge how far the unwonted luxury of gay clothing should have turned his head. Nice, smart, well-bred people like Beauclerk could see much to criticise in Goldsmith; but they are not forward to remember that much of what is objectionable might be called the scars of that conflict which he fought in the low, dark valley, unaided and alone, surrounded with slimy reptiles, gibbering ghouls, and mocking fiends, before he reached the serene heights where the god of day gives his countenance and joy.

With respect to a large portion of his literary work, one may say it was little better than bungling with unsuitable tools. He had neither the education nor perhaps the kind of capacity which would have rendered historical and scientific works valuable. But what then? Worse work, and more injurious, is daily done by others in toiling for their bread. Yet we should observe that even while moiling in such drudgery Goldsmith is a man of genius still; for even in *that* work we may discern some qualities which only a man of genius could give it. Were it only the power of selection we see in it, this remark would be vindicated. If there be anything that decisively indicates the superior mind as distinguished from the commonplace, it is the power of selecting what is really valuable in the presentation of a subject. The common-place mind is invariably encumbered with a crowd of useless or valueless details, amid which gleams of golden ore may be discernible by the gifted; but the whole will be delivered by the common-place writer or speaker with the same feeling of importance for each portion, and the effect on the mind of the reader or auditor is simply the return of chaos and old night. In view of such catastrophe, with which, alas, both readers and hearers are still too familiar, Goldsmith's power of selection, as seen, for example, in his histories, may be as greatly desiderated as genius itself.

And now, lest I should illustrate the opposite quality in this little history of mine, I shall quickly draw it to a close. I do so, I own, with some regret, the theme being tempting and the material abundant. When one gets among these genial fellows of the Literary Club, one likes to stay, having a peculiar interest in watching Goldsmith among them, but wishing also to appreciate the others, and to measure him by them. One goes back again and again to witness fine passes of wit amongst them in scenes which will not be forgotten wherever human beings congregate to speak the English tongue, certainly not in associations where literature is discussed. And whenever men think of those scenes they will remember that a great part of their attraction consists in the presence of the kindly, humourful, impulsive genius whom I have been trying to describe. Some of his associates, though eminent men and deservedly famous, are best remembered by a couplet which Oliver with a power (which is the true magic verse spell) affixed to each. You cannot now hear anyone talk five minutes about BURKE without getting from him Goldsmith's keen couplet applied to this father of politics:

'Who, born for the universe, narrow'd his mind,
And to party gave up what was meant for mankind.'

And GARRICK is at least as much remembered by Goldsmith's epigram as Goldsmith is by *his*:

'On the stage he was natural, simple, affecting;
It only was when he was off he was acting.'

REYNOLDS, too, has received from Goldsmith payment in kind, being made for ever memorable in this delightful little portrait:

'When they talked of their Raphaels, Correggios, and stuff,
He shifted his trumpet and only—took snuff.'

As long as thinking reading men remember the great lights of England in the eighteenth century, they will remember, also, these masterly portraits by Goldsmith in his poem 'Retaliation.'

Goldsmith teaches us to admire nature, simplicity, truth, and freedom; he teaches us to hate the insincerity of artificial manners, the mean pride that rises on the degradation of our fellow men, and the luxury that has debased those who are insensible to the fearful wants and woes of creatures made in the image of God. But how strange it would be if Goldsmith has now become one of those very luxuries which produce the direful effects deprecated in his melodious verse and genial prose! How strange if he has now become but one fine essence among the other exquisite perfumes of high life! if men now delight in him only as they do in so-called *generous* wine of about the same age! if they can now please their palates with sparkling draughts from his unfailing source, without one care, one earnest thought, for a more equal distribution of the blessings of heaven, and without any dread of the downfall of a selfish people dominated by luxury! Surely the influence of our prophets, heaven-illumined, like Goldsmith, will not grow so impotent among us. Let us hear him with more earnestness! and that the 'Northern Farmer'—or Ulsterman—may not have things all his own way, take as a set-off to *his* doctrine, this closing extract from Goldsmith on the evils of wealth:

> 'E'en now, methinks, as pondering here I stand,
> I see the rural virtues leave the land ;
> Down where yon anchoring vessel spreads the sail,
> That idly waiting flaps with every gale,
> Downward they move, a melancholy band,
> Pass from the shore and darken all the strand.
> Contented toil, and hospitable care,
> And kind connubial tenderness are there,
> And piety with wishes placed above
> And steady loyalty and faithful love!
> And THOU sweet Poesy! thou loveliest maid,
> Still first to fly where sensual joys invade,
> Unfit in these degenerate times of shame
> To catch the heart, and strike for honest fame,
> Dear charming nymph, neglected and decried,
> My shame in crowds, my solitary pride,
> Thou source of all my bliss and all my woe,
> That found'st me poor at first and keep'st me so,
> Thou guide by which the nobler arts excel,
> Thou nurse of every virtue, fare thee well!'

SHELLEY.

THOUGH all the writers I have treated in this book belong to one class over which the name Genius ought to be written, yet we feel constrained to attempt putting Shelley in a class by himself. In his essay on Bunyan, Lord Macaulay writes: 'The words bard and inspiration, which seem so cold and affected when applied to other modern writers, have a perfect propriety when applied to Shelley. He was not an author, but a bard. His poetry seems not to have been an art, but an inspiration.' Young men of genius like Shelley, Keats, and Chatterton, who flash on the world like fiery meteors and vanish, deserve to be considered in a class by themselves. They are not treated as examples for other young men to imitate. Indeed, there is little danger of their being imitated in every respect, and sensible young men feel that it is a poor matter when the imitation extends only to open shirt-collars, naked throats, and long-flowing hair.

It is not always remembered, amid the thunders of ecclesiastical machinery which he has roused, that Shelley was a very young man. We hardly expect any person, however great his genius may be, to have completed an original and irrefragable system of theology and philosophy at twenty-nine. Shelley was no older when he died; and as in his speculations he chose to cast off all authority in every sense of the word, and begin *de novo* as barely as Descartes himself, attempting a complete revolution of orthodoxy in all its shapes and kinds, the process demanded considerable trouble and no short limit of time. As Shelley was cut off ere half his days, his system, by reason of immaturity, if from no other cause, is not likely to be perfect. There was a strong antecedent probability that on some weighty points it would be found erroneous. Nevertheless, it may deserve to be studied by those who are competent, were it only that we might see its weakness, and be confirmed in the contrary truth. And poetry of a high order may be studied with little reference to its religious or philosophical doctrine. We do not agree with the religious views of Homer, or with the philosophical opinions of Sophocles, yet gravest bishops and most pious assemblies of divines wisely recommend these pagan authors as a means of mental culture in the preparation of young men for the most sacred duties. And though some of Shelley's speculative and religious opinions be no less pagan than those of any poet in ancient or in modern times, it is none the less certain that he now holds an unquestioned position as an English classic.

And it is my decided opinion that, notwithstanding all his paganism, there are a good many respectable professing Christians who might learn something from Shelley. Those who cannot tolerate Shelley may be found tolerating authors less out-spoken but more dangerous. No one doubts the simplicity of Shelley's aims or his unworldly benevolent character. No one doubts that he had an 'enthusiasm of humanity,' a passionate desire to right the wrongs and destroy the plagues of the world. Never was any soul more elevated above the base expedients of hypocrisy, and the narrow policy of selfishness. He was ever ready to open his purse or use personal efforts when a case of misery became known to him; he went to visit the distressed poor in their homes; he kept a list of the more deserving; he gave them his time and his advice as well as his money. Let no one mistake Shelley for one of our vulgar, sensual, heartless infidels. He was perfectly sincere in his opinions, which he had not adopted as a cloak for his vices. His life, as a whole, was morally pure, and resembled that of a studious hermit. The earnestness with which he adopted his speculative opinions is strikingly demonstrated by one fact—he thought the law of primogeniture a source of unhappiness to his fellow men, and *therefore*, as a first-born child, he actually consented to lose his large estate rather than give to that law his practical sanction. The word atheist sounds badly; but when we carefully consider what Shelley's opinions near the end of his brief life actually were, we see cause greatly to modify the meaning of that term in reference to him; for we find it is not materialism, but a subtle sort of spiritualism to which he is warmly attached. No man ever lived more constantly conscious of the orthodox poet's announcement:

'There lives and breathes
A soul in all things,'

and though he would have objected to the term 'theist,' he recognised the divineness of nature, and spoke of its Divine Source with a warmth of admiration and eloquence not common among those who are more orthodox. Whatever creed he had was no doubt somewhat vague and indefinite, but it is not for a moment to be compared to the bare materialism of some of the French *philosophes*. It was the antithesis of that. In fact, were the *name* of atheist removed, Shelley in his opinions could claim some respectable company. It would have been difficult to get Thomas Carlyle to subscribe any strictly defined system of theism: Tennyson probably would refuse to do so: and the author of 'Ecce Homo' (a book breathing strongly the Christian spirit) would possibly claim as wide a margin as any of these. One must own it is strange to see men who earnestly and manfully address themselves to the understanding of high theistic doctrines denounced or summarily judged by others, whose only merit is that they accept these doctrines thoughtlessly and without examination.

Hot controversialists do not always remember that it is one thing to deny God, and another to deny popular conceptions of Him. Calling on two fairly intelligent neighbours one day, I found them discussing with warmth the question, Whether God be possessed of human limbs and human shape? Still more amazing is it to find John Milton in his Latin system of theology attributing to God both human form and human feelings. Even in this nineteenth century of clearer intelligence, correct ideas on the nature of the Deity are by no means so common as may be supposed. I met one day a semi-clerical individual who took considerable pains to prove to me that God often changes His mind. In truth, instead of worshipping the Supreme Being, men too often worship what is in great part a creation of their own fancies. The knowledge of God is a large subject, yet it is wonderful how soon some are ready to cry they have attained and are already perfect therein. When we hear of anyone denying God, we should ask *what* God he denies, for there are still in the world gods many and lords many. It should also be remembered that for denying the gods of the heathen the first Christians were called atheists.

It is only fair to say that Shelley's atheism seems to be in great part directed against the ignorant conceptions of Deity which were prevalent in his day and are prevalent still. It is a truism to say that the Bible is a book much misunderstood. Shelley himself, though a constant reader and ardent admirer of the Bible, often misunderstood its representations of God, and taking figures of speech or anthropomorphic language too literally, fancied the God of the Bible was an evil being. Like many another fiery youth, he was too severely logical, and too little capable of suspending his judgment. He could not see that the subject might have hidden depths which he had never touched. Like a young Arab steed, he rushed forward to what seemed the direct logical conclusion, and became, not an unbeliever only, for it was not in his nature to rest in a cold negation, but an impassioned propagandist of the 'truth' which he thought he had found.

It is impossible to speak of Shelley without referring to these matters; for he was, first of all, a prophet, a reformer, a propagandist of opinion, however mistaken. His writings are chiefly grand and beautiful expositions of his social and religious creed. We cannot ignore his creed without ignoring the substance of a large part of his writings. His creed was liberty in the widest sense. 'Liberty,' he said, 'comprehends all other blessings.' Therefore he would begin by sweeping away the present organizations of society, abolishing the authority of kings and the sanction of religion, churches, the legal profession, the institution of marriage—all. He held there were no evils in the world but those which the human will had power to expel. 'Let us will it, my brothers,' he said; 'let us resolve society into its original elements. Behold, in all departments of life frightful, disgusting abuses have appeared! Let us abolish these ancient, outworn social arrangements, and begin the world anew!' Shelley was a Radical indeed—no half measures with him!

When under eighteen he had written 'Queen Mab,' a blank-verse poem inciting to such revolution, but he never published it. It was afterwards given to the world by a knavish publisher, who had fallen on a copy printed for private circulation; and then Shelley wrote to the *Examiner* disavowing its teaching, being now convinced that the tendency of the poem was to produce results directly opposite to those which he desired when he wrote it. These are his words: 'I am a devoted enemy to religious and political oppression; and I regret this publication not so much from literary vanity as because I fear it is better fitted to injure than to serve the cause of freedom. . . . I exonerate myself from all share in having divulged opinions hostile to existing sanctions, under the form, whatever it might be, which they assume in the poem.' Shelley was not like some dogmatic gentlemen who can never be brought to confess that they have erred. He has denied the faith, but he may surpass in charity some who are reputed great believers. St. Paul has discoursed much on the importance of faith, but he pronounces charity greater than either faith or hope. Consoling truth! The heights of speculation by which we ascend to faith are difficult—the ascent is perilous to some of the purest and tenderest, most loving, and most sincere. And is Jesus Christ the relentless, eternal enemy of such, if they, engaging to tread those dialectic intricacies, become helplessly thought-bewildered and speculatively wrong? Let us not think so of the Friend of publicans and sinners, Who propounded no difficult creed, but said: 'Ye are My disciples if ye do whatsoever I command you.'

One of Shelley's great objections to Christianity was that it threatens men into believing: it pronounces an awful penalty on those who do not believe. Shelley thought this as unreasonable as it would be to punish a juryman for failing to believe, against all the evidence, the prisoner to be guilty. But a juryman *should* be blamed if his prejudices prevented him from *listening* to the evidence produced. And Scripture condemns our want of faith, not because we fail to come to a conclusion on insufficient evidence, but 'This is the condemnation, that light has come into the world, and men have loved the darkness rather than the light, because their deeds were evil.' The man who shuns the evidence for fear he should feel its force—surely he is to be blamed for want of faith. It is different with earnest, sincere, though bewildered seekers for truth, who grope after it, if haply they may find it. Shelley, with all his faults, we recognise as one of these. 'A person of much eminence for piety in our times,' says Leigh Hunt in his autobiography, 'has well observed that the greatest want of religious feeling is not to be found among the greatest infidels, but among those who never think of religion except as a matter of course.' This testimony is true. We do not undervalue right beliefs; but if they are not really rooted in the soul, but only, as it were, stuck on or held by mechanical combination, they are little worth—they may be even worse than useless. If there were fewer sham beliefs of this kind, there would be fewer Shelleys.

There is an unsettled, chaotic stage of spiritual development through which the thinking young man must pass before he arrives at settled views and clear opinions: it should be remembered that a large portion of Shelley's writings belong to that stage. It was against his heart to denude the earth and the universe of a Divine Presence; hence, amid all his denials, his frequent and wondrous personifications of inanimate nature; and we hear from his friend Leigh Hunt that 'there was in reality no belief to which Shelley clung with more fondness than that of some great pervading Spirit of Intellectual Beauty.' We cannot say that he could be in every sense devoid of religion who wrote the noble hymn to which Hunt here alludes :

> 'The awful shadow of some unseen Power
>   Floats, though unseen, among us, visiting
>   This various world with as inconstant wing
>   As summer winds that creep from flower to flower.'

Let us remember the sincere opinion, the true emotion which enters into Shelley's poetry as we read his address to this Power :

> Thy light alone, like mist o'er mountains driven,
>   Or music by the night-wind sent
>   Thro' strings of some still instrument,
>   Or moonlight on a midnight stream,
>   Gives grace and truth to life's unquiet dream.
> Love, hope, and self-esteem like clouds depart
>   And come, for some uncertain moments lent ;
>   Man were immortal and omnipotent.
> Didst thou, unknown and awful as thou art,
> Keep with thy glorious train firm state within his heart,
>
> 'I vow'd that I would dedicate my powers
>   To thee and thine : have I not kept the vow?
>   With beating heart and streaming eyes even now
> I call the phantoms of a thousand hours
> Each from his voiceless grave. They have in visioned bowers
>   Of studious zeal, or love's delight,
>   Outwatch'd with me the envious night :
>   They know that never joy illumed my brow
>   Unlinked with hope that thou would'st free
>   This world from its dark slavery,
>   That thou, O awful Loveliness,
> Would'st give whate'er these words cannot express.
>
> 'The day becomes more solemn and serene
>   When noon is past : there is a harmony
>   In autumn and a lustre in its sky,
> Which thro' the summer is not heard nor seen,
> As if it could not be, as if it had not been.
>   Thus let thy power, which like the truth
>   Of nature on my passive youth

> Descended, to my outward life supply
> Its calm,—to one who worships thee,
> And every form containing thee—
> Whom, Spirit fair, thy spells did bind
> To fear himself and love all humankind.'

When we find such writing as this among Shelley's 'earlier poems,' we are justified, I think, in hoping from him in the long run something better than blank and comfortless atheism. We expect him to go on seeking further knowledge of that great 'Spirit of the world' or 'Soul of the universe' whom he already worships with such fervour. This was the opinion of Coleridge, who, if not Shelley's equal, was next to him in that great poetic age which produced also Wordsworth, Byron, and Keats. Referring to a visit which Shelley paid to the Lakes, Coleridge regrets it was Southey and not himself whom Shelley had the fortune to meet. Southey, who had neither head nor heart enough to sympathize with Shelley, 'treated him like a prig,' in the hard uncompromising way from which Shelley could derive no benefit. Coleridge says: 'The reverse of what would have been the case in ninety-nine instances in a hundred, I *might* have been of some use to him, and Southey could not; for I should have sympathized with his poetics and metaphysical reveries—and the very word metaphysics is an abomination to Southey—and Shelley would have felt that I understood him. His discussions tending towards atheism of a certain sort would not have scared *me;* for to me it would have been a semi-transparent larva, soon to be sloughed, and through which I should have seen the true image—the final metamorphosis. Besides, I have ever thought that sort of atheism the next best religion to Christianity; nor does the better faith I have learnt from Paul and John interfere with the cordial reverence I feel for Benedict Spinoza. As far as Robert Southey was concerned with him, I am quite certain that his harshness arose entirely from the frightful reports that had been made to him respecting Shelley's moral character and conduct—reports essentially false, but, for a man of Southey's strict regularity and habitual self-government, rendered plausible by Shelley's own wild words and horror of hypocrisy.'

Coleridge, who wrote of Shelley in this tolerant, candid, and judicious manner, had himself toiled up from the lowest region of doubt almost to the very summit of the Church's creed. How happy it would have been for Shelley if, instead of falling in with the acrid ungovernable Byron and the somewhat uninteresting pedantic Southey, he had become the companion of Coleridge. But the story of Shelley's encounter with Southey is worth relating. It is too good to be omitted. With a poor selfish vanity Southey, having first denounced Shelley's opinions, eagerly clutched him as a rare gratification for himself—a supposed sympathetic auditor of his lengthy bombastic poems. Having cunningly enticed Shelley upstairs to a private room in his house in Cumberland, having swiftly shut the door, locked it, and put the key in his pocket, Southey said to his visitor: 'Now you shall be delighted—but sit down.' Shelley, we are told, examined the windows; but as they gave no hope of escape, he sighed and resignedly took his seat. Instantly Southey brought forth his manuscript of the 'Curse of Kehamah.' The rest must be told in the language of Hogg: 'Charmed with his own composition, the admiring author read on, varying his voice occasionally to point out the fine passages and invite applause. There was no commendation, no criticism, all was hushed. This was strange. Southey raised his eyes from the neatly written manuscript—Shelley had disappeared. This was still more strange. Escape was impossible. Every precaution had been taken. Yet he had vanished. . . At length Southey discovered the insensible young Vandal lying buried in profound sleep underneath the table.' Shelley's biographer adds: 'No wonder the indignant and injured bard afterwards enrolled the sleeper as a member of the "Satanic School," and inscribed his name together with that of Byron on a gibbet.' Just so: the *odium theologicum* does not always light on a man through the simple operation of justice. Southey would not have shown such indignation at the doctrines of Byron and Shelley had he not been conscious they were spirits who had stronger sweep of wing than he.

'During my existence,' said Shelley, 'I have incessantly speculated, thought, and read.' He was born a baronet's heir, and, unlike many another literary genius, had at school and college the best education that England could afford. But genius can seldom be educated by ordinary methods, and severe discipline at school made him a rebel predisposed against all authority. It is perhaps not possible for the master of a large public school so clearly to discern the natures of all his pupils as to avoid all approach to tyranny. However this may be, 'old Keate,' Shelley's master at Eton, is represented as a tyrant, and the system of fagging existed in those days. There was in Shelley's nature that combination of extreme sensitiveness and impregnable obstinacy which made the effects of tyranny peculiarly bitter. And so it happened through a great part of his life, partly through circumstances and partly from his own sensitiveness, he was made to feel much as a hunted deer may be supposed to do when it turns to bay, facing its loud-voiced, sharp-fanged assailants. Let us hear some of his autobiographical singing. Other young men have felt as he did, but none have told their story so finely.

> 'I do remember well the hour which burst
> My spirit's sleep. A fresh May dawn it was
> When I walked forth upon the glittering grass
> And wept, I knew not why: until there rose
> From the near school-room voices that, alas!
> Were but one echo from a world of woes—
> The harsh and grating strife of tyrants and of foes.
>
> 'And then I clasped my hands and look'd around,
> But none was near to mock my streaming eyes,
> Which pour'd their warm drops on the sunny ground,
> As, without shame, I spake:—" I will be wise,
> And just, and free, and mild, if in me lies
> Such power; for I am weary to behold
> The selfish and the strong still tyrannize
> Without reproach or check." I then controlled
> My tears, my heart grew calm, and I was meek and bold.'

Though he much neglected the prescribed lessons, he was a voracious reader of forbidden books, on the principle that 'stolen waters are sweet,' and possibly on higher grounds. He continues his confession :

> 'And from that hour did I with earnest thought
>   Heap knowledge from forbidden mines of lore,
> Yet nothing that my tyrants knew or taught
>   I cared to learn : but from that secret store
> Wrought link'd armour for my soul, before
>   It might walk forth to war among mankind :
> Thus power and hope were strengthened more and more
>   Within me, till there came upon my mind
> A sense of loneliness, a thirst with which I pined.'

This, we must admit, is just the sort of youth likely to cause trouble to his superiors. One of the 'forbidden mines of lore' to which he refers was Hume's 'Essays,' from which and from some other works he drew out while at Oxford a short scheme in the form of a tract entitled 'The Necessity of Atheism,' which he had privately printed. This he enclosed to various divines and professors in letters in which he said he had found this tract but was not able to answer it. Would his correspondent kindly do so for him? There was a touch of boyish impertinence in this proceeding, besides something else much worse; yet we can hardly approve of the way in which the authorities dealt with it. They should have known that Shelley was not an ordinary youth; they should have known that in general he was an exemplary student. We hear that at that time there was much drunkenness among both professors and students at Oxford, but Shelley's habits were sober and free from vice. He was a hard reader, and at this time was passionately addicted to chemistry, from which science he hoped for marvellous results for the benefit of mankind. No doubt he and his fellow student Hogg excited some malicious feeling by keeping aloof from the other students, declining to join in their revels, and preferring the experiments and discussions of their private rooms; but unpopularity acquired in this way cannot justify the severity of the college authorities in dealing with these two youths. Shelley was suddenly summoned before the Council and asked if the tract was his. On declining to answer, he was told he must disown the tract or be expelled. He refused to do so, and instantly received the formal order of expulsion, which had been written out, signed, and sealed before he entered the council chamber. Hogg, vehemently exclaiming against this arbitrary proceeding, and affirming that if Shelley was guilty *he* was equally so, was expelled at the same time.

Could not some milder course, more honourable to the college and more helpful to Shelley, have been adopted ? We do not hear that any kindly old professor, remembering his own far-off days of doubt, came over quietly to Shelley to try the effect of friendly sympathy, and tell how *he* had 'fought his doubts and gathered strength,' or of some one else
'Perplex'd in faith, but pure in deeds,'
who at length 'beat his music out.' We do not even hear of anyone suggesting a good book on theism, or commending to his attention some piece of reading which his experience had found useful. As if they could hope for no change in a youth of seventeen,
'When time has sundered shell from pearl,'
and as if they wished to bind his opinions to him for ever in the bond of prejudice created by arbitrary harshness and intolerant pride, they instantly made him an outcast, marked on the forehead with the stamp of reprobacy at this early age !

The government at Oxford was not a paternal one, neither was that in Shelley's own home. His father disinherited him. His beautiful cousin, Harriet Grove, with whom he had fallen deeply in love, and who returned his affection, was induced by strong influence brought to bear on her to give him up because of his dangerous opinions. In the midst of these calamities, whose effect must have been excruciating on a mind so sensitive, Shelley was conscious of having done no wrong, unless accepting opinions which his reason seemed to warrant were wrong. A man who engages in a long mathematical calculation may without immorality come to an erroneous result. If you approach him in a friendly spirit, and go with him through all the stages of the calculation, point out his mistake, and thus lead him to the correct solution, he will thank you and you will deserve his thanks. But if you are one who do not know how to perform this mathematical calculation, but have only learnt the answer from some key, what is the use of denouncing your neighbour as a villain, because in one of those complicated processes he has made a mistake, and thus arrived at an erroneous result?

Shelley regarded his expulsion from Oxford somewhat in this light, and to a heart quivering with the pain of disappointed love, and a mind deeply sensitive to disgrace, orthodoxy in these circumstances did not assume a favourable aspect. It was in these circumstances he wrote some of the wildest passages in 'Queen Mab,' of which he was afterwards ashamed. But his afflictions did not end here. It was while he was in lodgings in London, an outcast from Oxford, and rejected by Harriet Grove, he met with another Harriet, whose maiden name was Westbrook. This young lady, who was at a boarding-school, evoked Shelley's sympathy by tales of tyranny which she said she was suffering, and finally cast herself on his protection. She, the daughter of a coffee-house keeper, and her wily old sister Eliza, seemed to have no fear of the result, should it be even to wed the ultimate heir of Castle Goring, with a baronetcy and £6,000 a year. Which actually happened, by Shelley's impulsiveness and romantic sense of honour. This precipitate step was followed by such results as the prudent can easily predict. Eliza ruled the household, that had to be managed on £200 a year, which Shelley's father, with some difficulty, was brought to grant. Eliza constituted herself her sister's indispensable friend and Shelley's perpetual torment. Introduced to Shelley by his wife as her most wonderful and most admirable sister, Eliza was found capable of just two things—the continual brushing of her glossy black hair, her sole ornament, and the management of her friends with the greatest possible amount of annoyance to all concerned. The plague of this sister first awoke the youthful pair to an acute sense of the unsuitableness of the arrangement that had been made so hastily; and when this was daily growing more apparent, the marriage was at length dissolved by mutual consent. Suicide, it seems, had always been a favourite idea of Harriet's, even in the happiest days after her marriage, and about a year after her separation from Shelley the final impulse to destroy herself came, but not from feelings connected with him, and was carried out. Shelley's second wife was the daughter of two celebrated writers and social reformers, Mary Wollstencraft and William Godwin. She inherited fine literary powers, with an intense enthusiastic nature, and was in every way a most suitable companion for Shelley. With her he lived the last eight years of his life in almost uninterrupted and ideal happiness. With her he might have developed into one of the best and most remarkable men that England or the world has produced. He was getting his style free from the froth of youthful fervour; he was spending his days in hard study of the highest kind; he was planning writings on the severest models of Greece, which would have been as immortal as those of Milton or Sophocles ;—but remorseless fate was at hand. He had already worn out some of his false theories and buried some fierce antipathies ; a happy domestic circle, with some noble-minded admiring friends, was gathering round him ; his refined simplicity of taste and his abstemious habits were settled and confirmed; he was doing gigantic literary work both in acquiring and producing, when—

> 'Comes the blind Fury with abhorrèd shears
> And slits the thin-spun life.'

The year before his death he had sung his beautiful lament over his friend John Keats—'Adonais'—the closing stanza o which seemed, after Shelley's own death, so strangely prophetic:

> 'The breath whose might I have invoked in song
> Descends on me; my spirit's bark is driven
> Far from the shore, far from the trembling throng,
> Whose sails were never to the tempest given ;
> The massy earth and spherèd skies are riven ;
> I am borne darkly, fearfully afar !

> Whilst burning thro' the inmost veil of heaven
> The soul of Adonais, like a star,
> Beacons from the abode where the eternal are.'

There are those who have had what seemed intimations more or less distinct of their death, but few have written of it beforehand as Shelley does here, whose ' boat' was some short months after actually ' driven far from the shore' of Italy, was foundered in a sudden storm, and Shelley, after some days, was washed on shore with a volume of Keats in the pocket of his wet clothes. Italy at that time renewed her classic lustre through the presence of famous Englishmen, and became more deeply interesting to all men by their lamented deaths. Keats had there been buried, mourned by Shelley, and shortly after the ashes of Shelley were interred in the same beautiful cemetery at Rome by Byron. How quickly these brilliant sons of genius succeeded one another, entering gloomy Sheol from those bright eastern shores! The noble poet who assisted in performing the last rites over Shelley's ashes, eighteen months later, was himself lying dead in that

> ' Clime of the unforgotten brave,
> Whose land from plain to mountain cave
> Was freedom's home, or glory's grave—'

that land of Greece for which he had lifted not only the pen, but the sword! Byron wrote no elegy on Shelley, as the latter did on Keats, but he wrote of him in plain prose, as the ' most high-minded, disinterested, and consistent man he ever knew.'

Shelley's manners and appearance were, unlike his principles, extremely aristocratic. 'Never did a more finished gentleman step across a drawing-room,' said one who had observed and could judge. With ladies, especially, Shelley was a high and universal favourite. It is said he never entered a house without exciting the instantaneous attention and exclusive admiration of every woman in it, from the housemaid up to the duchess, if such were there. Not that his face was what is called handsome, but when illuminated by his kindling soul it seemed beautiful, and there was a strange fascination in

his large, bright, wild eyes ; then there was always seen in him
a refined delicacy, a genuine modesty, and a nobleness of
thought that instantly won for him the hearts of the fair.
We hear of one high-born lady going so far as to say she
would willingly give the half of her large income just to have
him as an occasional visitor at her house, so delightful was the
influence of his fine spirit, so uncommon and wonderful was
his talk. All who approached him were impressed by his
exalted, pure, transcendent nature. No man was ever more
legitimately an object of enthusiasm among his fellows. Hogg,
his biographer and college friend, became an able barrister,
and a shrewd, keen, caustic man of the world, yet he constantly calls him his 'incomparable friend,' and disdaining
limits, asserts, 'he was better than everybody.' Leigh
Hunt's devotion and admiration are, if possible, even more
enthusiastic.

In Shelley we discover little of the vanity of the author ; even
the delight of the artist in his work is with him subordinate to that
momentous purpose to which he had devoted his life, and which
he would alone recognise as true ambition—the enfranchisement
and perfectioning of man. Even Napoleon he addressed scornfully as a 'most unambitious slave,' because he preferred a selfish
gratification, 'a frail and bloody pomp,' to establishing the
liberty and happiness of the people. Shelley's devotion to the
cause of the people, his intense interest in human welfare, is
well brought out in a characteristic story by Leigh Hunt. 'He
once came to me at Hampstead,' says Hunt, 'when I had not
seen him for some time ; and after grasping my hands with both
his in his usual fervent manner, he sat down and looked at me
very earnestly with a deep, though melancholy interest in his
face. We were sitting with our knees to the fire, to which he
had been getting nearer and nearer in the comfort of finding
ourselves together. The pleasure of seeing him was my only
feeling at the moment, and the air of domesticity about us was
so complete that I thought he was going to speak of some
family matter, either his or my own, when he asked me at

the close of an intensity of pause, what was the amount of the national debt.'

Another anecdote, abridged from Hunt's 'Autobiography,' will bring the living Shelley before us, and especially illustrate the kindness of his heart. It was a fierce winter night, with snow upon the ground, when Shelley, travelling on foot to Hunt's house in Hampstead, found a poor woman lying on the road in fits. Shelley, always promptest as well as most pitying on these occasions, knocked at the first houses he could reach, in order to have the woman taken in. At these genteel mansions the invariable answer was that they could not do it. He asked for an outhouse to put her in while he went for a doctor. Impossible! 'Shelley himself was no Christian; but,' says Hunt, 'the paucity of Christians is wonderful, considering the number of them.' Time flies; the poor woman is in convulsions, her son, a young man, lamenting over her. At last Shelley sees a carriage driving up to a house at a little distance. The knock is given; the warm door opens; servants and lights pour forth. 'Now,' thinks Shelley, 'is the time.' He puts on his best address, which anybody might recognise for that of the highest gentleman as well as of an interesting individual, and plants himself in the way of an elderly person who is stepping out of the carriage with his family. He tells his story. They only press on the faster. 'Will you go and see her?' 'No, sir; there's no necessity for that sort of thing, depend on it. Impostors swarm everywhere—the thing cannot be done. Sir, your conduct is extraordinary!' 'Sir,' cried Shelley, assuming a very different manner, and forcing the flourishing householder to stop out of astonishment, 'I am sorry to say that your conduct is *not* extraordinary! and if my own seems to amaze you, I will tell you something which may amaze you a little more, and I hope will frighten you. It is such men as you who madden the spirits and the patience of the poor and wretched; and if ever a convulsion comes in this country (which is very probable), recollect what I tell you: you will have your house, that you refuse to put the miserable woman into, burnt over your head!' 'God bless me, sir! Dear me, sir!' exclaimed the poor frightened man, and fluttered into his mansion. Shelley, we may add, had the poor woman brought at length to the dwelling of Hunt; whereupon—though Hunt was a married man with five children, in whose childish sports Shelley was accustomed to join with great zest—a report was circulated concerning a strange female whom Shelley (no Christian) brought to Hunt's house, and who was, of course, no better than she should be. *Which* was the true Christian—Shelley or one of these 'righteous' neighbours who *refused the woman and circulated the report?*

Our account of Shelley ought to include some reference to his visits to Ireland. The agitation for Irish Emancipation interested him, and, like a disinterested philanthropist as he was, he came over with a letter of introduction to Curran and deep sympathy for the miseries of Irishmen. We cannot say that in this *rôle* of political agitator Shelley achieved any great success. Byron once told him that his philosophy was 'too spiritual and romantic.' The good people of Dublin may have felt this, for they hardly understood him. Shelley came armed with a pamphlet containing his address to the Irish people, and he spoke at a great public meeting in the Rotunda with much earnestness, if not with much oratorical success. In dealing with the Irish people in his guileless, straightforward way, he used great plainness of speech—more, doubtless, than an experienced reformer would consider judicious. 'Irishmen,' he said, 'must reform themselves, not by force of arms, but by power of mind and reliance on truth and justice. No Irishman must swerve from the path of duty. Be open, sincere-single-hearted. O Irishmen, reform yourselves; desire peace and harmony, benevolence and a spirit of forgiveness; form habits of sobriety, regularity, and thought—before anything else can be done with effect these must be entered into and firmly resolved upon.' This was all good, but it was not exactly the kind of oratory to which Repeal meetings had been accustomed, and it was not popular. Shelley returned to

England disappointed. He spoke of being deeply pained with Irish poverty and wretchedness. 'The poor of Dublin,' he said, 'were the meanest and most miserable of all that he had seen.' Hogg's opinion of Ireland may be here given as a sign of the times. Having read while in Dublin the Irish newspapers, which he admitted were well written, and being asked what he thought of Irish grievances, Hogg replied: 'What I have read has entirely confirmed the only opinion I ever formed on the whole matter, that the Devil may mend it if he will, for full sure nobody else can.' Other Englishmen have been more hopeful of Ireland; but we should state in explanation that Mr. Thomas Jefferson Hogg, though Shelley's friend, was a high Tory.

Before proceeding to some criticism on Shelley's poetry, our remarks on his life may be well wound up with the following fine passage from De Quincy: 'The life of Shelley was "among the most romantic of literary history." From his childhood he moved through a succession of afflictions. Always craving for love, loving and seeking to be loved, always destined to reap hatred from those with whom life had connected him. If in the darkness he raised up images of his departed hours, he would behold his family disowning him, and the home of his infancy knowing him no more; he would behold his magnificent university, that under happier circumstances would have gloried in his genius, rejecting him for ever; he would behold his first wife, whom once he had loved passionately, through calamities arising from himself, called away to an early and a tragic death. The peace after which his heart panted for ever—in what dreadful contrast it stood to the eternal contention into which his restless intellect or accidents of position threw him like a passive victim! It seemed as if not any choice of his, but some sad doom of opposition from without, forced out as by a magnet struggles of frantic resistance from him, which as gladly he would have evaded as ever victim of epilepsy yearned to evade his convulsions! Gladly he would have slept in eternal seclusion, whilst eternally the trumpet summoned him to battle. In storms unwillingly created by himself he lived; in a storm cited by the finger of God he died. . . .

'His feud with Christianity was a craze derived from some early wrench of his understanding, and made obstinate to the degree in which we find it from having rooted itself in certain combinations of ideas that, once coalescing, could not be shaken loose; such as, that Christianity under-propped the corruptions of the earth, in the shape of wicked governments that might else have been overthrown, or of wicked priesthoods that, but for the shelter and shadow of spiritual terrors, must have trembled before those whom they overawed. Kings that were clothed in bloody robes; dark hierarchies that scowled upon the poor children of the soil—these objects took up a permanent station in the background of Shelley's imagination. . . . Can we imagine the case of an angel touched with lunacy? . . . Had not Shelley the excuse of something like monomania on the subject of religion? I firmly believe it. But words of deep meaning uttered by idiots or lunatics are said to execute themselves. . . . As a shepherd by his dog fetches out one of his flock from amongst five hundred, so did the *holy hurricane* seem to fetch out from the multitude of sails that one which carried him.'

There is no poem of Shelley's so characteristic, none more entirely beautiful and touching, than his 'Ode to the West Wind.' In the first three stanzas, with something like supernatural power, the effects of the 'West Wind' on the 'Earth,' the 'Air,' and the 'Ocean' respectively are described. Having spoken most wonderfully of its effects on the dead leaves, the clouds, and the waves, he closes the 'Ode' with two stanzas which present to my mind a better idea of Shelley than anything else that has been written:

> 'If I were a dead leaf thou mightest bear,
> If I were a swift cloud to fly with thee,
> A wave to pant beneath thy power and share
> The impulse of thy strength, only less free

> Than Thou, O Uncontrollable! if even
> I were as in my boyhood, and could be
> The comrade of thy wanderings over heaven,
> As then when to outstrip thy skiey speed
> Scarce seem'd a vision,—I would ne'er have striven
> As thus with thee, in prayer, in my sore need!
> Oh, lift me as a wave, a leaf, a cloud;
> I fall upon the thorns of life! I bleed!
> A heavy weight of hours has chained and bound
> One, too, like thee—tameless, and swift, and proud!
>
> Make me thy lyre, even as the forest is,—
> What if my leaves are falling like its own!
> The tumult of its mighty harmonies
> Will take from both a deep autumnal tone,
> Sweet though in sadness. Be thou, Spirit fierce,
> My spirit! be thou *me*, impetuous one!
> Drive my dead thoughts over the universe
> Like withered leaves to quicken a new birth,
> And by the incantation of this verse,
> Scatter, as from an unextinguished hearth
> Ashes and sparks, my words among mankind;
> Be through my lips to unawakened earth
> The trumpet of a prophecy. O Wind,
> If Winter comes, can Spring be far behind?'

Shelley himself defines poetry to be 'the record of the best and happiest moments of the happiest and best minds,' and one can easily recognise the truth of this definition in Shelley's own poetry. He is like his own skylark—

> 'That singing still dost soar, and soaring ever singest'—

which expresses happiness, no doubt, but also the constant *inspiration* and tendency towards the supreme, both in subject and manner, which strikes every reader. But it is affirmed that his poetry is often difficult to understand—that it is often no better than metaphysics with a poetic gilding. Still, this kind of poetry is found to have strong attraction for the finest minds, and the age which began by rejecting Tennyson's 'In Memoriam' as metaphysical has ended by accepting it as a great poem full of poetic beauty. After all, the difference between one who can read such poetry and one who cannot consists chiefly in attention. There are some eyes which apparently have not the faculty of seeing what they are looking at. Attention has been called genius, and certainly the power of close absorbing attention belongs to all who have genius. Some eyes seem to want the faculty of seeing the whole of the object placed before them. If we were not so hurried in this age of business—if we could give the mind full leisure to take in *all* the symbolical marks on the page before us with the full meaning of each, including every comma, dot, and dash, we should not so often complain that our poet is obscure or abstruse. Shelley's obscurity arises mostly from the nature of the subject, from the depth of his thought and feeling: his haziness is the 'dreamy ecstasy too high for speech in which his poetical nature—most subtle, sensitive, and voluptuous—delighted to dissolve and lose itself.' And Shelley by his marvellous power of *expression* has made striking and intelligible to the common reader thoughts that only students of philosophy were acquainted with. This is not an objection to Shelley with intenser natures, who love best the poet who 'stirs the spirit's inner deeps,' who expresses what had seemed inexpressible, who deals with thought in her remotest recesses, and who pictures by suggestion what cannot otherwise be indicated. What we might call 'essential poetry'—the undiluted poetic thought—abounds in Shelley. Hogg says: 'No poetry is so uniformly inspired as Shelley's.' It is eminently idealistic, yet it is far from the work of a vain visionary, but often practical and powerful—capable of catching the ear and moving the heart of the common world. His 'Julian and Maddalo,' a poetic record of a conversation between himself and Lord Byron, is as realistic and ably familiar as anything of the kind in Chaucer. His 'Letter to Maria Gisborne' is another beautiful instance of the same kind of writing. His lines to the Lord Chancellor, who separated from him the children of his first wife, are practical and intelligible enough:

> 'I curse thee by a parent's outraged love,
> By hopes long-cherished and too lately lost,
> By gentle feelings thou couldst never prove,
> By griefs which thy stern nature never cross'd,

> By all the happy see in children's growth,
> That undevelop'd flower of budding years,
> Sweetness and sadness interwoven both,
> Source of the sweetest hopes and saddest fears.'

It is in his shorter pieces that Shelley is happiest, *e.g.*, his 'Skylark,' than which there is nothing of the same length superior in any English poet, and the 'Cloud,' 'Arethusa,' 'Hymn to Apollo,' and many others whose poetry seems to me altogether unique and matchless. One who is able to imbibe the pure nectarean draught will find it there. The critic, like one amid a collection of splendid jewels, is at a loss which to fix on and hold up for admiration. Take the 'Hymn to Apollo': where, except in what has proceeded from Shelley's almost superhuman soul, can you find brilliance rich and precious and exalting as this?

You are to think of the Sun as a beautiful youth, Apollo, who speaks, alluding to his condition just before appearing above the eastern horizon: he is in his gorgeous bed, whose canopy is heaven's starry dome, the sleepless Hours as attendant nymphs surrounding him:

> 'The sleepless Hours, who watch me as I lie,
>   Curtained with star-enwoven tapestries,
>   From the broad moonlight of the sky,
>   Fanning the busy dreams from my dim eyes,
> Waken me when their mother, the grey Dawn,
> Tells them that dreams and that the moon is gone.
> 'Then I arise, and climbing heaven's blue dome,
>   I walk over the mountains and the waves,
> Leaving my robe upon the ocean foam;—
>   My footsteps pave the clouds with fire; the caves
> Are filled with my bright presence; and the air
> Leaves the green earth to my embraces bare. . . .
> 'I stand at noon upon the peak of heaven;
>   Then with unwilling steps I wander down
> Into the clouds of the Atlantic even;
>   For grief that I depart they weep and frown.
> What look is more delightful than the smile
> With which I soothe them from the western isle?'

Another of his shorter poems, 'Epipsychidion,' an able critic not given to enthusiasm pronounces to be for its wealth and fusion of all the highest things—of imagination, of expression, of music—one of the greatest miracles ever wrought in poetry. 'Epipsychidion' is like all that is best in Shelley, for he was essentially a lyric poet, autobiographical, relating various experiences and mistakes in his soul's voyage of discovery and attempt to find the supreme excellence of love, till at length 'Emily' (a beautiful Italian lady) crosses his path and he at once enters into blessedness. I confess this poem does not please me as much as those other shorter ones I have mentioned. It has fine passages, as the description of the Isle of Greece to which he proposed to convey Emily; but some are strained, and have not the genuine ring of the incorruptible and imperishable metal.

There is space for only a few brief remarks on Shelley's longer poems. These, however beautiful in parts, are not readable without considerable mental strain and even fatigue. They have the misfortune to require more time than can be often devoted to the *study* of poetry. 'Prometheus Unbound,' the greatest of Shelley's larger works, is not to be attempted in seasons of weariness, when the mind needs refreshment and relaxation: but it will repay severe study. It is a play somewhat after the manner of Sophocles, and so thoroughly had Shelley studied the Greek dramatist, that one fancies he can hear the ring of the Greek verse in Shelley's. It is a stronger and more elaborate expression of the spirit of rebellion against constituted authority and the ideas that sanction it than 'Queen Mab': it is a gorgeous triumphal pæan of Liberty on the fall of Despotism. Shelley's favourite idea, expressed in this drama, in 'Queen Mab,' in the 'Revolt of Islam,' and in other long poems, is that of a good man who, while oppressed by the evil principle of the world and by men, even good ones, through misconception, does not yield to the most terrible opposition and most cruel torture, but maintains the unequal war, until, as the truth he upholds gradually becomes influential, he at length conquers, and brings to nought all the monstrous forms of tyranny that afflict mankind.

This is, however, just the leading idea of Christianity, the system which Shelley charged with supporting the worst tyrannies of the world. But doubtless Shelley knew that Christianity; as it was conceived by Christ Himself, and Christianity as it has been embodied in certain organizations called churches, are very different things. There was, indeed, existing in Christ's day a system that in some respects closely resembled that of our churches, but *that* was the system on which Jesus made war, and by which he was crucified—the system of the Pharisees. Christianity, as originally conceived, was benevolent—was beautiful—was divine; but formalized Christianity, like sweet wine changed to vinegar, had just the opposite qualities. Shelley treats the God whom Christians worship as if he were the Devil; but he may have done so on the principle that the so-called Christians of these days are really modern Pharisees. And if this were so—and to a large extent it *is* so—Shelley was not so far wrong. To those outwardly respectable, self-satisfied, spiritually proud people, whose attention to Divine worship was so ostentatious and elaborate, a Greater than Shelley gave this clear and infallible information: 'Ye are of your father the Devil.' The sin of the Pharisees was precisely that for which, in the opinion of many, Shelley is condemned. They affirmed that the author of the 'good works' was the Evil One. This is for ever 'unpardonable.' To recognise the working of the Good Spirit, to hate it when recognised, and in malignant bitterness call it by the *worst* name, is the last proof of reprobacy, and the sure sign of hopeless depravity. But a man should not be charged with this simply on account of his use of *names*. It is for the way in which his heart treats the *things*—the Good and Evil principles in their manifestation—that he is condemned in the sentence, 'Woe unto them that call evil good, and good evil.' Were the ideas which ignorant men attach to the name of God really Satanic, though so well disguised that their true nature could not be discerned by the multitude, *then* it would not be blasphemy to speak against such a being, whatever name he might be known by: and there can be no doubt that in Shelley's day many of the popular ideas of God were, to say the least, incorrect. We may hope things are somewhat better in our own time; and if they are, it is not by the lazy acquiescence of those who fear to get into trouble by disturbing the popular notion, but by the bravery and earnestness of men who scorned half-truths and apparent truths, whose minds could never rest till they touched reality, and who were willing to revolutionize the world rather than allow its foundations to rest on a lie. It is *this spirit* in Shelley, not his positive teaching, that has made him of value in the world. We heartily agree with J. A. Symonds that 'the real lesson of his life and writings is not to be sought in any of his doctrines, but rather in his fearless bearing, his resolute loyalty to an unselfish and, in the simplest sense, benevolent ideal.'

TENNYSON.

THE 'IN MEMORIAM.'

OUR 'introduction' to Tennyson and illustration of his genius will be confined for the present to an exposition of the 'IN MEMORIAM.'

Of that delightful pensiveness which Milton has described under the name of 'Melancholy,' there can be found no higher instance than the 'lofty rhyme' built by Tennyson as his friend's memorial. Milton's 'Penseroso' is conversant with the highest and purest joys, as well as the most elevating and instructive thoughts; and, like him, Tennyson, while he sorrows,

> 'Hears the Muses in a ring
> Aye round about Jove's altar sing';

chooses for his chief companion

> 'Him that yon soars on golden wing,
> Guiding the fiery-wheelèd throne,
> The Cherub Contemplatïon';

wishes to 'unsphere

> 'The spirit of Plato, to unfold
> What worlds or what vast regions hold
> The immortal mind, that hath forsook
> Her mansion in this fleshly nook';

and desires to feel the instructive, consolatory power of all forms of beauty in earth and sky,

> 'Till old experience do attain
> To something like prophetic strain.'

If we ought ever to expect a revival of the 'prophetic' function in modern days, it might surely be in circumstances like those in which 'In Memoriam' was written. The man of genius, with his mind full of the deep questions and discussions of modern thought, deeply sympathizing with the highest spiritual struggles of the time, developed under the highest culture, and refined to the utmost delicacy of feeling, suddenly receives the most dreadful blow which the hand of fate can inflict. By an unlooked-for 'rush of blood to the head,' he loses his dearest and most valued friend, whose endowments he thought superior to his own. Startled and stirred to its depths, his soul grapples with the fearful reality of death; his best and bravest thoughts wrestle with it; as Paul fought with beasts he fights with it; and, chiefly by the inspiration and power of his great and wonderful love, he *conquers* it at last, singing his pæan in words like these:

'Dear heavenly friend, that canst not die,
Mine, mine FOR EVER, EVER mine!'

To one of the deepest thinkers of old, Philosophy was but 'a meditation of death,' and even common minds have noticed that in the presence of the 'awful shadow' some important subjects appear in a new and clearer light; for our thinking is most earnest then, and attacks with vigour those great questions which are concealed by the 'veil of life,' but assume imposing forms as they crowd around the grave. In the present instance, that earnestness of thinking which is nearest inspiration, which produces consolatory light for common minds, which is at once original and orthodox, which faces doubt and fights it fairly, and by which we are relieved to see

'Large elements in order brought,
And tracts of calm from tempests made,'

has wrought in Tennyson for the production of a MONUMENT which will serve the purpose of a BEACON-LIGHT for many an age to come!

Is it possible to build any memorial more enduring than one composed of true poetic words? Hear what Shakespeare says:

'Nor marble, nor the gilded monuments
Of princes shall outlive this powerful rhyme,
But you shall shine more bright in these contents
Than unswept stone besmear'd with sluttish time;
When wasteful war shall statues overturn,
And broils root out the work of masonry,

> Nor Mars his sword, nor war's quick fire shall burn
> The living record of your memory,
> 'Gainst death and all-oblivious enmity
> Shall you pace forth; your praise shall still find room
> Even in the eyes of all posterity,
> That wear this world out to the ending doom;
> So, till the judgment that yourself arise,
> *You live in this* and dwell in lovers' eyes.'

It has been sometimes said that Shakespeare was himself unconscious of the great power manifested in his writings; but those who are acquainted with his sonnets know this to be a mistake. He too had in contemplation a task similar to that which Tennyson has set before him—the preserving by immortal verse of his friend's admirable endowments—and he had far more confidence in this than in the most enduring stone or metal:

> ' Since brass, nor stone, nor earth, nor boundless sea,
> But sad mortality o'ersways their power,
> How, with his rage, shall beauty hold a plea,
> Whose action is no stronger than a flower? . . .
> O fearful meditation! where, alàck,
> Shall Time's best jewel from Time's chest lie hid?
> Or what strong hand can hold his swift foot back?
> Or who his spoil of beauty can forbid?
> O, none, unless this miracle have might,
> That in black ink my love may still shine bright!'

It was a memorial of this kind that Tennyson designed for his friend; not a few verses cut on his tomb, but a book which will live, which men 'will not willingly let die.' We cannot indeed say that Tennyson's friend has a tomb at all so magnificent as that in which, according to Milton, Shakespeare himself lies 'sepulchred'—his own imperishable dramas:

> ' Thou, in our wonder and astonishment,
> Hast built thyself a livelong monument, ...
> And so sepulchred, in such pomp dost lie,
> That kings for such a tomb would wish to die.'

But we believe that no man has raised for another a nobler monument of verse, or built a loftier rhyme, than that raised by Tennyson for his friend Arthur Henry Hallam, son of the celebrated historian and critic.

Arthur was born in London, in the year 1811, and was therefore a year older than his friend Tennyson. He died, during his third visit to the continent, at Vienna, at the early age of twenty-two. The son of the author of the 'Literature of Europe' was naturally expected to be somebody; and the following record, by one who knew him well, and was no mean judge, will serve to indicate the reputation which this young man left behind him:

'I have met with no man his superior in metaphysical subtlety; no man his equal as a philosophic critic on works of taste; no man whose views on all subjects connected with the duties and dignities of humanity was more large and generous and enlightened.'

His fellow students at Cambridge, Tennyson among the rest, looked up to him as a master spirit. His father tells us that from his earliest years his son was distinguished by clearness of perception and firm adherence to his sense of what is right and becoming. At eight years of age he learnt to read Latin with ease in a single year. He was early enamoured of the old English poets, but 'in Shakespeare alone he found the fulness of soul which seemed to slake the thirst of his own rapidly expanding genius for an inexhaustible fountain of thought and emotion.' He published exquisite poetry of his own at sixteen. He went to Italy, and there—like a second Milton—wrote Italian sonnets which Italian critics admired. Dante became his second master, and from him he learnt disdain of flowery redundance, and aspiration after what is better and less fleeting than earthly things. He knew French literature almost as well as that of his own country. He had not (says his father) a prompt or accurate memory for dates or mere details: but he could remember anything connected with an idea. He learned much in society, and was always surrounded by minds of the first intelligence, who desired above all things the knowledge of truth and the perception of beauty. Before he was twenty-one he had written three little books, on Petrarch, Voltaire, and Burke, respectively, manifesting an ability marvellously mature and versatile. Leaving

Cambridge, he turned to the study of law; but, shortly after, his death occurred at Vienna, caused, it was thought, by weakness of the cerebral vessels and want of energy in the heart, producing a sudden access of blood to the head. His father (from whose beautiful little memoir these facts are taken) speaks of his disposition as faultless, of his calm self-command, of his genuine love to God and man. 'He seemed to tread the earth as a spirit from some better world,' writes the elder Hallam, whose calm and graceful narrative hardly conceals the tender paternal feeling which trembles under his polished and dignified style.

As contributing along with these facts to illustrate 'In Memoriam,' a short specimen of Arthur Hallam's poetry may be interesting; and we select a sonnet addressed to his mother, referring to his season of doubt, that 'Slough of Despond' through which all earnest young thinkers must pass:

> 'When barren doubt, like a late-coming snow,
> Made an unkind December of my Spring,
> That all the pretty flowers did droop for woe,
> And the sweet birds their love no more would sing,
> Then the remembrance of thy gentle faith,
> Mother belov'd, would steal upon my heart;
> Fond feeling saved me from that utter scáthe,
> And from *thy* hope I *could* not live apart.
> Now that my mind hath pass'd from wintry gloom,
> And on the calmèd waters once again
> Ascendant faith circles with silver plume,
> That casts a charmèd shade, not now in pain,
> Thou child of Christ, in joy I think of thee,
> And mingle prayers for what we both may be.'

Before turning to look at some of the many touching and beautiful things which Tennyson has written of this young man, one might like to know what *he* thought of Tennyson. We are able to gratify this wish, for young Hallam wrote, in one of the reviews of the day, a critique on Tennyson's first poetry, which had just appeared in a small volume. From this criticism, which is so interesting both on account of its writer and its subject, we present the following sentences:

'One of the faithful Islâm, a poet in the truest and highest sense, we are anxious to present to our readers. He sees all the forms of nature with an instructed eye; and his ear has a fairy fineness. There is a strange earnestness in his worship of beauty which throws a charm over his impassioned song, more easily felt than described, and not to be escaped by those who have once felt it. . . . This author imitates nobody; we recognise the spirit of his age, but not the individual form of this or that writer. . . . We have marked five distinctive excellences of his own manner. First, his luxuriance of imagination, and at the same time his control over it. Secondly, his power of embodying himself in ideal characters, or rather modes of character, with such extreme accuracy of adjustment, that the circumstances of the narration seem to have a natural correspondence with the predominant feeling, and, as it were, to be evolved from it by assimilative force. Thirdly, his vivid picturesque delineation of objects, and the peculiar skill with which he holds all of them *fused*, to borrow a metaphor from science, in a medium of strong emotion. Fourthly, the variety of his lyrical measures, and exquisite modulation of harmonious words and cadences to the swell and fall of the feelings expressed. Fifthly, the elevated habits of thought implied in these compositions, and imparting a mellow soberness of tone, more impressive to our minds than if the author had drawn up a set of opinions in verse and sought to instruct the understanding rather than to communicate the love of beauty to the heart.'

This surely is wonderful writing for a youth of twenty. The justness of the criticism will be appreciated by those who have read Tennyson's earlier poems, and no less by readers of the greater work, of which the critic himself, by his lamented death, was so soon to be the occasion.

'In Memoriam,' though a poem, or series of poems, occasioned by death, is not gloomy—does not read like an additional chapter of 'Hervey's Meditations among the Tombs.' It is because it contains so much of the spirit of the age—that is, the better spirit of the age; because so many modern questions of universal human interest gleam up in its poetic light; because it combines truth with tolerance, and elevated habits of thought with sweetest human enjoyment; because it contains the vindication by an exalted soul of truths which degraded or commonplace minds cannot see, and therefore deny; and, lastly, because of its rare and genuine poetic beauties, that I have chosen it out of the large mass of modern verse as deserving special attention.

Consider, first of all, the reality of the poem. Poetry is not necessarily fiction, but is often simply a fuller and truer account of the fact than what is given in prose. The character portrayed in this poem is certainly not fictitious, but real, with all the reality and manifoldness of nature; and this being so, we have in it what is highly important, but rarely created, in any age—a noble ideal or copy for inferior souls. From various parts of the poem we have placed together the following portrait, which is a picture that cannot be too frequently set before our young men :

> ' High nature, amorous of good,
>   But touch'd with no ascetic gloom,
>   And passion pure in snowy bloom
> Thro' all the years of April blood.
> A love of freedom rarely felt,
>   Of freedom in her regal seat
>   Of England : not the school-boy heat,
> The blind hysterics of the Celt;
> And manhood fused with female grace,
>   In such a sort the child would twine
>   A trustful hand unasked in thine,
> And find his comfort in thy face. . . .
> On thee the loyal-hearted hung;
>   The proud was half disarm'd of pride,
>   Nor cared the serpent at thy side
> To flicker with his double tongue.
> The stern were mild when thou wert by,
>   The flippant put himself to school
>   And heard thee, and the brazen fool
> Was softened, and he knew not why.
> While I, thy dearest, sat apart
>   And felt thy triumph was as mine ;

And loved them more that they were thine,
The graceful tact, the Christian art. . . .
For who can always act? but he
To whom a thousand memories call,
Not being less, but more, than all
The gentleness he seemed to be,
Best seem'd the thing he was, and join'd
Each office of the social hour
To noble manners, as the flower
And native growth of noble mind.
Nor ever narrowness or spite,
Or villain fancy fleeting by,
Drew in the expression of an eye
Where God and nature met in light.
And thus he bore without abuse
The grand old name of gentleman,
Defamed by every charlatan,
And soil'd with all ignoble use.'

'In Memoriam' is directly an expression of grief—of deep, poignant sorrow, but indirectly it is a eulogium of Arthur: for we are told to judge of his character by the sorrow which his death has caused:

'I leave thy praises unexpress'd
In verse that brings myself relief,
And by the measure of my grief
I leave thy greatness to be guess'd.'

The poem opens with the thought, often expressed, that the soul's present suffering may afterwards prove its gain; but, asks the poet, who that grieves deeply can comfort himself with the thought of that effect in the future? 'For grief like mine,' says he, 'its cause is a better defence than its effect, and I would rather bear this great crushing grief than be possessed of such a nature as would be incapable of the love which causes it. Let me keep both the grief and the love, since now the absence of the one would imply the absence of the other. I prefer the deepest sorrow, the most un-alleviated gloom, yea, even that dreadful levity of grief which is akin to madness, to the degradation which I should feel could it be said that time had worn my love away.'

'Let Love clasp Grief, lest both be drown'd,
  Let darkness keep her raven gloss ;
Ah, sweeter to be drunk with loss,
  To dance with death, to beat the ground,
Than that the victor Hours should scorn
  The long result of love, and boast,
  "Behold the man that loved and lost,
But all he was is overworn."'

Shakespeare, we may remark, has expressed a similar belief in, and reverence for, the love that dwelt in his own great soul :

'Love's not Time's fool, tho' rosy lips and cheeks
  Within his bending sickle's compass come ;
Love alters not with his brief hours and weeks,
  But bears it out even to the edge of doom.'

Longfellow's 'Ladder of St. Augustine,' a beautiful little poem setting forth the idea that men's misfortunes, and even vices, may be made to serve as steps towards excellence, is probably that which is referred to in the opening stanza of 'In Memoriam' :

'I held it true, with him who sings
  To one clear harp in divers tones,
  That men may rise on stepping stones
Of their dead selves to higher things.'

We quote the first and last stanza of Longfellow's poem—we would like to quote it all :

'Saint Augustine ! well hast thou said,
  That of our vices we can frame
A ladder, if we will but tread
  Beneath our feet each deed of shame. . . .
Nor deem the irrevocable past
  As wholly wasted, wholly vain,
If rising on its recks at last
  To something nobler we attain.'

With this thought in his mind, we imagine the poet beginning to write on the great theme of which his heart is so full. We seem to see him, like that afflicted Arabian, sitting silent on the ground for seven days, and then at length breaking the silence by pouring forth a flood of melodious sorrow, which makes his affliction for ever memorable. We know with what exquisite song Milton, in similar circumstances, mourned the loss of his fellow-student, the young poet 'Lycidas;' we know the beauty of David's lament over the young prince Jonathan; we know also the generous and melodious verse with which Shelley honoured his dead 'Adonais;' and we would think it a truly interesting and delightful study to compare Tennyson's elegy with these. Shelley, and especially Milton, have rather given us fine poems than that earnest expression of real grief which is felt in reading Tennyson, whose manner is more like David's : 'I am distressed for thee, my brother Jonathan; very pleasant hast thou been unto me : thy love to me was wonderful, passing the love of women.'

With the thought of a 'dead self'—the feeling of one who has left his former self in a past age, and is now no longer the same man which he was in the days of his great friendship—and with a vague, faint hope that even by the aid of this dead self, used as a 'stepping stone,' he may rise higher in the scale of being, he tries in thus bringing together loss and gain to sum up even a little comfort. In vain. Who can live so far away in the future

> 'Or reach a hand thro' time to catch
> The far-off interest of tears?'

In the 'first dark day' of sorrow the impression of a 'dead self' predominates, the resultant 'higher things' are dimly discerned afar. Therefore the mourner, drawn to the graveyard, feels its sad emblems congenial, and is especially fascinated by an old yew-tree; and while he considers how its roots are grasping the skulls beneath the sod, he grows sick and displeased, thinking of its age, and how many lives *its* life is equal to, till, benumbed by sorrow and lost in thought, he almost loses consciousness of the difference between himself and that leafy emblem of woe :

> 'I seem to fail from out my blood
> And grow incorporate into thee.'

Out of this benumbed condition the mourner's soul awakes to a keener sense of the ruin which has been wrought, and we have a poem which might be headed 'The Unbelief of Sorrow' (III.) Grief may be defended by its cause, the great love without which it could not exist, or it may be defended by its effect, 'the far-off interest of tears;' but how can we defend it if it denies the existence of all goodness and good Providence? Yet such is the mental confusion which Arthur's death has produced, he seems to hear the voice of Sorrow telling him that all nature is dislocated and ruined, that the stars have now no intelligent guide, but run blindly in their courses, and that though a cry ascends from the ruins of the world, there is no access to heaven; but Sorrow is herself the sole remaining Deity in expiring nature, and all nature's music is a hollow echo of hers. The poet knows the folly of these whispers from Sorrow's 'lying lip'—he knows that he has been unconsciously communicating to the universe the gloom of his own mind; and though he has defended his sorrow on account of the love in which it is rooted, he half desires to crush it by his reason, as he would an improper desire the moment it arose:

> 'And shall I take a thing so blind,
> Embrace her as my natural food,
> Or crush her as a vice of blood
> Upon the threshold of the mind?'

Wearied with such questions, sleep at length comes to the sorrow-laden soul—not the sound slumber of the healthy mind, but one in which he has still a dim consciousness of loss, with a fear to make it more clear.

> '*Something* it is which thou hast lost,
> Some pleasure in thine early years,'

he says to himself in this troubled dream, but fears to inquire farther. How touchingly the reality of his sorrow is here laid open! Few of us have been so fortunate as to be utterly unable to understand this.

We next see the Delicacy of true sorrow, when he says:

> 'I sometimes hold it half a sin
> To put in words the grief I feel.'

Words do it wrong: they only 'half reveal' while they 'half

conceal' it. Shakespeare has a similar idea (Sonnet XVII.), where he speaks of his verse being

> 'But as a tomb,
> Which hides your life, and shows not half your parts.'

The great masters of expression have all felt this. 'As in the centre of your lamp's flame there is a portion which is said to be perfect darkness, so even the most expressive words will sometimes darken almost as much as they reveal. So does nature reveal, yet conceal, the designing Mind; and the Prophet who is sure of Him must at times exclaim, 'Verily thou art a God that hideth Thyself!' For while the heavens declare His glory and the earth showeth His handiwork, we feel that still nature itself interposes between Him and us. The language of the poet is, like the language of the skies, at best an imperfect revealer of the hidden spirit, and he sometimes 'holds it half a sin' to wrong his grief by clothing it in these poor words. But the 'sad mechanic exercise' of versemaking soothes one: as 'some poor beggar exposed to the cold would take refuge in the coarsest clothes, I take refuge in my poor rhymes: and as only a rough outline of the beggar's form could be seen, so is my large grief imperfectly expressed in what I write.'

Like others, the poet receives letters of condolence, and is told, as Hamlet was told, that loss 'is common.'

> 'And common is the commonplace,
> The vacant chaff well meant for grain.'

The thought that so many suffer but adds to his affliction. Even while a father is pledging his son, that son is lost to him in the far-off battle. Even while a mother is praying for her sailor-boy,

> 'His heavy-shotted hammock shroud,
> Drops in his vast and wandering grave.'

'And I was looking for Arthur home, and keeping for him something I had written, when *he* was taken.' Then he adds an illustration which comes nearer his own case than the father of the soldier or the mother of the sailor does. It is so good a specimen of Tennyson's perfect picture-making that I venture to present it entire. In thought he now addresses a betrothed maiden expecting her lover:

> 'O somewhere, meek unconscious dove,
>   That sittest ranging golden hair,
>   And glad to find thyself so fair,
> Poor child, that waitest for thy love!
> For now her father's chimney glows
>   In expectation of a guest,
>   And thinking, "This will please him best,"
> She takes a riband or a rose;
> For he will see them on to-night,
>   And with the thought her colour burns,
>   And having left the glass she turns
> Once more to set a ringlet right.
> And even when she turn'd the curse,
>   Had fallen, and her future lord
>   Was drown'd in passing thro' the ford,
> Or killed in falling from his horse.
> O what to her shall be the end?
>   And what to me remains of good?
>   To her perpetual maidenhood,
> And unto me no second friend.'

There is a saying by the elder Hallam, that 'there is a weakness and folly in all misplaced and *excessive* affection.' It is to be feared that practical people who have heard me so far are beginning to object to Tennyson's love and grief as excessive. Knowing the pressure of life, and that they cannot give much thought or feeling to some events on which a poet might write a book, on behalf of serious work they here enter a protest. Tennyson thinks of such objections as he writes. He fancies he hears those who criticize his singing. One says:

> 'This fellow would make weakness weak,
>   And melt the waxen hearts of men.'

Another accuses him of parading his pain in order to get the praise of constancy. A third, a greater man than the other two, apparently some great politician or philosopher, reproves the poet for wasting his time at a barren song of private sorrow, forgetful of the public cause, and how the rising tide of democracy endangers the chairs of authority. Or if the poet has no taste for politics, there is Science! Should he not be ashamed to lie buried in his private grief, while science works her miracles unheeded? Is this

> ' A time to sicken and to swoon,
>   When Science reaches forth her arms
>   To feel from world to world, and charms
>   Her secret from the latest moon?'

Perhaps when we hear the poet's answer to these apparently reasonable objections, we may be inclined, on the whole, to let him have his own way. As will be afterwards seen, this poet is by no means indifferent to the claims of science or politics; but for the present he appeals to nature and the inestimable worth of the departed to justify his song, and he asserts that those who talk as these objectors have done, are ignorant of the truth that genuine poetry is, like the music of the grove in spring, the effect of nature:

> ' Behold, ye speak an idle thing,
>   Ye never knew the sacred dust;
>   I do but sing because I must,
>   And pipe but as the linnets sing:
>   And one is glad; her note is gay,
>   For now her little ones have ranged;
>   And one is sad, her note is changed
>   Because her brood is stolen away.'

This is certainly a modest way of speaking of his poetry, but it is sincere, for it is the true view of the matter, and it is followed by a still more graceful similitude and apology. A lover, leaving the home of his mistress on finding her absent, sees the place suddenly divested of interest; 'so,' says Tennyson, 'I find all places desolate where Arthur and I used to meet'; and then he adds the apology which becomes a triumph :

> ' Yet as that lover, wandering there
>   In those deserted walks may find
>   A flower beat with rain and wind,
>   Which once she foster'd up with care ;
>   So seems it in my deep regret,
>   O my forsaken heart, with thee
>   And this small flower of poesy,
>   Which, little cared for, fades not yet.

> But since it pleased a vanish'd eye,
> I go to plant it on his tomb,
> That if it can it there may bloom,
> Or dying, there at least may die.'

But the poet has another, a sharper way of dealing with his critics, by which he forces deep self-knowledge on those who are capable of receiving it, and develops further the important principle with which the poem begins. You may wonder at his grief—call it 'excessive'; you may pity the too sensitive poet—he pities you! He says he envies not the tame linnet that never beats its cage, nor the beast that has never had a twinge of conscience; he chooses the nobler nature, though it be attended with greater pain. Though his great love has become great sorrow, still he is thankful it was given him to love so greatly and so purely; and were his life to begin again, he would love Arthur again, though he foresaw the sad result:

> 'I hold it true, whate'er befall;
> I feel it when I sorrow most,
> 'Tis better to have loved and lost
> Than never to have loved at all.'

Here is a thought for the very sensible people who pooh-pooh what they consider 'excessive' feeling, and value themselves on preserving their equanimity and being moderately comfortable under every circumstance. 'I envy not,' says Tennyson, 'the heart that never plighted troth,'

> 'Nor any want-begotten rest.'

If you find your heart incapable of any noble, elevating emotion, it is bad enough—do not go on to worse—to sneering at those who have felt what you cannot feel. It is well enough to see people preserving their equanimity and being always moderately comfortable; but why should they set up for being the greatest and wisest of the earth on that account? What if it be only the absence of some noble feeling or endowment that keeps them so calm? And what if their 'rest' is 'begotten' of that 'want'? As there is something nobler in the spirit of freedom possessing the wild bird of the mountain than in the tameness of the little creature that has always been accustomed to its cage; as there is something nobler in the endowment of conscience, even when it brings Macbeth's terrors to the bosom, than in mere brute sensation, however self-satisfied; so a soul which has been possessed by a great and deep and holy love, however wretched it may become, has nothing to be ashamed of beside some stolid or superficial nature which is incapable of such depth of feeling. This is the poet's preaching, needful for the age, and daily becoming more needful.

Even should there be worse than present loss—should there be no future meeting; still, he would rather have loved than not. He would not lose the elevation of soul—the pure heights of being—'the ennobling stir in which he feels himself exalted,' for fear of any pang, however poignant, or any gloom, however deep—yea, should there be no future state !

The dark suggestion leads to the highest speculations of the poem—not, of course, to questions of theology, which would be inconsistent with the true idea of art; but to guiding thoughts and wise imaginings on awful subjects, such as an earnest and gifted and purified soul that has freed itself from the shackles of all the systems may arrive at and announce. You may be able to detect a certain scepticism in Tennyson, but it is not of the school of Byron or Shelley. He constantly and deeply feels, what these poets seem never to have rightly felt, the value of reverence as the companion of research, and of the purest love as co-mate of the highest knowledge. The piece farther on, which we might call the grand Hymn of Universalism, shows his thought to be sufficiently free and unfettered; but he never rudely shocks men by striking at opinions evidently based on their nobler instincts, like Shelley: his countenance never wears the ferocious God-defying scowl of 'Cain.' Some lovers of poetry still prefer the bolder, but more brutal and more fiendish style of writing; they are welcome to their taste; but I think their favourites have nothing on this subject of doubt at once so moderate and so good, so wise and so delicate, as that part of 'In Memoriam' which we are now approaching. I refer to the touching appeal to a free-thinking brother on behalf of his believing sister. The discrimination and delicacy here and elsewhere manifested was a new thing in the world's poetry when it appeared. I wish all our sceptical or 'advanced' young men would commit the following advice to memory; it would make them, not indeed believers, but in this respect perfect gentlemen:

> 'O thou that after toil and storm
>   Mayst seem to have reached a purer air,
>   Whose faith hath centre everywhere,
> Nor cares to fix itself to form,
> Leave thou thy sister when she prays
>   Her early heaven, her happy views,
>   Nor thou with shadow'd hint confuse
> A life that leads melodious days.
> Her faith thro' form is pure as thine,
>   Her hands are quicker unto good:
>   Oh, sacred be the flesh and blood
> To which she links a truth divine
> See thou that countest reason ripe
>   In holding by the law within,
>   Thou fail not in a world of sin,
> Even for the want of such a type.'

But Tennyson is no bigot: he does not fail immediately to deal with the other side of this question. This pure and gentle creature — this tender-hearted, benevolent, believing sister — may instinctively discover that her brother is not a believer as she is; and great will be the alarm and indignation at the discovery. She may become dogmatic and denunciatory, and disastrous consequences may ensue. It is indeed well to warn the brother not to wantonly disturb his sister's faith; but should not the sister also be instructed and advised? Yes; and Tennyson devotes one of his little cantos to this: namely, that widely celebrated one containing these two proverbial lines:

> 'There lives more faith in honest doubt,
>   Believe me, than in half the creeds.'

The gentle, pure-hearted, believing sister whose suspicions are roused must be instructed thus: That doubt is not always evil; that it is not always what she calls it, 'devil-born.' 'I knew a man,' says our poet, referring doubtless to Arthur 'who earnestly sought to lay the foundation of his faith in reason, and entered into many a subtle question to this end. At first he was unsettled, even filled with unhappy uncertainty; but because he earnestly and honestly dealt with the questions that came before his mind, sparing no pains to discover the truth, he found light, and was soon on his way to a more solid happiness than he had ever possessed : he

> 'Touch'd a jarring lyre at first,
> But ever strove to make it true,
> Perplext in faith, but pure in deeds,
> At last he beat his music out.'

The gentle believing sister whose suspicions are roused must hear something of this, lest she become ungentle and intolerant : and truly the severity of gentle believing sisters—like the rage of a mother-bird when its young are attacked—is something terrible.

> 'Sweet-hearted, you, whose light-blue eyes
> Are tender over drowning flies,
> You tell me doubt is devil-born.'

That from the lady is pretty strong; but now, since her suspicions are aroused, she must be taught—that, once a doubt is started in a man's mind, it must be laid by the exercise of reason, and not by hoodwinking reason; that the man who flies from these 'spectres of the mind' is far more cowardly than the one who faces them fairly; and that the man who fights his doubt earnestly and fairly is nobler than he who dismisses it carelessly or silences it sophistically. The appeal to the believing sister should be 'committed,' as well as the other to the 'advanced' brother :

> 'You tell me, doubt is devil-born.
> I know not; one indeed I knew
> In many a subtle question versed,
> Who touch'd a jarring lyre at first,
> But ever strove to make it true.
> Perplext in faith, but pure in deeds,
> At last he beat his music out;
> There lives more faith in honest doubt,
> Believe me, than in half the creeds.

> He fought his doubts and gather'd strength;
> He would not make his judgment blind.
> He faced the spectres of the mind
> And laid them; thus he came at length
> To find a stronger faith his own:
> And Power was with him in the night,
> Which makes the darkness and the light,
> And dwells not with the light alone.'

It is implied that the Power who made both light and darkness may sometimes be with doubt as well as with faith. And some who are condemned as doubters may have more real faith than the full professors of creeds. As too often our creeds are accepted in a formal, perfunctory or traditional way, it may be that much of what is called orthodoxy is not real or earnest faith, and there may even be more real faith in those who are not professedly orthodox, because what amount of belief they have accepted is earnest and living, and they are on their way to higher attainments.

Let us not, however, mistake Tennyson, as if he encouraged or approved of doubt, because he manifests this wise and eminently Christian tolerance, in which so many good people are deficient. He at length rejoices over the destruction of the doubt which was born of his great sorrow, or arose from the mental confusion caused by it: and to him, not doubt, but the faith fairly won from it, constitutes human greatness and blessedness. In dealing with religious doubt, he has, he says, been chiefly helped by the instinctive suggestions of his own great love for the departed, especially when it was put in comparison with the short life of his friend. He has been brought to feel that such love is by its own nature immortal, and he accepts the promise that it gives of a future meeting with Arthur. It is by the native intuitions of his soul, rather than by any creed, by the spontaneous suggestions of his better nature, rather than by systematic theology, that he acquires faith in God and in immortality. Truth has come to him, he says, with his full manhood; he finds it 'deep-seated in his mystic frame.' He has not to search afar; there is a light that lighteth every man; the word is nigh him; in his heart and in his mouth. Yet he is ready to pay a reverent tribute to CHRIST as the great Revealer, and he acknowledges His transcendent power especially in this, that He has made those great truths which once only the deeper and nobler natures could get a glimpse of, open and evident to the commonest and least educated minds; surely a beautiful passage this :

> ' We yield all blessing to the name
> Of Him who made them current coin.
> And so the Word had breath and wrought
> With human hands the creed of creeds,
> In loveliness of perfect deeds,
> More strong than all poetic thought :
> Which he may read that binds the sheaf,
> Or builds the house, or digs the grave,
> Or those wild eyes that watch the wave
> In roarings round the coral reef.'

It is wonderful how naturally all the various subjects of the poem are connected with Arthur, preserving thus its unity. His faith is rooted in his love to Arthur; and when he is visited, like others, by a season of depression and darkness, then does he especially long for the presence of his departed friend, who used to help him with his difficulties. *Could* he come back? He dares not say it is impossible, but thinks we may be sometimes unaware of such blessed presence by reason of our own impurity :

> ' They haunt the silence of the breast,
> Imaginations calm and fair,
> The memory like a cloudless air,
> The conscience as a sea at rest.
> But when the heart is full of din,
> And doubt beside the portal waits,
> They can but listen at the gates
> And hear the household jar within.'

Nevertheless, though unworthy, he prays earnestly that Arthur's spirit may be 'near him' in the sad seasons of ill-health and doubt with which he is wont to be visited. And here we have that touching invocation, which is at the same time a powerful description of a state of the modern intellect, which accounts for so much of the weakness and inconsistencies of spiritual life—in which he desires Arthur's spirit may be near him in seasons when the light of his soul is low and bodily pains get a momentary victory over faith; when the soul, through her darkened windows, sees men crowding on the earth as if they were buzzing, waspish insects laying their eggs, stinging one another, building cells and perishing; when all the product of Time appears like a fortuitous concourse of atoms ('Time a maniac scattering dust'); when life seems to be given to human beings at haphazard, often where it is likely to cause the greatest agony ('Life a fury slinging flame') :

> 'Be near me when my light is low,
>   When the blood creeps and the nerves prick
>   And tingle; and the heart is sick,
>   And all the wheels of Being slow.
> Be near me when the sensuous frame
>   Is rack'd with pangs that conquer trust,
>   And Time a maniac scattering dust,
>   And Life a fury slinging flame.
> Be near me when my faith is dry,
>   And men the flies of latter spring,
>   That lay their eggs, and sting, and sing,
>   And weave their petty cells and die.
> Be near me when I fade away,
>   To point the term of human strife,
>   And on the low dark verge of life
>   The twilight of eternal day.'

Thus Tennyson, strong and believing, lets the weak and faithless know he understands their case, and establishes a fellow-feeling that makes them willing to listen to him when he speaks words of encouragement and hope. When the darkened eye of the poet's soul begins to clear, he looks again at the world and at himself, and finds order where he saw confusion :

> 'I see in part
>   That all, as in some piece of art
>   Is toil co-öperant to an end. . . . .
>   And all is well, tho' faith and form
>   Be sunder'd in the night of fear ;
>   Well roars the storm to those that hear
>   A deeper Voice across the storm.'

Be hopeful, then, ye strugglers for reform ! be not discouraged by reason of your own infirmities, or because of the follies and stupidities of the race among whom ye labour ! Independent of all instruments, there is a mighty Power moving forward human beings—yea, should worst revolutions be imminent and confusions more tremendous than any the world has yet seen ; should the 'September days' of Paris be thrice repeated ; should the 'spires of ice' topple down, the sustaining crags tremble, and the mountains be cast into the sea, that mighty Power moves onward to its gracious ends, that 'deeper Voice across the storm' is heard—

> 'Proclaiming social truth shall spread
> And justice, even tho' thrice again
> The red fool-fury of the Seine
> Should pile her barricades with dead.'

Too distressingly at times one feels the imperfection of all earthly things—even this great love to Arthur has flaws in it which, in moments of severe introspection, make the poet dissatisfied, and he exclaims :

> 'I cannot love thee as I ought,
> For love reflects the thing beloved.'

But one may catch a gleam of hope even from that 'wild oats' theory—the 'sober man among his boys' who was a wild youth once—which is so liable to be abused; one may hope for a more perfect love and a more perfect world when time shall ' sunder shell from pearl '; and so, from a heart struggling with its sadness, and at last victorious, come those great earnest strains of Universalism :

> ' Oh, yet we trust that somehow good
> Will be the final goal of ill,
> To pangs nature, sins of will,
> Defects of doubt, and taints of blood.'

With the true spirit of our century, the poet feels he cannot be dogmatic even about this, and, after soaring a little on the wings of his faith and hope, his music falls with a touching sense of weakness :

> 'So runs my dream: but what am I?
> An infant crying in the night,
> An infant crying for the light,
> And with no language but a cry.'

We follow with unflagging interest these diary-like records of the ups and downs of his spiritual man; for there is substantial thought as well as deep feeling and beautiful poetry in all: there is also a subtle principle of unity running through all these detached entries. Some of the finest pieces we have passed over as well known, and not needing either notice or comment; but we must not conclude without a reference to that 'noble passage' in which Hugh Miller long ago saw 'the sagacity of the poet—that strange sagacity which seems so nearly akin to the prophetic spirit.'* Holding by his faith in immortality, but not blind to the results of science, our poet has stumbled—as who has not?—at seeing the waste of life in nature, which, while careful of the type, is careless of the individual. And what if *he*—what if *Arthur* should be that 'single life' of which nature seems so careless? But there is a worse doubt at hand. Geology shows that nature is not careful of the type either: the rocks testify that whole genera, almost whole animal kingdoms, have become extinct. This thought wakes in the bosom of the poet a horrible fear, which rouses all his spiritual strength to struggle with the doubt. The result is the canto which Miller has so highly praised. The difficulty of the doctrine which denies a future state has never been more forcibly or more effectively stated; and the oft-quoted passage may bear quoting again:

> 'And he, shall he,
> Man, her last work, who seem'd so fair,
> Such splendid purpose in his eyes,
> Who roll'd the psalm to wintry skies,
> Who built him fanes of fruitless prayer,
> Who trusted God was love indeed,
> And love Creation's final law—
> Tho' Nature, red in tooth and claw
> With ravine shriek'd against his creed—

---

* 'Testimony of the Rocks,' p. 113.

> Who loved, who suffer'd countless ills,
> Who battled for the True, the Just,
> Be blown about the desert dust,
> Or seal'd within the iron hills?
> No more? A monster, then, a dream,
> A discord. Dragons of the prime,
> That tare each other in their slime,
> Were mellow music match'd with him.'

Such earnestness, such effort of the nobler nature, such high illuminating thoughts, such fadeless records of true genius, resulted to Tennyson from the 'distressful stroke which his youth suffered.' We see a noble soul further ennobled and purified by that desolating blow, so that it rises to more real sympathy with men and the great questions which concern the race, and to put forth unselfish, energetic efforts which the untroubled and self-satisfied forget or decline to do. So it has always been with the world's prophet benefactors. They have been made perfect through suffering. In the agony of their private sorrows they have risen to true and vivid conceptions of the evils of the world. From struggles to get rid of the shadow on their own souls, they have gone on to earnest desires and labours to cause the great shadows of ignorance and sin, of self-deception and injustice, of unfaithfulness and unbelief, to pass from off their land and their race.

THE END.

Elliot Stock, Paternoster Row, London.

www.ingramcontent.com/pod-product-compliance
Lightning Source LLC
Chambersburg PA
CBHW031933230426
43672CB00010B/1911